About the editors

Sonja Novkovic is a professor of economics at Saint Mary's University, and academic co-director in the Co-operative Management Education programme. Currently, she is the chair of the International Co-operative Alliance Research Committee and academic co-lead of the Measuring the Co-operative Difference Research Network in collaboration with Co-operatives and Mutuals Canada.

Tom Webb is an adjunct Professor at Saint Mary's University School of Business and is program manager of the master's degree in the Management of Co-operatives and Credit Unions (MMCCU).

More praise for *Co-operatives in a Post-Growth Era*

'The timing of this book is perfect! The findings from the 2012 Imagine Conference summarize ways to create prosperity and stability in this new economic, social and environmental reality. Leading economic thinkers provide critical insights in how the co-operative enterprise model meets the growing complex global problems while building a better world. Kudos to Webb and Novkovic for making this happen.' *Denyse Guy, executive director, Co-operatives and Mutuals Canada*

'Imagine 2012 has been the silver lining behind the cloud for those who believe that co-ops are enterprises to build a better world.' *Jean Louis Bancel, president, Crédit Coopératif*

'The ideas about economics in this book will help co-operative leaders move co-operative development forward.' *Nelson Kuria, CEO, Co-operative Insurance Company, Kenya*

'A unique collection of essays that offers both theoretical arguments and practical insights into how co-operatives can provide the basis for a more socially and environmentally sustainable economy. This should be required reading for all students in business and economics, and a must read for all interested in the future of the planet.' *Darryl Reed, York University Canada*

'When markets fail, co-operatives bring needed products and services, competition and opportunity for people. Building a global co-operative economy will ensure fewer economic crises and greater food security around the world.' *Paul Hazen, executive director, US Overseas Cooperative Development Council*

CO-OPERATIVES IN A POST-GROWTH ERA

CREATING CO-OPERATIVE ECONOMICS

edited by Sonja Novkovic and Tom Webb

Zed Books
LONDON

Fernwood Publishing
HALIFAX | WINNIPEG

Co-operatives in a Post-growth Era: Creating co-operative economics was first published in 2014 by Zed Books Ltd, 7 Cynthia Street, London N1 9JF, UK

www.zedbooks.co.uk

Published in Canada by Fernwood Publishing, 32 Oceanvista Lane, Black Point, Nova Scotia, BOJ 1BO and 748 Broadway Avenue, Winnipeg, Manitoba, R3G 0X3

www.fernwoodpublishing.ca

Fernwood Publishing Company Limited gratefully acknowledges the financial support of the Government of Canada through the Canada Book Fund and the Canada Council for the Arts, the Nova Scotia Department of Communities, Culture and Heritage, the Manitoba Department of Culture, Heritage and Tourism under the Manitoba Book Publishers Marketing Assistance Program and the Province of Manitoba, through the Book Publishing Tax Credit, for our publishing program.

Set in Monotype Plantin and FFKievit by Ewan Smith, London
Index: ed.emery@thefreeuniversity.net
Cover designed by Dougal Burgess

A catalogue record for this book is available from the British Library
Library of Congress Cataloging in Publication Data available
Library and Archives Canada Cataloguing in Publication
    Co-operatives in a post-growth era / edited by Sonja Novkovic and Tom Webb.
Includes bibliographical references and index.
ISBN 978-1-55266-690-6 (pbk.)
    1. Cooperative societies. 2. Economic development. 3. Social entrepreneurship. I. Novkovic, Sonja, editor II. Webb, Tom, 1946-, editor
HD2963.C6739 2014   334   C2014-905464-5

ISBN 978-1-78360-078-6 hb (Zed Books)
ISBN 978-1-78360-077-9 pb (Zed Books)
ISBN 978-1-55266-690-6 pb (Fernwood Publishing)

MIX
Paper from
responsible sources
FSC
www.fsc.org   FSC® C013056

Printed and bound in Great Britain by
TJ International Ltd, Padstow, Cornwall

CONTENTS

TABLES AND FIGURES

Tables

Figures

INTRODUCTION: CO-OPERATIVE ECONOMICS, WHY OUR WORLD NEEDS IT

Tom Webb and Sonja Novkovic

The decision to hold a conference on co-operative economics during the International Year of Co-operatives in 2012 had its roots in the thinking about co-operatives and co-operation that spurred the creation of the Co-operative Management Education programmes in the Sobey School of Business early in the first decade of the new millennium. The impetus to create these programmes in turn was stimulated by the thinking of Sidney Pobihushchy, a long-time board member of Co-op Atlantic and a seminal co-operative thinker. Together we developed the Initiatives for Renewal, a far-reaching vision that imagined co-operatives, and Co-op Atlantic in particular, playing a leading role in economic renewal in the Atlantic Canada region. Those ideas, while ahead of their time, bear interesting similarities to the Co-operative Blueprint now being imagined globally by the International Co-operative Alliance.

Those of us excited about co-operatives found co-operatives exciting, in large measure, because of our discomfort with prevailing economic thought. The economy, for us, was about the relationships people created to provide themselves with the goods and services they needed to live meaningful lives. It was not about the narrowly measured efficiency of investor-owned business, or about growth of output, but about how well the economy met the needs of people and communities. Those needs were seen as being inclusive of a healthy environment and healthy communities in a healthy society. It seemed clear that both the state socialist and capitalist models of the twentieth century left much to be desired.

Our hope for a better economy based on the co-operative business model was founded on fundamental differences between co-operatives and the dominant investor-owned model, which has concentrated power in the hands of a wealthy few on the one hand

and the bureaucratic state-owned firm on the other, where power was concentrated in the hands of a small political elite. Co-operatives are different. They spread power. The purpose of the business is different. Its purpose is to meet member and community need rather than to maximise the wealth of shareholders. The people who use a co-operative business – workers or producers or consumers or small business people – own the business. In setting it up as a co-operative, they buy into the ideas, values and principles of co-operation; otherwise we can assume that they would have chosen a different business model. Members or managers, several generations later, may have forgotten or not be aware of the meaning of co-operation but that is a failure of education and a loss of identity.

What sets co-operatives apart from employee stock ownership plans (ESOPs), social enterprise, or investor-owned business? Co-operatives comprise a unique form of businesses that can be found around the world. They cross ethnic, cultural, linguistic and religious differences. They cross almost every line that divides humanity. There are four key pillars of the co-operative business model that set the co-operative family of businesses apart: 1) the purpose of the business; an internationally accepted framework of both values (2) and principles (3); and 4) a founding ethic of fairness or social justice.

The co-operative model is people-centred, while the investor-owned model is wealth-centred. The co-operative manager has an obligation to meet member and community need. The investor-owned business manager has a (perceived) fiduciary responsibility to maximise shareholder value. The co-operative business purpose resonates with the human spirit with its blend and balance of individual and social needs. This is a business model that reflects the fullness of the human spirit rather than simply the acquisitive slice of individualism.

If the purpose of the co-operative is to meet member and community need, then the question 'Who are the members?' is vital to understand the different types of co-operatives and their governance. In a co-operative, the residual power lies with the members. The matrix of possibilities set out in Table 0.1 opposite is useful in this regard.

This is clearly a flexible and adaptable business model. As noted above, it has been adopted by peoples around the world, across a wide diversity of human culture and circumstance. While often

TABLE 0.1 Types of co-operative and their members

Type of co-operative	Members
Consumer co-operative	Consumers of various commodities such as food, insurance, funerals, financial services, travel services, etc. This model would include mutuals.
Small business (producer) co-operative	Small and medium businesses such as farmers, fishermen, woodlot owners, plumbers, electricians, retail shop owners, hotel owners, etc. These are usually family-owned businesses.
Workers' co-operative	Those who work in the business. This could be in any industry, including food, agriculture, retail sales of goods or services, social services, etc. This model would include collectives,[1] although most workers' co-operatives would not function as collectives.
Solidarity[2] co-operative	There are different classes of members, who could include consumers, workers, community representatives, investors, suppliers, etc., and who could be engaged in any type of business, such as food, agriculture, retail sales of goods or services, social services, etc.
Community co-operative	People drawn from and representing a community.
Exceptions	Almost every country has examples of some co-operatives that defy simple classification into the above categories but that are clearly democratically governed co-operatives.

Notes: 1. Collectives are non-hierarchical working groups with decision-making by consensus. 2. Also termed 'multi-stakeholder' co-operatives in the literature.

seemingly invisible, the magnitude of co-operative business, on focused examination, is significant and important. The statistics below illustrate the scale of co-operative business around the world:

- In the United States, 30,000 co-operatives provide more than 2 million jobs (NCBA 2013).
- Co-operatives and credit unions have more than a billion members around the world (ICA 2013).
- Co-operatives provide over 100 million jobs around the world, 20 per cent more than all the world's multinational enterprises put together (ILO 2014).
- The United Nations estimated in 1994 that the livelihood of nearly 3 billion people, or half the world's population, was made secure by co-operative enterprise (ICA 2013).

- In Kenya, 63 per cent of the population derive their livelihoods from co-operatives. Approximately 250,000 Kenyans are employed or gain most of their income from co-operatives (Coop Africa 2009).
- Almost 350 million people in the Asia-Pacific region belong to co-operatives (ICA 2013).
- The 300 largest co-operatives in the world have a combined annual turnover or revenue of US$2 trillion, which is more than the gross domestic product (GDP) of Italy, the world's seventh economy (UNSDN 2013).
- Between 2007 and 2010, European co-operative banks' assets grew by 14 per cent (Birchall 2013).
- Co-operative financial institutions did not produce any of the 'toxic' paper that destabilised the global economy.
- In the economic downturn, credit unions and co-operative banks did not require bailouts, the value of co-operative shares remained stable, and most co-operatives experienced modest growth and continued to extend credit to members, including businesses, in the midst of global credit shrinkage.

The co-operative business model's differentiating purpose, values and principles, when operationalised, have far-reaching consequences for what co-operatives do and how they do it. The implications for managers and governance are profound. For example, a consumer co-operative would be expected to share all information it has about the products it sells to the members who own it. Also, because co-operative members benefit based on their use of the co-operative rather than on the value of their shares, a co-operative, unlike its investor-owned counterpart, does not need to maximise its return on investment.

It was as a result of this train of thought that a group of co-operative leaders in the mid-1990s began to work on developing management education programmes for co-operatives.[1] Their initiative was based on the understanding that managing a co-operative was different and more challenging than managing an investor-owned firm. The programme was successfully created with the added leadership of President Dr Colin Dodds and Management Department Chair Dr John Chamard, of Saint Mary's University in Halifax, Nova Scotia. The core idea was to develop a programme for managers of co-operatives, at a master's level, in which every course and topic reflected the impact of the co-operative purpose, values and principles on the dynamics and operation of the business. A catchphrase was: 'I know how this is done in an investor-owned firm, but how would it be done differently in a co-operative that understood and respected its co-operative identity?' The programme founders believed that the co-operative difference was a business advantage. This pervasive application of co-operative purpose, values and principles to every aspect of managing a co-operative was unique. There was simply no other programme like it.

The programme[2] looked at marketing as though co-operative values and principles mattered. It looked at accounting and asked: if its purpose and goals are significantly different, what is it a co-operative needs to account for? How would just using standard accounting, with its primary focus on return on investment for shareholders, impact on a co-operative's performance? Would it focus boards and managers on the goals of investor-owned firms rather than on co-operative goals? If the purpose of the co-operative is people-centred rather than capital-centred, should co-operative managers learn about human resource management or people development? The programme developed distinctive approaches to 'co-operative accounting', 'co-operative marketing' and 'co-operative people development'. Every course reflected the co-operative management difference.

A key question was what to do about economics? We knew that if we went back to early economic thinkers such as John Stuart Mill[3] and Alfred Marshall[4] – and even Adam Smith's ideas about community and responsibility in his less cited work *The Theory of Moral Sentiments* (1759) – there was a rich vein of economic thought that fitted well with the ideas of co-operation. We also knew that a growing number of modern economic thinkers were proposing ideas and theories that were an expression of concern about economic trends and ideas and at the same time fitted with co-operative theories and ideas. We were also keenly aware that much of mainstream economics was increasingly failing to reflect reality – destructive overuse of measures such as GDP (see Chapter 3) and assertions such as the 'tragedy of the commons' (Chapter 13) – and that much of current conventional economic thinking was actually hostile to co-operative thought and endeavour. Ideas such as Milton Friedman's 'the business of business is business' and the George Soros observation, when asked about the havoc his currency speculation caused to Far Eastern economies in the crash of 1997, 'As a market participant, I don't need to be concerned with the consequences of my actions' (Clark 2003) were fundamentally at odds with the ideas of co-operation.

What economics do we use?

A typical neoclassical definition of the economy and economics would be:

- The economy is a system in which scarce resources are allocated among competing uses.
- Economics is the study of the use of scarce resources to satisfy unlimited human wants.

The key tenets of the approach to economics promoted by the Chicago School saw unrestricted markets and the publicly traded joint stock company as producing the most efficient use of resources. The shares of the most efficient companies would command a higher value in the marketplace and an efficient economy would be the result.

This neoclassical conceptual framework is an uncomfortable fit for co-operatives whose shares are not publicly traded and whose purpose is not to maximise return on investment but to meet member and community need. The alternative definitions below (see also Chapter 2) would be a far better fit for the co-operative business model:

- The economy is the complex set of relationships that people use to provide themselves with the goods and services they need to live meaningful lives in their communities.
- Economics is the study of how effective the economy is at meeting human needs in a manner that allows people to live meaningful, happy lives as an integral part of a healthy planet.

These definitions, while tentative, would provide a sound basis for what we could call co-operative economics. If capitalism is the ordering of human activity for the benefit of the capital owner, or wealth creation using the investor-owned firm as its tool or techno-logy, we might regard neoclassical economics as a system of thought developed to provide an explanation and justification for capitalism. In contrast, co-operative economics at the macro scale would focus on the effectiveness of the economy in meeting human need and providing scope for human aspirations, and, at the micro level, on how effective co-operative firms are at these tasks.

There were also other tendencies in neoclassical economic thought that were uncomfortable for co-operatives. These included:

- examining economic considerations in isolation, as if economic action did not produce environmental and social impacts and as if environmental impacts and social action did not have economic impacts;
- the idea that the economy and business activity were 'amoral' and 'value free';
- the separation of economics and common sense (the funda-mentals of the economy may be seen as sound even if 6 million children starve to death or GDP growth resulted from oil spills);
- ignoring the set of interlocked social, environmental and political crises that an increasing number of 'alternative' economists had documented and analysed (financial instability, environmental overshoot, income inequality, energy uncertainty, nation states in crisis, erosion of democracy, etc.), with the result that too much economic thought was not based in reality and growing instability in the global economy was not dealt with;
- viewing financial gain as the only real motivator of human action, creating another reality gap; and
- thinking based on hyper-individualism rather than on a more balanced social–individual continuum.

There are some fundamental questions for co-operative economics to explore. What are the significant socio-economic trends and issues that co-operative managers need to be aware of to successfully man-age their co-operatives? Are the prevailing neoclassical economics and the inherent incentives in the structure and purpose of investor-owned firms fuelling income inequality, poverty, food crisis, climate change and other negative socio-economic trends and exacerbating these problems? Do the fundamental differences in the co-operative business model based on purpose, values and principles (ICA 1995) offer the promise of ameliorating these macro-level tendencies and issues? At the micro level, are they living up to that potential and how does their performance compare with that of investor-owned firms?

A significant challenge facing the Co-operative Management Education programme was identifying the 'new' economic thinkers whose work was meaningful to co-operatives building a co-operative economy. What became clear as the economic curriculum emerged was that few economic thinkers in the 'new economy' had considered how co-operatives might relate to their work. Most of them clearly identified serious issues and problems, but solutions to those issues, when offered, were expressed in terms of changes in the economic behaviour of investor-owned firms or public policy relating to investor-owned firms. Even when a problem was one where the co-operative business model clearly performed better by its design (for example, the salary gap between the lowest and highest paid people in a firm), the words 'co-operative' and 'credit union' rarely appeared in the table of contents or the index of books by the new economists.

Having developed a suitable initial curriculum and recognised the need to review and update it yearly, the idea emerged that we needed to think about what a co-operative economy would look like. We understood corporate globalisation, but what would global co-operation entail and how might co-operatives make it a reality?

Early in the development of the programme we were fortunate to connect with the Master of Co-operative Economics programme located at the University of Bologna, the world's oldest university. This connection made it much easier to make the leap to the concept of co-operative economics. Rooted in the significant economic success of co-operatives in Emilia Romagna, the Bologna master's programme has pulled together several first-rate economists who know, understand and have studied and researched co-operatives. The Italian co-operative experience is rich and varied. Both Vera Negri Zamagni and Stefano Zamagni are central players in the Bologna programme and both have made substantial contributions to the field, the Imagine 2012 conference, and this book.

Those of us involved in the Saint Mary's programme were enormously excited by the declaration of 2012 as the International Year of

Co-operatives. The best contribution we could make to the year was to organise an international conference on co-operative economics. In bringing together leading economic thinkers who were engaged in the emerging new economics and leaders of co-operatives from around the world, our aim was twofold: to have the co-operative leaders leave the conference with a profound understanding of the importance of co-operatives in creating a new economy and a better world; and to have at least a small group of world-class economic thinkers develop a much greater understanding of how the co-operative business model could make a significant contribution to solving growing economic problems. Imagine 2012: International Conference on Co-operative Economics was the result (www.imagine 2012.coop). With major support from the Desjardins Group, the conference took place in Quebec City in October 2012 in conjunction with the first International Summit of Co-operatives.

The extent to which the conference achieved its objectives will not be clear for some time. This book and other related materials from the conference will have an impact. The writing of those who presented at the conference may also make a significant contribution. Our hope is that these ideas will coalesce and take shape in the months and years to come. We hope that co-operatives will imagine what a global economy shaped by co-operative ideas – global co-operation – would look like and that increasingly economists will reflect on the promise of a business model whose purpose is to meet human need. We can imagine a world in which co-operative leaders, economists and public policy-makers will create the expectation that the co-operative business model should live up to the potential contained in its purpose, values and principles.

The structure of the book

This book is in two parts. In Part One, chapters tend not to focus on co-operatives or on the potential of co-operatives to have a positive impact on the economic issues raised. Why did we pick these authors? We picked them because their work has relevance for an economy focused on meeting human need. As they concentrate on the needs of people rather than capital, co-operatives include a concern for community among their principles. Communities exist within the context of the natural world. To be relevant for co-operatives and for the ideas of co-operative human relations, consideration of the economy has to include how economic functioning and processes impact on the natural world and on human society more broadly. Co-operative economics cannot be insular. It cannot embrace an assumption that by focusing on economic functions that benefit capital the needs of people will be served. In choosing presenters and authors for the Imagine 2012 conference and for this volume, we looked for economic thinkers who were addressing the issues that were relevant to a co-operative economy, although they may not have studied co-operatives.

The second part of the book comes from economic thinkers who have studied and written about co-operatives and co-operation. Some chapters present current and potential co-operative contributions to the economy, while others add to the co-operative economic paradigm, having debunked the mainstream economic thinking about efficiency, collective ownership, employee ownership and management, and about the impact of trust and reciprocity on economic behaviour and society.

As you go through the first part of this book, challenge the ideas presented with questions: if co-operatives lived up to their ideas and ideals, could they contribute to positive change on this issue, and transform communities and the global economy? We think they could.

Notes

1 The initial group included Dr Sidney Pobihushchy from Co-op Atlantic, Dennis Deters of The Co-operators, Gerard Duggan of the Credit Union Central of Prince Edward Island, Jack Christie of Northumberland Co-operative Dairies, Peter Podovinikoff of Delta Credit Union, and the author.

2 The Co-operative Management Education programme has expanded to include a graduate diploma.

3 See Chapter 10.

4 Marshall was one of the founders of the discipline of economics and was president of the UK Co-operative Congress in Ipswich in 1889.

References

Birchall, J. (2013) *Resilience in a Downturn: The power of financial cooperatives*. Geneva: International Labour Organization (ILO), p. 27.

Clark, N. (2003) 'NS profile – George Soros'. *New Statesman*, 2 June. www.newstatesman.com/economics/economics/2014/04/ns-profile-george-soros (accessed April 2014).

Coop Africa (2009) 'Cooperative governance project in Kenya'. Geneva: International Labour Organization (ILO). www.ilo.org/public/english/employment/ent/coop/africa/download/knfc.pdf (accessed April 2014).

ICA (1995) 'Statement of Co-operative

Identity'. International Co-operative Alliance (ICA) website. http://ica.coop/en/whats-co-op/co-operative-identity-values-principles (accessed June 2014)

— (2013) 'Co-operative facts & figures'. International Co-operative Alliance (ICA) website. http://ica.coop/en/whats-co-op/co-operative-facts-figures (accessed April 2014).

ILO (2014) '100 million jobs: the contribution of cooperatives to employment creation'. Geneva: International Labour Organization (ILO). www.ilo.org/wcmsp5/groups/public/@ed_emp/@emp_ent/documents/publication/wcms_101313.pdf (accessed April 2014).

NCBA (2013) 'What is a co-op?' National Cooperative Business Association (NCBA) website. http://ncba.coop/what-is-a-coop (accessed April 2014).

UNSDN (2013) 'Cooperatives newsletter, December 2013'. United Nations Social Development Network (UNSDN) website. http://unsdn.org/?p=12957#_ftn1 (accessed April 2014).

PART ONE

WHAT IS THE NEW ECONOMY AND WHY DO WE NEED IT?

1 | THE WORLD ON A COLLISION COURSE AND THE NEED FOR A NEW ECONOMY[1]

Manfred Max-Neef

Preamble

In October 2008, at the same time as the Food and Agriculture Organization of the United Nations (FAO) was reporting that hunger was affecting 1 million people, and estimated that US$30 million annually would suffice to save those lives, the concerted action of six central banks (USA, EU, Japan, Canada, the United Kingdom and Switzerland) poured US$180 billion into the financial markets in order to save private banks. The US Senate approved an addition of US$700 billion. Two weeks later another US$850 million were approved in the United States. That not being enough, the rescue package continued to grow, reaching an estimate of US$17 trillion by September 2009.

Faced with such a situation, we are confronted with two alternatives: to be a demagogue or to be a realist. If, based on the law of supply and demand, I say that there is a greater demand in the world for bread than for luxury cruises, and much more for the treatment of malaria than for haute couture apparel, or if I propose a referendum asking the citizens if they prefer to use their monetary reserves to save lives or to save banks, I will be accused of being a demagogue. If, on the contrary, I accept that it is more urgent, more necessary and more convenient and profitable to all to avoid an insurance company or a bank going bankrupt, instead of feeding millions of children, or giving aid to victims of a hurricane, or curing dengue fever, it will be said that I am a realist.

That is the world in which we are – a world accustomed to the fact that there is never enough for those who have nothing, but there is always enough for those who have everything. The obvious question arises: where was that money? For decades we have been told that there are not enough resources to overcome poverty, yet there are more than enough resources to satisfy the wants of speculators. US$17 trillion divided by the US$30 billion the FAO estimates as enough for overcoming world hunger, instead of saving private banks, could generate 566 years of a world without hunger. Would not a world without misery be a better world for everyone, even for the banks?

What are we facing in our world today?

The quadruple convergence[2]

1 Exponential increase of human-induced climate change affecting all regions of the world.
2 The end of cheap energy, with dramatic effects on societies.
3 Extensive depletion of key resources basic to human welfare and production, such as fresh water, genetic resources, forests, fisheries, wildlife, soils, coral reefs and most elements of local, regional and global commons.
4 The gigantic speculation bubble that is fifty times larger than the real economy of exchange of goods and services.

The root causes are:

1 the dominant economic paradigm, which poses rapid economic growth at any cost and stimulates corporate greed and accumulation;
2 the uncontrolled use of fossil fuels to feed that obsessive economic growth;
3 the promotion of consumerism as the road to human happiness;
4 the decimation of traditional cultures, in order to impose conventional economic industrial models, which determines the loss of cosmovisions, languages and values that differ from those of the dominant culture;
5 disregard of planetary limits in relation to resource availability, consumption, waste generation and absorption; and
6 overpopulation: the population's eventual growth beyond the capacity of the Earth to sustain it.

Consequences The conditions mentioned above may bring about unprecedented and dangerous environmental and social costs:

1 Climate chaos and global warming imply a loss of much productive land, storms, rising sea levels, massive dislocation, desertification and economic and social problems, especially in poorer countries.

2 The depletion of inexpensive oil and gas supplies has a direct impact the world over, threatening future industrial development. This will make industrial food systems and urban and sub-urban systems increasingly difficult to sustain, as well as many commodities that are basic to our accustomed way of life, such as cars, plastics, chemicals and refrigeration. This is all rooted in the assumption of an ever-increasing inexpensive energy supply.

3 There will be shortages of other resources, such as fresh water, forests, agricultural land and biodiversity; we are facing the possible loss of 50 per cent of the world's plant and animal species over the next decades.

Crisis or crises?

It should be stressed that what we are facing today is not simply an economic and financial crisis, but a crisis of humanity. Probably never before in human history have so many crises converged simultaneously to reach their maximum level of tension. Rather, what used to happen was one crisis followed by another. Now we have them all together, which represents a monumental challenge.

Apart from the aspects already mentioned, we can add increasing political, economic, religious and sports corruption; the consolidation of greed as a fundamental value; gigantic enterprises exclusively concerned with their own benefits; judicial systems that forget justice; obsession with growth at any cost; the destruction of nature and disdain for planetary limits; decadence of the school and health systems; hyper-consumerism; hyper-individualism; global warming; climate change; eagerness for power; and disdain for life – colossal convergences that can only result in equally colossal outcomes.

Solutions Solutions imply new models that, above all else, begin to accept the limits of the carrying capacity of the Earth and a move from efficiency to sufficiency and well-being. Also necessary is the solution of the present economic imbalances and inequities. Without equity, peaceful solutions are not possible. We need to replace the dominant values of greed, competition and accumulation, for those of solidarity, co-operation and compassion.

This paradigm shift requires us to turn away from economic growth at any cost. The transition must be towards societies that can adjust to reduced levels of production and consumption, favouring localised systems of economic organisation. We need again to look inward.

We need, however, to understand why the dominant economic model has become so strongly ingrained in our world and in our everyday life. We shall see that its strength rests on mythology.

The myths that sustain the dominant model[3]

Myth 1: Globalisation is the only effective route to development Between 1960 and 1980 the majority of developing countries, especially in Latin America, adopted the principle of 'import substitution', which allowed for significant industrial development. During that period, per capita income in Latin America grew 73 per cent and in Africa 34 per cent. After 1980, economic growth in Latin America came to a virtual halt, increasing, as an average, not more than 6 per cent over twenty years, while growth in Africa declined by 23 per cent.

The period from 1980 to 2000 annihilated import substitution and replaced it with deregulation, privatisations, elimination of international trade barriers and full openness to foreign investments. The transition was from an inward-looking economy to an outward-looking one. The results indicate that the poorest countries went from a per capita growth rate of 1.9 per cent annually in the 1960–80 period, to a decline of 0.5 per cent a year between 1980 and 2000. The middle group of countries did worse, dropping from annual growth of 3.6 per cent to just under 1 per cent after 1980. The world's richest countries also showed a slowdown.

Countries such as South Korea and Taiwan, frequently given as examples to be emulated, achieved their development through trade barriers, state ownership of the big banks, export subsidies, violation of patents and intellectual property, and restrictions to capital flows, including direct foreign investment. It would be absolutely impossible for any country to replicate these strategies today without severely violating the regulations of the World Trade Organization (WTO) and the International Monetary Fund (IMF).

Myth 2: Greater integration into the world economy is good for the poor Poor countries must adapt to a number of rules and restrictions established by international organisations. The result is that poor countries divert human resources, administrative capacities and political capital away from more urgent development priorities such as education, public health and industrial capacity.

In 1965, the average per capita income of the G7 countries was twenty times that of the seven poorest countries. In 1995 it was thirty-nine times larger, and today it is over fifty times larger. In practically all developing countries that have adapted to rapid trade liberalisation, income inequality has increased, and real incomes have declined between 20 per cent and 30 per cent in Latin America.

Today, more than eighty countries have a lower real per capita income than one or two decades ago. The paradox is that precisely the more marginal countries are the ones that have integrated themselves more completely into the global economy.

Myth 3: Comparative advantage is the most efficient way to ensure a prosperous world One of the unquestioned principles of modern politics is the need for global free trade. To doubt its benefits is an act of heresy. However, in spite of its supposed greater efficiency, compared with other systems of economic organisation, global free trade is notoriously inefficient in real terms. By giving greater priority to large-scale production for export purposes, instead of to small- and medium-scale production for local needs, and by generating competitive pressures that confront communities the world over, the prices of consumer products may decrease, but at an enormous social and environmental expense.

There is still a dominant belief about the benefits of adhering to comparative advantages. However, according to the model of David Ricardo (creator of the concept), the system functions as long as there is no transnational mobility of capital. Internally, capital searches for the most adequate niche that gives it the comparative advantage. However, when capital is granted full transnational mobility, it will look for absolute advantages in countries that allow for lower salaries, lower taxes and fewer environmental regulations. As noted by John Gray (1998):

> When capital is (transnationally) mobile it will seek its absolute advantage by migrating to countries where the environmental and social costs of enterprises are lowest and profits are highest. Both in theory and practice, the effect of global capital mobility is to

nullify the Ricardian doctrine of comparative advantage. Yet it is on that flimsy foundation that the edifice of unregulated global free trade still stands.

Take an example: Nike Corporation (makers of footwear), in order to remain competitive, needs to reduce its standards. So it moves to Indonesia, where, through independent contractors, the shoes are made by young girls who are paid around 10 to 15 US cents per hour. As David Korten (1995) comments:

> Most of the outsourced production takes place in Indonesia, where a pair of Nikes that sells in the United States and Europe for $73 to $135 is produced for about $5.60 by girls and young women paid as little as fifteen cents an hour. The workers are housed in company barracks, there are no unions, overtime is often mandatory, and if there is a strike, the military may be called to break it up. The $20 million that basketball star Michael Jordan reportedly received in 1992 for promoting Nike shoes exceeded the entire annual payroll of the Indonesian factories that made them.

Myth 4: More globalisation means more jobs According to the International Labour Organization (ILO), one-third of the world's working force was unemployed or underemployed in 2000. The situation, as noted by the ILO, tends to deteriorate further.

Outsourcing, as described in the previous section (myth 3), is a necessity of the big corporations in order to remain competitive. It goes without saying that such a process generates unemployment in the place of origin, and underemployment in the country of arrival.

Myth 5: The World Trade Organization is democratic and accountable
> Many decisions affecting people's daily lives are being shifted away from local and national governments and are instead being made by a group of unelected trade bureaucrats sitting behind closed doors in Geneva. They are now empowered to dictate whether the EU has the right to ban the use of dangerous biotech materials in the food it imports, or whether people in California can prevent the destruction of their last virgin forests, or whether European countries have the right to ban cruelly-trapped fur (Lucas and Hines 2002).

According to the rules of the WTO, if a transnational corporation investing in a given country concludes that there are certain national laws or regulations considered to be inconvenient to its interests, the country is forced to abolish them, or adapt them to the satisfaction of the investor. This means that, under WTO rules, the race to the bottom (described in myth 3) is not only in social and environmental standards, but also in democracy itself.

The WTO has no rules whatsoever about child labour or workers' rights. Everything in its constitution is shaped to the advantage of corporations. During the discussions that gave origin to the WTO, known as the Uruguay Round, the controversial issue of intellectual property rights, for instance, was put on the agenda by thirteen major companies, including General Motors and Monsanto. In the negotiations that followed, ninety-six of the 111 members of the US delegation working on property rights were from the private sector. It should be obvious to conclude that the final agreement serves corporate interests and undermines poor people's access to knowledge and technology. A dramatic case in point is that poor countries are not allowed to produce their own inexpensive generic pharmaceutical products, but are forced to buy the ones produced, at much higher prices, by the pharmaceutical corporations. The consequences have been particularly tragic in the case of HIV in Africa, where corporate prices are far beyond the purchasing power of the great majority of the suffering population.

In short, the WTO should be recognised not for what we are told it is, but for what it really is: an institution whose main purpose is to make the corporations rule the world.

Myth 6: Globalisation is inevitable Renato Ruggiero, former director general of the WTO, used to say that 'trying to stop globalisation is tantamount to trying to stop the rotation of the earth'. Bill Clinton pointed out that: 'Globalisation is not a political option; it is a fact.' Tony Blair identified globalisation as 'irreversible and irresistible'. Margaret Thatcher immortalised the sentence 'There is no alternative.' All such statements are evidence of the degree of fundamentalism of the defenders of the system. As a result, the model amounts to a pseudo-religion.

Alternatives are obviously possible. The point is that the dominant model has been the product of the systematic renunciation, on the part of the majority of countries, of their right to control economic processes for their own benefit. Yet any condition that originates in political decisions is obviously reversible.

It may most probably be argued that any change would mean a choice between the present economic rules, on the one hand, and chaos on the other. This is, of course, absurd. A fundamental change could be an increased re-localisation of the economy, designing new rules that bring production and consumption nearer. A human-scale economy.

A new economy

A possible alternative is a new economy based on five postulates and one fundamental value principle:

- *Postulate 1*: The economy is to serve the people, and not the people to serve the economy.
- *Postulate 2*: Development is about people and not about objects.
- *Postulate 3*: Growth is not the same as development, and development does not necessarily require growth.
- *Postulate 4*: No economy is possible in the absence of ecosystem services.
- *Postulate 5*: The economy is a subsystem of a larger and finite system, the biosphere, hence permanent growth is impossible.
- *Value principle*: No economic interest, under any circumstance, can be above the reverence for life.

Going through the list, one point after the other, it is not difficult to conclude that what we have today is exactly the opposite. Yet it would be absurd to assume that an economy based on these postulates is not feasible. It is already being practised in many countries at the local, regional and municipal levels. The Swedish movement of eco-municipalities is a conspicuous case in point.

The most important contribution of a human-scale economy is that it may allow for the transition from a paradigm based on greed, competition and accumulation, to one based on solidarity, co-operation and compassion. Such a transition would allow for greater happiness not only among those who have been marginalised, but also among those responsible for those marginalisations, despite what they may believe.

Some of the new rules may include the following:

1 Establish monetary localisation, so that money flows and circulates as much as possible in its place of origin. It can be shown by economic models that if money circulates at least five times in its place of origin, it may generate a small economic boom.
2 Produce everything possible locally and regionally, in order to bring consumption closer to the market.
3 Protect local economies through tariffs and quotas.
4 Introduce local co-operation in order to avoid monopolies.
5 Impose ecological taxes on energy, pollution and other negatives. At present we are taxed for *goods* and not for *bads*.
6 Establish a greater democratic commitment to ensure effectiveness and equity in the transition to local economies.

Foundations of the new economy

Postulate 1: The economy is to serve the people, and not the people to serve the economy The effects of the outsourcing described in myth 3 illustrate a clear case of humans being used for economic interests. Any corporation that outsources its production according to the principles consecrated by the WTO produces unemployment in the place of origin and underemployment in the place of arrival. A great many cases of this sort could be listed.

More dramatic is the case of child and slave labour. It is unbelievable that today, in the twenty-first century, there are more slaves than there were before the abolition of slavery in the nineteenth century, at least two-thirds being children. The fact that such a situation does not even reach the news reveals the degree of perversity that the dominant economic model has been able to impose.

As noted by David Sirota (2009):

> Those of us pushing for serious trade policy reform have argued for years that businesses are aiming to create global economic policies that allow them to troll the world for the most exploitable forms of labor. As General Electric CEO Jack Welch famously said, corporations want laws that allow them to 'have every plant you own on a barge' – one that can move from country to country

looking for the worst conditions to exploit. Such an international economic regime would (and now does) allow the worst governments to create artificial comparative economic advantages through bad/immoral policies.

Global business has so far opposed every effort to put labour, environmental and human rights standards into the so-called 'free trade agreements', and is doing everything in its power to weaken the laws barring products made with child slave labour. It knows that the fewer rules exist, the more cost-cutting exploitation it can engage in, and that is what 'good business' is all about.

Postulate 2: Development is about people and not about objects In relation to this postulate, I quote extensively from my book *Human Scale Development* (Max-Neef 1991):

The acceptance of this postulate leads to the following fundamental question: How can we determine whether one development process is better than another? In the traditional paradigm, we have indicators such as the Gross Domestic Product (GDP) that is in a way an indicator of the quantitative growth of objects. Now we need an indicator of the qualitative growth of people. What should that be? Let us answer the question thus: The best development process will be that which allows the greatest improvement in people's quality of life (wellbeing). The next question is: What determines people's quality of life? Quality of life, or wellbeing, depends on the possibilities people have to adequately satisfy their fundamental human needs. A third question arises: What are those fundamental human needs, and/or who decides what they are?

It is traditionally believed that human needs tend to be infinite, that they change all the time, that they are different in each culture or environment and that they are different in each historical period. It is suggested here that such assumptions are inaccurate, since they are the product of a conceptual shortcoming.

A prevalent shortcoming in the existing literature and discussions about human needs is that the fundamental difference between needs and satisfiers of those needs is either not made explicit or is overlooked altogether. A clear distinction between both concepts is necessary.

Human needs must be understood as a system: that is, all human needs are interrelated and interactive. With the sole exception of the need of subsistence, that is, to remain alive, no hierarchies exist within the system. On the contrary, simultaneities, complementarities and trade-offs are characteristic of the process of needs satisfaction.

We have organized human needs into two categories: existential and axiological, which we have combined and displayed in a matrix [see Table 1.1]. This allows us to demonstrate the interaction of, on the one hand, the needs of Being, Having, Doing and Interacting; and, on the other hand, the needs of Subsistence, Protection Affection, Understanding, Participation, Idleness, Creation Identity and Freedom.

From the classification proposed, it follows that food and shelter, for example, must not be seen as needs, but as satisfiers of the fundamental need of Subsistence. In much the same way, education, study, investigation, early stimulation and meditation are satisfiers of the need for Understanding. Health schemes may be satisfiers of the need for Protection.

There is no one-to-one correspondence between needs and satisfiers. A satisfier may contribute simultaneously to the satisfaction of different needs or, conversely, a need may require various satisfiers in order to be met. For example, a mother breastfeeding her baby is simultaneously satisfying the infant's needs for Subsistence, Protection, Affection and Identity. The situation is obviously different if the baby is fed in a more mechanical fashion where only the need for Subsistence would be satisfied.

We can now add two principles. First: Fundamental human needs are finite, few and classifiable. Second: Fundamental human needs are the same in all cultures and in all historical periods. What changes, both over time and through cultures, are not the needs, but the way or the means by which the needs are satisfied.

It must be added that needs are satisfied within three contexts: a) with regard to oneself (Eigenwelt); b) with regard to the social group or community (Mitwelt); and c) with regard to the environment (Umwelt).

It should be the purpose of every political, social and economic

TABLE 1.1 Matrix of needs and satisfers

Needs	Being (qualities)	Having (things)	Doing (actions)	Interacting (settings)
Subsistence	Physical, emotional and mental health	Food, shelter, work	Work, feed, procreate, clothe, rest/sleep	Living environment, social setting
Protection	Care, adaptability, autonomy	Social security, health systems, rights, family, work	Co-operate, plan, prevent, help, cure, take care of	Living space, social environment, dwelling
Affection	Respect, tolerance, sense of humour, generosity, sensuality	Friendships, family, relationships with nature	Share, take care of, make love, express emotions	Privacy, intimate spaces of togetherness
Understanding	Critical capacity, receptivity, curiosity, intuition	Literature, teachers, educational and communication policies	Analyse, study, meditate, investigate	Schools, families, universities, communities
Participation	Adaptability, receptivity, dedication, sense of humour	Responsibilities, duties, work, rights, privileges	Co-operate, propose, dissent, express opinions	Associations, parties, churches, neighbourhoods
Idleness	Imagination, curiosity, tranquillity, spontaneity	Games, parties, spectacles, clubs, peace of mind	Daydream, play, remember, relax, have fun	Landscapes, intimate spaces, places to be alone, free time
Creation	Imagination, boldness, curiosity, inventiveness, autonomy, determination	Skills, work, abilities, method, techniques	Invent, build, design, work, compose, interpret	Spaces for expression, workshops, audiences, cultural groups
Identity	Sense of belonging, self-esteem, consistency	Symbols, language, religion, values, work, customs, norms, habits, historical memory	Get to know oneself, grow, commit oneself, recognise oneself	Places one belongs to, everyday settings, maturation stage
Freedom	Autonomy, passion, self-esteem, open-mindedness, tolerance	Equal rights	Dissent, choose, run risks, develop awareness, be different from, disobey	Temporal/spatial plasticity (anywhere)

Note: The matrix does not contain any material elements. So, in the 'Having' column, there are no objects, only principles, institutions, norms, traditions, etc. In conventional economics we have two links: wants and goods. In human-scale development theory we have three links: needs, satisfiers and goods. For instance, there is the need of Understanding, whose satisfier is literature, whose good is a book.

system to generate the conditions for people to adequately satisfy their fundamental human needs. This is a paramount condition if a new economy is to be coherent with the problems of the twenty-first century.

Postulate 3: Growth is not the same as development, and development does not necessarily require growth It is generally assumed that the more an economy grows, the more successful it is. The main indicator is, of course, the GDP, on the behaviour of which political decisions are made. A possible formula for the indicator is:

GDP = C + Y + Gex + X – I

Where C is consumption, Y is investment, Gex are government expenditures, X is exports and I is imports. It thus represents the flux of goods and services that are traded in the market through producers and consumers.

GDP has a number of shortcomings that are normally not taken into consideration when it comes to policy-making. First, everything is added, regardless of whether the impacts are positive or negative. The costs of traffic accidents or of diseases are added in the same way as investments in infrastructure or education. There is no difference between goods and bads. Second, it does not include the value of unpaid work, thus discriminating against household and voluntary work, which are fundamental in a society. Third, it considers only that which can be expressed in monetary terms. Fourth, nature and ecosystem services have no value at all.

If one considers such limitations, it is obvious that no assessment of quality of life or welfare can be made using GDP. If we accept what has already been proposed, that development is about people and not about objects, and that that development is best where the quality of life improves the most, we must look for a different indicator – an indicator that should disaggregate GDP into two accounts: a national benefits account and a national costs account.

A number of studies concerning this problem were carried out by the author and colleagues some twenty years ago in different countries, using the human needs matrices in order to assess quality of life and/or welfare. In the process certain unexpected evidence began to show up, which led us to propose what we called 'a threshold

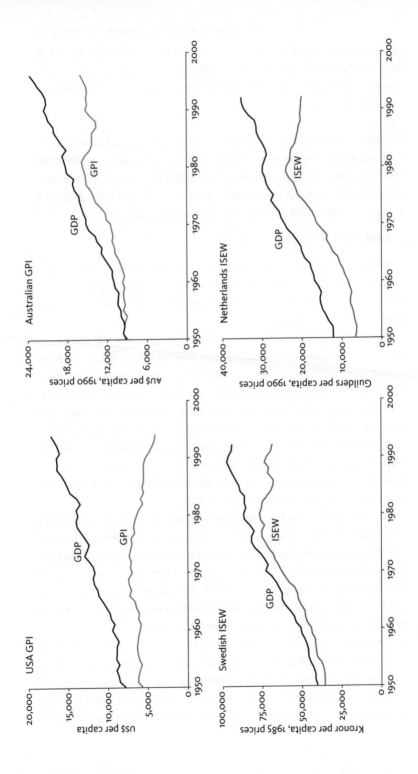

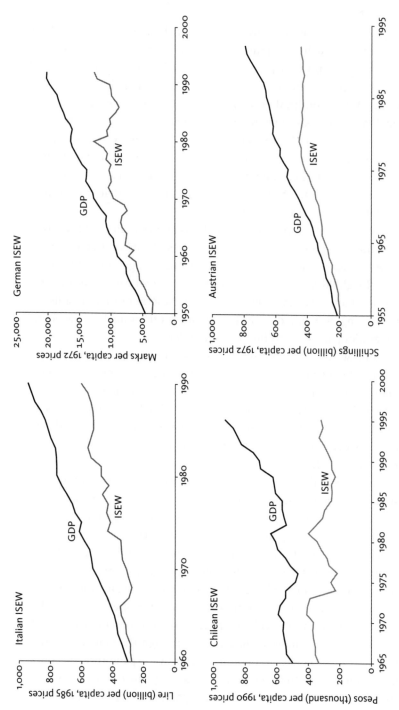

1.1 Genuine Progress Indicators (GPIs) and Indices of Sustainable Economic Welfare (ISEWs) for selected countries (*source:* Friends of the Earth UK: www.foe.co.uk/community/tools/isew/international.html).

hypothesis' stating that: 'In every society there is a period in which economic growth contributes to an improvement of the quality of life, but only up to a point, the threshold point, beyond which if there is more economic growth, quality of life may begin to deteriorate.' A few months after we proposed the hypothesis, based on our qualitative analysis, a study was published by Daly and Cobb (1989) in which a new indicator was proposed – the Index of Sustainable Economic Welfare – where positives and negatives are disaggregated. Applied to the United States for the period 1950–90, it shows a parallel increase with GDP up to 1970, and a decline after that year despite a continuous increase in GDP.

As a result of our proposed hypothesis and Daly and Cobb's paper, a number of groups organised themselves in different countries in order to repeat the studies using the methodology of the US paper. The threshold began to appear in practically all cases, provoking a great debate between many economists. Several of them dismissed the findings as methodological errors, while others made constructive suggestions in order to improve the index.

After twenty years, improvements have been made, and the indicator has changed its name, becoming the Genuine Progress Indicator. Many more studies have been carried out that confirm the threshold. Although there are still some economists who dismiss the results, it can be stated that the threshold hypothesis is a robust hypothesis that has become fundamental in the field of ecological economics. Results for eight countries can be seen in Figure 1.1.

If we accept that the threshold hypothesis is coherent with reality, some significant changes should be expected in development theory.

The fundamental question is: how does the economy function before the threshold point and how does it function after that point? Much analysis is still required, but a few assumptions can already be made. For instance, if there is poverty in a country that has not reached its threshold, it is legitimate to point out that in order to overcome poverty more growth is necessary. However, after the threshold, such arguments no longer hold up, because the economy has reached a point at which the costs of growth outweigh the benefits. In the language of ecological economics, defensive expenditures become dominant. Hence the overcoming of poverty must be the result of specific policies addressed to that purpose, since growth alone can no longer do the trick. We can identify the pre-threshold period as a quantitative economy and the post-threshold as a qualitative economy. Economic laws that function in one segment no longer function in the same way in the other segment. Much is still to be done and investigated in order to fully understand the characteristics of post-threshold economies.

Postulate 4: No economy is possible in the absence of ecosystem services It is disturbing that the economy that is still being taught in most universities represents a system closed within itself that has no relations with any other system. It is just a flow of goods and services, through the market, between firms and families, expressed in monetary terms, which has no relationship with the environment, and which ignores the physical impacts and consequences of economic activity.

As a matter of fact, if one goes through the index at the end of any of the most important textbooks of economic theory, words such as 'ecosystem', 'biosphere', 'nature' and 'thermodynamic laws' are nowhere to be found.

Figure 1.2 represents the economy as it is taught and understood in conventional economic thinking.

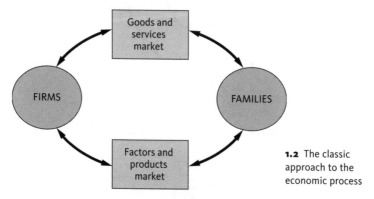

1.2 The classic approach to the economic process

Circular flow of money in a closed system that does not have relations with the environment and ignores the physical consequences of economic activity

Figure 1.3 represents the economy as it is interpreted and understood according to ecological economics.

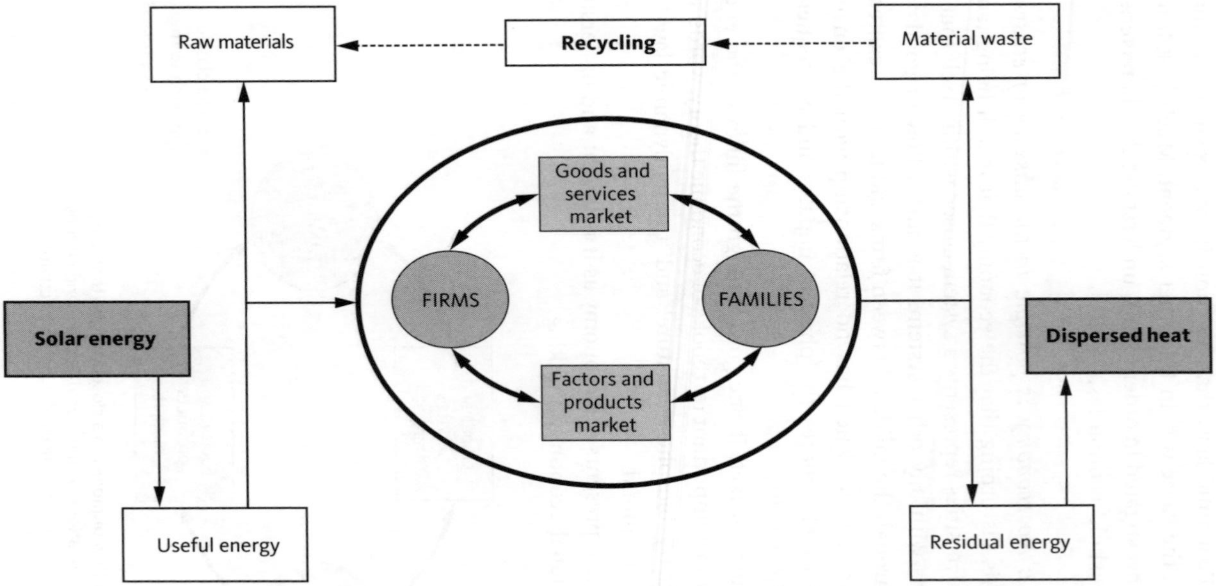

Raw materials
Recycling
Material waste
Goods and services market
FIRMS
FAMILIES
Factors and products market
Solar energy
Dispersed heat
Useful energy
Residual energy

1.3 The ecological economic approach

While the economy depends on services provided by the biosphere – such as the supply of energy and materials, and the capacity to absorb residues and the maintenance of biodiversity – at the same time it produces impacts on the biosphere in terms of dispersed energy, degraded materials, pollution and residues, an increase of entropy, global warming and, as a consequence, climate change. This being the case, it is high time that economists developed a systemic vision of economic processes and their relations with all those components of the biosphere that are responsible for the maintenance of life.

There are ten planetary boundaries (Rockström et al. 2009), all of which are affected by economic activity. They are: climate change, rate of biodiversity loss, nitrogen cycle, phosphorous cycle, stratospheric ozone depletion, ocean acidification, global fresh water use, change in land use, atmospheric aerosol loading, and chemical pollution. Of these ten boundaries, three have dangerously crossed their acceptable limits. In relation to climate change, the proposed boundary of carbon dioxide concentration (parts per million by volume) is 350 and the current status is 387, while the pre-industrial value was 280. In addition, the proposed boundary for change in radiative forcing (watts per square metre) is 1.0 and the current status is 1.5, while the pre-industrial change was 0.0. In relation to biodiversity loss, the proposed boundary for extinction rate (number of species per million species per year) is 10 and the current status is over 100, while the pre-industrial rate was 0.1 to 1.0. With regard to the nitrogen cycle, the proposed boundary for the amount of molecular nitrogen removed from the atmosphere for human use (millions of tonnes per year) is 35 and the current status is 121, while the pre-industrial amount was zero. The remaining boundaries are slowly approaching their limits as well.

This being the case, it is inconceivable that such fundamental conditions for the maintenance of life – conditions that are deeply affected by economic processes – are totally absent in the economics curricula. This is the result of the absurdity that in the twenty-first century, facing problems that have no historical precedent, we are still teaching nineteenth-century economic theories as if there were no alternatives. No surprise that there are so many economists doing marvellous abstractions with their economic models, but who do not understand the real world in which we are living.

Postulate 5: The economy is a subsystem of a larger and finite system, the biosphere, hence permanent growth is impossible Sustainability is essentially a matter of scale. That means that we must accept that we have only one planet that is finite, within a biosphere that is also finite. If in addition we recognise that anything and everything we produce can be reduced to an amount of land necessary to produce it, then the question that must be answered is: what amount of renewable and non-renewable ecologically productive land area do we need in order to support the resource demands and to absorb the wastes of a given population or specific activities? The answer is the ecological footprint, which, as a consequence of years of analysis and calculations, reveals that in order to maintain the resilience of our planet we must not go beyond 1.8 hectares per person. Yet, as Figure 1.4 shows, we have one planet, but in 1986 we crossed the threshold and are, at this stage, using one planet and a quarter. This means, among other things, that the renewable resources we use in twelve months are regenerated by nature in eighteen months. That is obviously not sustainable.

Despite this evidence, which is known to economists, we continue with more of the same. There is no doubt that the great Kenneth Boulding was right when he said that 'those who believe that economic growth can go on forever in a finite planet are either mad or are economists'.

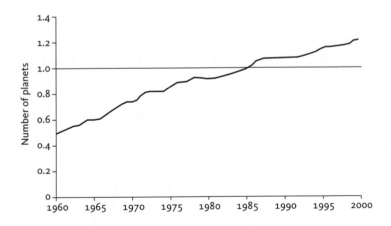

1.4 Humanity's ecological footprint, 1961–2001

It is not only the ecological footprint that shows that we are already overdrawn. If we evaluate economic processes in terms of energy units, instead of monetary units, we reach similar conclusions. If we know what the land budget per person is, we now need to know what the energy budget per person should be.

Searching for the answer, I proposed years ago the name ecoson (an abbreviation of ECOlogical perSON) for the per capita energy budget. At the time it was not clear to me how to calculate it. The answer came from German physicists Ziegler (1992) and Dürr (1993), who, using the loss of biodiversity as a consequence of human impact on a given ecosystem as an indicator for environmental over-stress, suggested a *critical value of anthropogenic primary energy flow per unit area and time* that should not be surpassed of about:

$$14 \pm 2 \text{ GJ/km}^2 \text{ day} = 160 \pm 20 \text{ kW/km}^2 = 0.16 \text{ W/m}^2$$

An appropriate extrapolation yields that an anthropogenic world throughput of primary energy of 9 terawatts is the limit in order not to exceed the carrying capacity of the biosystem of the Earth. These 9 terawatts amount to 20 per cent of the natural flow of the energy of the sun that goes through the continental biosystem.

If we divide 9 terawatts by 6 billion inhabitants, what we get is:

$$1 \text{ ecoson} = 1.5 \text{ kW/h/pp or } 13{,}000 \text{ kW/h/yr/pp}$$

which is the energy budget per person that should not be surpassed in order not to exceed the carrying capacity of the biosystem.

The main importance of establishing the ecoson is that we can reconceptualise some demographic considerations, showing that: 1 person is not = 1 person. If we classify all countries according to their per capita income, what we get is shown in Table 1.2.

The first line shows all countries with per capita income below US$1,000, which amount to a total population of 390 million people yet only 13 million ecosons, meaning that those inhabitants are far below the 1.5 kilowatt energy budget. The first three lines represent countries with more people than ecosons, whereas in the next three lines the situation is reversed and we have countries with more ecosons than people. Of all countries, the one with the greatest gap between people and ecosons is the United States: with 300 million inhabitants, it has almost 4,000 million ecosons.

TABLE 1.2 World population, per capita income and number of ecosons

Income (US$)	Population (millions)	Ecosons (thousands)
<1,000	390	13,000
1,000–1,999	1,370	274,000
2,000–3,999	1,920	1,152,000
4,000–7,999	840	1,624,000
8,000–15,999	240	528,000
≥16,000	760	3,851,000

What is the importance of all this? It can be explained in very simple terms: the baby just born in Boston Central Hospital is not the same as the baby just born in a hut in Sierra Leone. They are not the same because their weight in terms of impact on the biosphere will be dramatically different. In fact, one American baby may be equivalent to ten or fifteen Sierra Leone babies. Hence, if we are concerned with sustainability, it is much more important to know, for each country, the number of ecosons, because they represent the true weight of the population. To illustrate how dramatic this new way of understanding demography is, Table 1.3 shows the true size of the United States in comparison with other countries.

TABLE 1.3 The real size of the United States

Country	Ecosons (thousands)	USA/p
USA	1,938,956,000	
India	206,540,000	9.4
China	696,591,000	2.8
Indonesia	56,973,000	34.0
Brazil	99,224,000	19.6

The United States, with its 300,000,000 inhabitants, is nine times bigger than India, three times bigger than China, and so on. It follows that, for conventional economics, India and China are much bigger than the United States. However, when seen from the perspective of ecological economics, the United States is immensely larger than India and China. For those who favour population control, the message should be to control not people but ecosons.

The calculations reveal that 6,000,000,000 ecosons is the global energy budget in order not to upset the carrying capacity of our biosystem. According to available statistical information, the present global energy consumption amounts to 8,000,000,000 ecosons. Therefore, just as in the case of the ecological footprint, here again we detect an overdraft of 30 per cent; that is, we are living on 1.3 planets, but we have only one.

To evaluate economic processes in terms of energy instead of money is much more revealing if our concern is sustainability.

Value principle: No economic interest, under any circumstance, can be above the reverence for life No examples are required. The degree to which this fundamental principle is systematically violated is so overwhelming that one can only hope that, after a probable gigantic catastrophe provoked by the insistence on more of the same, a dramatic cultural shift may occur – one that leads us from an anthropocentric world of greed, competition and accumulation to a biocentric world of solidarity, co-operation and compassion with all forms of life.

Notes

1 This chapter is reprinted from Manfred Max-Neef's 2010 article 'The world on a collision course and the need for a new economy', published in *AMBIO: A Journal of the Human Environment* 39(3): 200–10, and available online at www.ncbi.nlm.nih.gov/pmc/issues/210334/.

2 Ideas for this section have been taken from Mander (2007).

3 Pieces of information for this section have been taken from Lucas and Hines (2002).

References

Daly, H. and J. Cobb (1989) *For the Common Good: Redirecting the economy toward community, the environment, and a sustainable future*. Boston, MA: Beacon Press.

Dürr, H.-P. (1993) 'Sustainable, equitable economics – the personal energy budget'. In P. B. Smith, S. Okoye, J. de Wilde and P. Deshingkar (eds), *The World at the Crossroads: Towards a sustainable, equitable and liveable world. A report to the Pugwash Council*. London: Earthscan Publications.

Gray, J. (1998) *False Dawn: The delusions of global capitalism*. London: Granta.

Korten, D. (1995) *When Corporations Rule the World*. West Hartford, CT: Kumarian Press.

Lucas, C. and C. Hines (2002) 'Time to replace globalisation: a green localist manifesto for the World Trade Organization Ministerial'. The Greens/European Free Alliance in the European Parliament.

Mander, J. (ed.) (2007) *Manifesto on Global Economic Transitions*. San Francisco, CA: International Forum on Globalization.

Max-Neef, M. (1991) *Human Scale*

Development: Conception, application and further reflections. New York, NY: The Apex Press.

Rockström, J., W. Steffen, K. Noone et al. (2009) 'Planetary boundaries: exploring the safe operating space for humanity'. Ecology and Society 14(2): 32. www.ecologyandsociety.org/vol14/iss2/art32/.

Sirota, D. (2009) 'Business Aims to Relax Bans on Products Made with Child & Slave Labor'. World News Daily website. www.informationclearinghouse.info/article23951.htm.

Ziegler, W. (1992) 'Zur Tragfähigkeit ökologischer Systeme'. Wissenschaftliche Zeitschrift der Technische Universität Dresden 41: 17–20.

2 | THE NEW ECONOMY

Neva Goodwin

As human economies have overshot the capacity of the ecosphere to serve our demands and absorb our wastes, it is becoming necessary to figure out how a non-growing – even a shrinking – economy can still provide human well-being, while beginning to restore the health of the natural world. Twentieth-century economic theory is not well able to conceptualise this problem, especially since it sees well-being dependent on income, income dependent on jobs, and jobs dependent on growth. What changes are needed in theory for the twenty-first century if the economics profession is to make positive contributions to conceptualising and realising the needed changes?

Introduction

Prices affect our lives in many ways, often very significantly. People tend to associate that fact with two beliefs: prices are set by markets; and only markets should set prices. I am going to argue that markets, in fact, don't do a very good job of setting some of the prices that are most important in our lives; and that other social forces should, and can, take more intentional control in some areas of some price-setting.

This conclusion is not quite as radical as it sounds, for in reality many prices are already set by a much more complex set of factors than just market-determined supply and demand. The reason why we are not generally aware of this is that our perceptions are shaped by an economic theory that has gone too far in defining a particular kind of ideal economy, and then in setting out what we must and must not do – or believe – for this ideal to be realised. Which, in fact, it never is.

When you want to make sense of a really knotted tangle, you need to figure out which threads to pull on. I will list the intertwined issues I have been trying to unscramble in thinking about the new economy, and then I will take hold of the threads that seem to me most likely to lead to constructive new ways of understanding.

1 First of all is the issue of scale in the relation between economic activity and ecological health. The global economy has probably gone beyond a scale of economic activity that is ecologically sustainable, let alone beginning on the long job of ecological restoration. This suggests the need to find an alternative to growth as a goal, especially for the rich countries.

2 Next, there is the relation between economic activity and human well-being on the consumption side – raising the questions of what kinds of outputs contribute to human well-being, and how to refocus economic activity, including systems of production, towards an enhancement of well-being.

3 With regard to the relation between technology and work, the burning questions are: will technology raise labour productivity, hence wages, faster than they are reduced by resource degradation and depletion? And will technology in concert with a shrinking economy reduce the number of jobs that are needed?

4 Next comes the relation between work and well-being in a reoriented, post-growth economy. What, aside from a pay cheque, are the values of work? Are there goals other than full employment that should be considered? What is the importance of leisure in our rethinking of work and well-being?

5 The huge, unexpected demographic shift that is taking place is a slowing of population growth, followed by a reversal into population decline. This is predictable or already under way in much of the world.

6 With all of these complex interrelations in mind, the great practical challenge for all of us is to work out the least painful – maybe even the most exciting – ways of making the transition from existing economic systems to systems that are socially and environmentally just, sustainable and satisfying. If we do not manage to plan an orderly U-turn from our present growth dependence, the result will be ecological – hence economic and social – disaster on an almost unimaginable scale. To quote the subtitle of Peter Victor's path-breaking book on the subject, our best hope is 'slower by design, not disaster' (Victor 2008). In stating this challenge I both

suggest the basic elements of the new economy – it must be *socially and environmentally just, sustainable and satisfying* – and implicitly state why we need it: because these words do not characterise the economy we have now.

For the long run, the scale of the economy is the most critical element on this list, but you can't get to the long run in one jump, even when this long run is not so very far away – it will occur not only in the lives of our children and grandchildren, but probably also in our own lives. To get there, conceptually and practically, I believe that we have to go through some short-term issues around work. But these, too, have been very hard to get a grip on because of the theoretic assumptions pulling against us.

Again, I want to emphasise that, while the theoretical issues are relevant for the whole world, the practical conclusions and suggestions I draw later will be addressed expressly to the rich countries. Some of the suggestions will also be relevant for developing countries, but in many ways their circumstances are so different that this would all need to be rewritten quite substantially in order to address their situation.

Scale and growth – or not?

Let us start by considering the idea that we need to reduce greatly the throughput of materials and energy in the global economy – recognising that this will probably mean a reduction in economic growth, at least as we now understand that term. A cessation of economic growth, as it is now measured and understood, may be expected to come about through a combination of two principal factors:

1   On the demand side, unless technology can provide an extraordinarily dramatic rescue operation, products, and the physical inputs (including energy) required to make them, will become more expensive relative to incomes from work. This will be the result of ecological constraints making themselves felt through rising resource costs and/or through deliberate social action designed to prevent the depletion and degradation of valuable, scarce resources. It would likely result in a decline in wages, and hence in effective household demand.

2 On the supply side – specifically in relation to the supply of labour
   – in most of the world demographic shifts will shrink the proportion of the population that is of working age relative to those who
   are too old or too young to work.

Some possible outcomes for jobs and incomes In terms of jobs and
incomes, there are several quite different outcomes that could be
traced from the unfolding of these factors (Table 2.1).

TABLE 2.1 Six possible scenarios

	Plenty of jobs	Not enough jobs
Reduced productivity of labour	A) Wages go down; general decline in GDP	B1) Job-sharing: a generalised decline in material standards of living B2) No job-sharing: some do well, while most suffer severe reductions in their standards of living
Technology rescues labour productivity	C) Wages remain about the same; GDP changes little (however, demographic shifts may lower per capita GDP – hence lower household incomes)	D1) Job-sharing: standards of living may stay flat or decline D2) No job-sharing: some do very well, while others suffer the effects of unemployment

Source: Neva Goodwin.

There might be enough jobs available for all or most of those
who want them; or there might be a decreased market demand for
labour, resulting in either massive unemployment or job-sharing
(whether this is achieved through a growth in co-operatives or by
some other means). A decline in resource quality and quantity might
make labour less productive, resulting in lower wages;[1] or technology might come to the rescue, maintaining or increasing labour
productivity, and therefore not reducing labour income. Scenario
C, in which technology rescues labour productivity without cutting
jobs, is the one that most people would hope for – although, as I
will discuss at the end of the chapter, scenario D1, with reduced work
hours, could also be very appealing. Frankly, though, I am not very
optimistic about technology rescuing productivity. Even if it does,

there is also the issue of whether a reduced workforce, relative to the total population, can maintain per capita output at today's levels.

Issues of resource scarcity and quality

However, I will start from a different perspective, with a few remarks on the potential for a technological rescue in terms supplied by Howard Brown, one of the most optimistic business people I know, and one of the smartest. He co-founded a company called dMASS, Inc. – a name that refers to the reduction of resource mass through design. The goal of dMASS is naked value. *Naked Value* – the name of the excellent short book he wrote with two of his colleagues – is defined as 'the essence that remains in a product or service after stripping away all unneeded resources. It's the pure benefit customers seek, without waste and without material resources that don't contribute to wealth or well-being' (Brown et al. 2012: 3). The reason why it is so important to concentrate on naked value is that the world is facing lower quantities and inferior quality of many essential resources. The British Geological Survey now publishes a 'Risk List' ranking fifty-two economically important elements based on the risk that the supply will not be able to meet current expectations and patterns of use, and a recent McKinsey report states:

> A number of factors are conspiring to create a risk that we might be entering a new era of high and volatile prices over the next two decades. Up to three billion people could join the middle class, boosting demand at a time when obtaining new resources could become more difficult and costly. The stress on the resource system is likely to be compounded by increasing links between resources that mean that price shocks in one can swiftly transmit to others. In addition, environmental deterioration, driven by higher consumption, is making the supply of resources – particularly food – more vulnerable (Dobbs et al. 2011).

As Richard Heinberg explains in his book *The End of Growth*:

> When the quality of an ore drops the amount of energy required to extract the resource rises. All over the world mining companies are reporting declining ore quality. So in many if not most cases it is no longer possible to substitute a rare, depleting resource

with a more abundant, cheaper resource; instead the available substitutes are themselves already rare and depleting (Heinberg 2011: 161).

Howard Brown similarly notes that:

Growing demand in the face of constrained supplies creates resource price volatility and conflict over unreliable supplies. So, while your markets grow, and perhaps demand for your products grows, the resources you need to operate your business become more expensive and less accessible (Brown et al. 2012: 310).

The good news from Brown is that there are technological and smart-thinking solutions that will make it possible to shrink the throughput of materials and energy in our economies while improving the functionality of the total output. He says: 'For any business today, the central goal should be figuring out how to deliver the benefits people need in new ways with as little resource mass as possible' (ibid.: 36). And he cites as examples companies that are 'developing products that deliver light without light bulbs, portable power without batteries, warmth without thick insulation or boilers, bacteria-safe surfaces without chemicals, and clean clothes without detergent' (ibid.: 4–5). The less good news from McKinsey is that:

the capital needed each year to create a resource revolution will rise from roughly $2 trillion today to more than $3 trillion. However, the benefits could be as high as $3.7 trillion a year if carbon had a price of $30 per tonne and governments removed substantial resource subsidies and taxes. Even this would not be sufficient to prevent global warming and provide universal access to resources, which could cost in the region of another $350 billion a year (Dobbs et al. 2011).

Environmentalists such as Heinberg assume that the rich world will need to greatly reduce its consumption. Brown's optimistic twist on this is that, yes, we will need to reduce greatly the use of materials and energy used in production, but it will be possible to end up producing equal or better outcomes for consumers. The McKinsey report similarly assumes that the technology is there, if the money and the will can be found. As for whether any of this means an end to economic growth as we know it, that may depend on how we measure growth. Maybe consumers will consent to spend as much on the naked value of oral hygiene without the packaging and materials now used for a tube of toothpaste. However, if the reduction in input mass occurs faster than the rise in input costs, the net result will be reduced production costs. Then market competition should bring down the price for which this good – or service – can sell.

We thus have a picture that is both attractive and scary: our economies might retain or increase their ability to produce what people want, but less money will change hands as businesses spend less on inputs, and consumers spend less to get the real values they seek. The alternative is a picture that is scary but unattractive: businesses do not manage to reorient their conception of the naked value they are selling, or do not manage to reduce sufficiently the energy and materials required to produce that value, and a shift away from growth occurs, not because of human cleverness, but because of binding ecological constraints.

The meaning for economic theory – and production

Without trying to predict which path will be taken, I will now consider the issues for economic theory that arise when contemplating the likelihood of the required major changes in economic systems occurring. This will not be as boring as you might expect; the relationship between theory and reality is dramatically overdue for a realignment. In the twentieth century, economic theory, regardless of its realism, was allowed to direct policies – some self-fulfilling, and some disastrously different from their announced intentions. We must move to a theory that not only is based on observed reality, but also pays attention to what kind of economy is necessary, possible and desirable.

Therefore the first challenge to the old economic theory is the question: what are the goals for the economy? The existing theory claims no overt goals, but it has implicit ones: economic growth, for macro-economics; and maximisation of consumption, for micro-economics. Second is the critical point that the scale of an economy must not exceed its supporting ecosystem. This is related to the third point: that an economy is embedded in and completely dependent on its ecological and social context. The economy is a subsystem of a human social system; and that, in turn, is a subsystem of the ecological context. Each of these systems affects, and is affected by, the others.

Those first three points relate to how we think about the economy. The next point is about action as much as it is about theory. The requirement for a transition to a post-growth economy begins with constraints on supplies of goods and services. It is critical, at this juncture, for humanity to join with nature in restricting those products whose production requires a throughput of the kinds of materials and energy that are ecologically damaging, or that are becoming depleted in ways that threaten future ecological and economic sustainability. This is not a new idea: there are always supply constraints, which normally feed, through markets, into prices. What I am talking about, however, is not adequately recognised in twentieth-century economic theory. It is about constraints that are based on projections regarding limitations that will be more binding in the future than they are now. Such projections are well documented in scientific literature, but they are not translating adequately into current prices: the various futures markets are either too short-sighted, or not knowledgeable enough, or not powerful enough to perform this translation. Therefore, a major challenge to economic theory that will emerge from this situation is the question of how to insert scientific knowledge of future constraints into short-term behaviour, when market-derived price signals have proven inadequate to do so.

Using prices to achieve goals

A proposal to set prices by something other than market mechanisms, although breathtakingly heretical in the current economic ideology, is not, of course, really new in the history of Western economics. As one example, during World War II, John Kenneth Galbraith oversaw a system of price controls designed to ensure that priority would be given to resources that were needed for the war effort.

That heresy of Galbraith's was significantly different from John Maynard Keynes' earlier argument that the federal government must act as a major generator of demand, for labour and for the products of labour. The Keynes era, which is reluctantly (but increasingly) accepted by modern economists as a rational response to severe economic recession, was similar to the present in two important respects: it accepted without question the desirability of economic growth; and it supported this growth through the market, using government as an engine of demand. The government accepted responsibility for increasing the demand for labour, with a resulting increase in household income. Markets responded to rising household incomes, hence rising consumer demand, with price signals that enticed investors and producers to increase their activity.

The Galbraith price-control system, in contrast, could be said to have overridden the market, rather than using it – and for this reason it is hardly remembered today as part of economic history. While Galbraith did not at that time imagine a situation when it might be necessary or desirable to end or reverse economic growth as we know it,[2] he was notable for his casual attitude towards the markets – compared with the reverence accorded them by, for example, Milton Friedman and his disciples. Galbraith did not see any reason to believe that markets would generate the prices needed to direct production appropriately, at least not within the urgent time frame required for the war effort. Among the things that Galbraith and Keynes did share, however, was the broad recognition that market prices can generate suboptimal results, whether in terms of a national aim, such as war production, or in terms of maintaining the level of demand for output that would ensure full employment.

A third example of price-setting outside the markets is perhaps even more telling, as it continues into the present, with little attention paid to the fact that critical prices are being determined by other-than-market forces. Countries that decide to increase exports and decrease imports regularly regard the exchange rate of their currency as a tool for persuading their citizens and people in other countries to change their buying patterns. This may fail if the country in question is inflation-prone, but otherwise it often succeeds in changing the price of the currency as desired. The alternatives to a central government taking charge of a country's exchange rate are either to simply peg the exchange to some other currency – in recent years a number of Latin American currencies have been pegged to the US dollar – or to allow it to 'float'. The latter is, indeed, a choice to leave the decision to international markets; but, for strong economies, some degree of currency manipulation is an accepted way of influencing prices.

The point of these examples is simply to illustrate that the magic of the market is not always sufficient, without strong guidance, to achieve desired results through internally generated price signals. That observation challenges the economic theories of the twentieth century, which, ignoring examples such as these, maintained a never-meddle-with-the-market ideology.

This raises the next great challenge to an economic theory that, for most of the twentieth century, has claimed to be value-free. Using markets as well as other means, we need to find ways to set prices that will appropriately recognise human values, including equity, ecological realities, and present and future needs.

Twentieth-century economics' claim to a purely objective, value-free theory has worn very thin. The theory, as taught in universities and as used in policy-making, implicitly accepted the goal of maximising efficiency, so that the pursuit of self-interest could deploy the available resources to achieve '*the most desired results*'. Please note the values assumed in 'most desired'. The phrase raises the question: desired by whom? There is an answer to that question: when efficiency is pursued through the price system, the only kinds of self-interested motives that the system works to maximise are those that go through the market – specifically, the consumer's desire to make purchases and the producer's desire to make profits. Only these desires – *and only if they are backed up by money*, which allows the economic actor to participate in the market – benefit from the efficiency characteristics of the system. In the 'one-dollar, one-vote' price system, the market minimises recognition of the needs, wants and values of those who have few dollars with which to express them. Since standard economic theory has no way of formally recognising the validity of needs and wants that cannot achieve market expression, the emphasis on efficiency crowds out attention to issues of equity.

I am making the claim that markets cannot always be left alone to set prices that are fair, that take account of the future, that will guide human behaviour to desired results, or that adequately reflect human values. There is an automatic response to this: at least the market is objective; if we step outside the market to set prices, who will choose between subjective values? I have proposed some preliminary answers to this. First, market prices are not simply objective: they reflect the wishes of the rich and powerful much more than those of the poor; and, second, the government is an appropriate meddler in markets in times of national emergency, such as war, deep recession or economic catastrophe, present or future, or in subjects of broad national interest such as exchange rates.

I will go beyond this, however, to talk about a particular kind of price: wages. This topic turns out to be the essential background for understanding how an economic system that is ecologically sustainable – that is, a post-growth economy – can provide good lives for people. The conundrum that is often the stopping point for this conversation is the perceived need for economic growth in order to keep providing enough jobs.

Work

The topic of 'jobs' is a subset of the topic of 'work', which is, in fact, a much larger topic. Not all work is done in a context that is defined as a job: some of the most important work, for the survival and well-being of our species, is done without pay, in homes and communities, where children are raised and care is given to major aspects of people's socialisation, health, rest, comfort and entertainment. Therefore, I will pay some attention to the broad subject of work before getting to its subset of jobs.

There are two essential keys to a good, post-growth society: the issues of how work is rewarded, and how children and others who cannot work are supported. Social democratic societies in northern Europe provide plenty of good models for achieving the second essential. At this point, I will take a detour from theory to focus on the first critical issue – how work is rewarded.

Work has three main positive functions:

• It provides an income for the worker, when the work is done as a job with a wage or salary attached.
• It creates goods and services that are valuable for those who use them. (In the case of paid work, users are often referred to as consumers; users of the outputs of unpaid work constitute a varied category, with no standard name, and sometimes include the worker, for example in the case of food produced for household use.)

- Work itself can have positive meaning for the worker, whether because it is done with other people, creating positive relationships, or because the worker enjoys the feeling of 'a job well done', or is happy to be producing something of value to others, or because it satisfies creative urges. (Standard economic analysis treats work itself as bad – something that people do only out of necessity.)

Not all work has all three of these functions: it may create valuable goods and services, or provide positive meaning to the worker, with or without generating income for the worker; and it may generate income while producing nothing of value, or while being a net psychic negative for the worker. For at least a century economics students have been told that the only relevant reward to labour is the wage. That is the first error: important though wages are, work has other positive rewards that should not be neglected. The second error is in fitting our understanding of wages entirely within standard price theory, with the neat intersection of supply and demand put forward as *the* determinant. To be sure, it is one important determinant, but many other elements intervene to affect why one type of work, or one type of worker, receives a higher wage than another. The third error is to ignore the large amount of economically and socially important work that is done without the lure of a wage. In fact, there is not just one but two large categories for the work that is done in any society: either it is defined as a job, resulting in monetary income, or it is unpaid work. The second category produces results that, in monetary terms, have been valued at the equivalent of one-third or more of gross domestic product (GDP).[3]

The discussion of labour in economics textbooks normally focuses on the function of income-generation. However, modern economies are entering a period of enormous transition, when systems that have worked in the past to produce rising standards of living, accompanied (up to a certain point) with rising well-being, are due for re-examination. The systems that characterise modern industrialised economies are increasingly producing 'ill-being' along with wealth. Some of the problems – as well as some potential solutions – can be seen in an examination of the three functions of work listed above. A major problem, and also an opportunity, arises from the realisation that the first and second functions do not necessarily go together: work may provide income while not creating net social value. And, of course, it may create social value without generating a monetary income.

The work involved in making cigarettes, or financial instruments with hidden risks, are examples of work that produces things that actually harm those who use them. In a similar category, meat may be a health-giving part of the human diet, but not when it is raised in ways that lace the meat with antibiotics or growth hormones. Products may diminish net well-being by engendering frustration and annoyance that far outweigh their utility to the user: for example, products designed for obsolescence, or so poorly made that early failure is likely. Aside from these specific cases of the production of 'bads' rather than 'goods', there is much evidence that a rich country such as the United States has reached saturation in many areas of consumption: additional purchases do not increase the well-being of the purchaser.

More broadly, virtually all production has some degree of negative environmental consequence, in the throughput of energy and materials. Of course, this last point does not mean that all production is bad; however, it reinforces the idea that it is increasingly important, at a time of growing resource constraint, to prioritise among productive activities and to find ways – whether through incentive or regulation – to direct society's resources towards the most valuable outputs. For that, we need to find new ways – other than who can pay more than others – to define what is of value.

The ideal economy

To get to the long-term issue of the place of the economy within the larger ecosystem, we need to address several tensions within the subject of work – tensions, that is:

- between work that produces relatively little well-being but is well paid and the need for much work that receives little or no monetary compensation – the latter includes the production of food as well as the 'caring work' that is often done by women, in basic healthcare, childcare and home activities;
- between the need for income and the fact that many jobs are not

useful to society – any newspaper you pick up makes it clear that people in our society are heavily dependent on having paying jobs, even though many of those jobs produce things that should not be produced (for any of the reasons adduced above); and

• between the working time offered by employers and workers' preferences about working time – many people work less than they want (usually because they would like to earn more, but sometimes – especially in the case of retired people – because they are bored or feel disconnected from society), while many others wish they had longer vacations or shorter daily or weekly working hours.

When this picture is looked at in the abstract, the logical conclusion is that it would be desirable to discover or invent some better organisation of the economy so that:

1 all children would have the means to develop their capabilities through nurturing love, quality education, nutritious food, clean water, secure healthcare and adequate shelter – and this would be achieved regardless of the earning capacities of their parents;

2 all adults would have access to basic survival and security;

3 conditions of work would be such as to maximise the positive psychic rewards and to minimise, or share fairly, the work that is disagreeable;

4 incentives and rewards to work would recognise the value of the work that is done and the investments required to train people to do that work, as well as any disagreeable aspects;

5 all the work that is needed would get done; and

6 work that produces unneeded or harmful things would not get done.

If the first two conditions were fulfilled (as they now are in the US, partially, but insecurely, through a patchwork of government 'safety nets', public education, etc.), this would reduce the pressure for jobs, jobs, jobs – hence making it more possible to consider implementing condition number 6. The last two conditions are the crux of the issues that need to be addressed: getting the necessary work of society done, while not wasting resources or burdening the natural environment with useless production.

Why is this all so hard to bring about? The condition that would require the most dramatic change from the economic system we have now is point number 4. This takes us back to the sixth challenge for the new economy that was set out at the start of the chapter, which is also a challenge for the theory that will underpin such an economy. The new economy must find ways to set incentives and rewards for work that recognise, at least much better than at present, the social value, the requirements for investing in human capital, and the intrinsic rewards or distastefulness of different kinds of work.

How standard wage theory must adapt

Standard economic theory has at its core the idea that prices – including wages – are set by the intersection of supply and demand. Wages are described as being set at the intersection where people supply their work by choosing how much (and where and how) to work, while the demand for labour is derived from the demand for the products of that labour. The theory is further simplified by the assumptions that employers select workers based only on well-founded expectations of their ability to contribute to the productive effort and that workers have good information about all the possible jobs they could have. The conclusion from this reasoning is that all workers receive their just deserts: their pay reflects precisely what they add to the firm's receipts.

This picture contains some realistic points about supply and demand, along with a number of unwarranted assumptions. Normally neither the workers nor the employers have as much knowledge as is assumed, about either the product market or the job market. While wages are nearly always an important consideration, many workers give equal or nearly equal weight to a number of other factors in their selection of a job, including such issues as location, opportunities for learning and advancement, image and status associated with the job or the particular employer, or the social value of the product. (The latter concern is a major motivator for many people who choose to go into often low-paying jobs with non-profit organisations, or into areas such as social work.) While both the lack of perfect knowledge and the presence of personal preferences receive some acknowledgement in the old model, these complications are not really factored in: the conclusion is that the stringent assumptions of perfect knowledge and simply modelled goals are *good enough* so that, *on average*, the labour market works as described, with all workers receiving exactly what they deserve.

Other social sciences have pointed to masses of data showing labour markets having rather different outcomes. Perhaps it is safe to conclude that the old model goes about halfway in predicting outcomes. The simple twentieth-century theory – powerful because it is simple, but also wrong because it is simple – ignores other factors that, in many circumstances, are at least as important in determining wages. These include power, externalities, history and culture. Due to the lack of space, I will talk about only one of these.

Power in society is often connected with legal status. Individuals or groups who have the standing that allows them to raise, or to resist, legal challenge have significantly greater power than those who lack such standing. A good example is provided by the case of illegal immigrants in the United States. They are vulnerable to threats of exposure to immigration authorities; and, if they are mistreated or underpaid, they cannot take their case to law, as that would, again, expose their status to the immigration authorities.

Unions confer on their members the legal status that makes them more effective in protesting about unfair treatment. John Kenneth Galbraith famously referred to unions as the salutary 'countervailing power' against excessive corporate power in the United States. However, since the 1970s, union membership in the US has declined dramatically. The reasons include the threat that companies can replace union labour with lower-cost illegal immigrant labour; the threat that union demands can cause companies to source their production overseas, where wages are lower and unions are not a problem (China is notable for blocking attempts to legalise unions); and the growth of corporate political and economic power combined with ever decreasing countervailing power.

When workers lack bargaining power, gains in worker productivity can be diverted into profits rather than wages. It is increasingly widely recognised that the gains in labour productivity that were achieved during the last quarter of the twentieth century mostly resulted in increased corporate profits, with little going to raise wages.

Another set of issues under the heading of power concerns gender and ethnicity. To summarise this, any type of work that is predominantly associated with a group that lacks political, cultural or economic power in the wider society will have lower status and lower pay.

Conclusions

I have suggested that human values should lead the way in setting important prices, using markets only as appropriate to achieve the desired valuations. While the prices of scarce resources or of more or less destructive energy sources are of huge importance at this critical moment in human history, how work is organised and compensated is equally important, not least for the political reason that the concern about jobs is making it difficult to face environmental realities.

Moving towards some conclusions, let us imagine that, by ten years from now, economics, in hand with ecology, technology and a variety of other fields of human knowledge, has progressed to a point where it is capable of identifying the types and amount of throughput that can safely be processed, given ecological constraints. This determination, of course, depends on priorities for output, as well as on the technologies to be used – that is, how far technology has progressed towards stripping production down to the naked value.

Out of these calculations comes a conclusion regarding how many, and what kind of, labour hours are needed in the formal economy. Note an important point that was suggested earlier: the total number of labour hours demanded will be *greater if average labour productivity is low*, but lower if productivity does not decline, or if it continues to increase. And then there is the important question of whether society has managed to organise work in ways that allow shorter working weeks for those who want them – an achievement that would, in itself, represent a critical recognition of the importance of unpaid care work, for such social organisation would leave more time for that.

The conclusion that was suggested as scenario C (in Table 2.1) will probably win the most votes. The 'naked value' versions of all the things we want – health, nutrition, education, transportation, communication, home with all its comforts, and a sufficient variety of entertainment – could be produced within the envelope of ecological constraints and resource limitations. It would be even better if 'all the things we want' had somehow been redefined to exclude things that do not contribute to well-being – reducing the amount of work society demands by excluding the kinds of outputs I described earlier when talking about 'unproductive work'. In the best case, this could dovetail with demographic trends, so that the workforce declines as a proportion of total population just as household demands are reduced, to focus on real contributions to well-being. Thus, per capita GDP and average household incomes could simultaneously decline without a reduction in well-being.

If this redefinition of wants was indeed achieved, scenario D1 could also be quite rosy; this scenario supposes that, while technology has kept labour productivity high, it has also streamlined production so that it requires decreased labour inputs along with less material and energy. Indeed, this is the picture painted by Juliet Schor in her book *Plenitude* (2010); all well-being wants are served within nature's constraints, while leisure time is greatly increased.

Those are very appealing images. How do we get there?

To start with, as noted earlier, we have relevant models to draw on, of countries where sensible tax policies give governments the means to achieve the first requirement in the ideal economy: to support everyone, especially those who are unable to work, or who cannot find work. However, all the welfare states I know of still need to focus more attention on work that is not done through the formal job market. There is movement in this direction in countries where governments provide support that allows parents to care for their own children. The alternative – to pay only for day care that permits parents to do other, market work – is hugely inefficient, ignoring the tremendous value to society of good parenting. (My feminist friends have a number of different points of view on this.) There are other unpaid or volunteer activities that could add a great deal more to the quality of life if they received a little more support. An example is time banking, a system of exchange in which time, not money, is the currency that allows the connection to be made between unused capacities and unmet needs. Time-banking systems have generally been most successful in retirement settings, where there are so many human capacities with no good outlet. However, Edgar Cahn, a prime inventor and mover behind such systems, has recognised that if they are to endure they require a consistent manager, who probably needs to do this as a paid job.

Not everything we want to achieve can be done by just adapting existing models, but a great deal can be. Taxation is a well-known way of changing prices. Those who do not want to admit that government is or should be in the business of changing incentives will defend taxes, if at all, only as a way of raising income for the government. But whether or not we like the current regime, we might as well admit the reality, and work to use taxes to bring about the results we want rather than the results we don't want. Constructive examples would include sumptuary or luxury taxes, set high enough to help discourage status consumption, and graduated income taxes that would begin at a high level and could be designed to bring the compensation of the highest paid executives into some reasonable relation to the compensation of the lowest paid workers in their firms. While we're at it, capital gains taxes should be set at a high level, to get away from the present situation in which unearned income is taxed at a substantially lower rate than income from work.

There are plenty of other existing government programmes that could be reformed to align better with ecological realities and human well-being. Subsidies are a good example. According to a Bloomberg New Energy Finance report of July 2012, subsidies that promote consumption of fossil fuels, such as below-market gasoline prices, totalled $557 billion worldwide in 2008. This number was well over twelve times the global renewable energy subsidies of that year – and the fossil fuel figure did not even include production subsidies. Again, this exemplifies the current situation where prices are being very effectively manipulated, but since the theory/ideology doesn't believe that this should happen, it is done without due public attention being paid to whose values are served by the manipulation. Even if we did not increase the degree to which prices are now skewed by government action, we could move much closer to the ideal world by shifting that effort towards the real values that need to be expressed.

Much is said about public–private partnerships. A critical area for doing this right is investment in research and in productive activities that will most benefit society while respecting nature's limits. Suppose we were to start from a concept of restorative development: not just keeping us where we are, as in the notion of sustainability, but rebuilding the health of ecological and social systems that have been damaged over the last century. Perhaps there needs to be an academic discipline of restorative development, or some organisation, similar to the Intergovernmental Panel on Climate Change, that can outline ways of identifying activities that will promote restorative development. Such activities would presumably include implementation of renewable energy, infrastructure, education and health, as well as research in all of these areas.

The price of capital – the expected return that can attract it to one place rather than another – is not the only thing that decides where it flows: the existing distribution of wealth, fashions of thought, expectations and egos all play large parts here, as in other areas of price-setting.

The Bank of North Dakota is a very successful example of an alternative approach. It holds state funds as well as deposits from individuals and institutions; it invests these in ways that are good for the people of the state, and that have turned out to be much more secure than the investments of strictly profit-oriented banks.

On a range of scales, both much smaller and much larger than the state of North Dakota, there is a need to prioritise constructive investments. The next step is to find ways to attract investment funds into these areas and away from destructive activities. Credit unions and co-operative banks have traditionally played a constructive role in this regard. Rich Rosen, at the Tellus Institute in Boston, suggests using public utility commissions as models for how to better target and direct the use of new capital investment. As he has noted, the world cannot rely on traditional capital markets to properly prioritise the future need for capital among and within key industries.[4] Rosen's colleague, Paul Raskin, has described the situation we should be moving towards as one where:

> Publicly controlled regional and community investment banks, supported by participatory regulatory processes, recycle social savings and tax-generated capital funds. To receive funds from these banks, capital-seeking entrepreneurs must demonstrate that their projects, in addition to financial viability, promote larger social and environmental goals (Raskin 2012).

This would be good news for co-operative worker ownership systems, which have often faced difficulties in raising capital.

I have given just a few concrete examples of areas where some of the knottiest problems can be solved through conscious attention to how prices are set. These examples include:

- implementing a more well-being-oriented welfare state;
- enhancing support for the non-profit organisations and co-operatives that are making it possible for people to do the work needed by society;
- shifting how taxes and subsidies are set;
- recognising that investment is a public good, which should prioritise sustainable well-being and restorative development; and
- most deeply, reordering how work is organised, which implies basic shifts in our economic and political understanding of the roles of paid work, unpaid work, the markets, and the large and important areas of our economy that operate mostly or entirely outside those markets.

It becomes possible to think about these options when we recognise that prices are not set by God or by nature: they are the result of human decisions. Those human decisions can be made on a strictly individual basis, in which case the results are skewed towards the decision-makers with the most money and the most power, or they can be made communally.

The question behind all of these questions is: who decides? We need to figure out how to elect people whom we might trust, which means getting money out of politics. Trust is a significant driver of human affairs. We should withdraw our trust from corporations that purely seek profit, to the exclusion of the social good. Markets can be an important part of many solutions, and governments are never perfect, but we should not trust the economists who tell us that markets have all the solutions.

When we focus solely on that knotty issue of economic scale and growth, the problems seem virtually impossible to solve by design – we'll just have to wait for disaster. But when we have untangled the knot, pulling on the price theory thread and the work thread, we can begin to see the paths we must take.

Notes

1 Labour income is determined not just by productivity, but also by the share of the surplus generated that accrues to labour. Since the 1980s, the share going to capital has steadily increased so another scenario (in which co-ops could play an important role) is changing how profits are divided between labour and capital. This could make it possible to sustain more jobs even if the money value circulating in the economy remained unchanged. However, if the decline in resource quality or quantity were to continue past the point where the wage/profit division had reached an acceptable and sustainable balance, then the decline in jobs and/or wages would resume.

2 However, Galbraith wrote one essay near the end of his life in which he considered the possibility that there could be a limit to how much consumption is needed for a good life. See 'Afterword: A Japanese social initiative' in Harris and Goodwin (2003) and also, of course, Keynes' famous essay 'Economic possibilities for our grandchildren'.

3 The leader in this field has been Marilyn Waring.

4 See www.corporation2020. org/corporation2020/documents/ Papers/2nd-Summit-Paper-Series.pdf.

References

Bloomberg (2012) *Global Corporate Renewable Energy Index (CREX) 2012*. Copenhagen: Bloomberg New Energy Finance and Vestas Wind Systems. www.bnef.com/InsightDownload/7210/pdf/.

Brown, H., K. Aldred Cheek and K. Lewis (2012) *Naked Value: Six things every business leader needs to know about resources, innovation & competition*. Guilford, CT: dMASS Media.

Dobbs, R., J. Oppenheim, F. Thompson, M. Brinkman and M. Zornes (2011) *Resource Revolution: Meeting the world's energy, materials, food, and water needs*. New York, NY: McKinsey Global Institute. www.mckinsey.com/insights/mgi/research/natural_resources/resource_revolution.

Harris, J. and N. Goodwin (eds) (2003) *New Thinking in Macroeconomics: Social, institutional and environmental perspectives*. Cheltenham and Northampton, MA: Edward Elgar Publishing.

Heinberg, R. (2011) *The End of Growth: Adapting to our new economic reality*. Gabriola Island, Canada: New Society Publishers.

Raskin, P. (2012) 'Scenes from the great transition'. *Solutions* 3(4): 11–17. www.thesolutionsjournal.com/node/1140.

Schor, J. B. (2010) *Plenitude: The new economics of true wealth*. New York, NY: Penguin Books.

Victor, P. A. (2008) *Managing without Growth: Slower by design, not disaster*. Cheltenham: Edward Elgar.

Waring, M. (1988) *If Women Counted: A new feminist economics*. San Francisco, CA: Harper & Row.

3 | THE WORLD WE NEED

Richard Wilkinson and Kate Pickett

Reducing carbon emissions and moving towards sustainability are usually regarded as requiring a sacrifice of living standards – either through forgoing future economic growth, or by reducing current levels of consumption. However, many of those at the centre of the environmental debate now think this assumption is mistaken. They suggest that the kind of transformation of social and economic life we need to reach sustainability is likely to involve substantial improvements in the real quality of human life. The difference in opinion is rather as if most of us were still in the position of Malthus in the late eighteenth century: he failed to see that, instead of trapping humanity in endless misery, population pressure on resources would lead instead to the innovations of the Industrial Revolution that transformed the quality of human life.

At the centre of the story is the still largely unrecognised weakness of the relationship between economic growth and well-being. Take life expectancy. It is a central component of well-being, not only because longevity is in itself crucial, but also because life tends to be short in societies where its quality is poor.

The cross-sectional relationship between life expectancy and gross national product per capita (GNPpc) is shown in Figure 3.1, which appears to show that life expectancy in the rich countries has ceased to rise with increases in GNPpc. However, this relationship has several interpretations. Replacing GNPpc on the horizontal axis with the log of GNPpc would show that, throughout the long course of economic development, life expectancy remains close to a linear function of the log of income, even in the rich countries. If we were to assume causality, this means that a doubling of incomes in rich countries would buy the same increase in life expectancy as a doubling of incomes in poor countries: in other words, each additional year of life expectancy in the rich countries

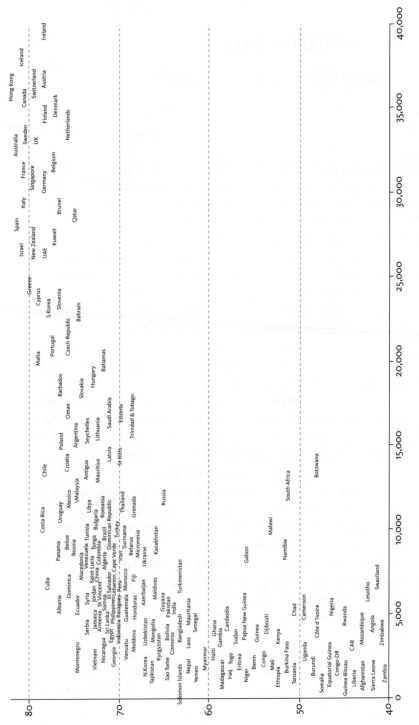

3.1 Income per head (us$) and life expectancy (years) in rich and poor countries (*source:* Wilkinson and Pickett 2009)

would cost up to fifty times as much as an extra year of life in poorer counties.

However, the curve in Figure 3.1 does not trace out a path in which rising life expectancy occurs during the course of economic growth over time. The real gains in longevity are much greater at all stages of economic development than the increases in gross national income per capita (GNIpc) (logged or not) would suggest. As Sam Preston showed in 1975, the curve (Figure 3.2) shifts up vertically over time so that each level of income appears to buy more life expectancy than it did previously. In the rich countries, life expectancy continues to increase by two to three years with every decade that passes, as it has done for over a century (Preston 1975).

Looking at international data from the 1930s to the 1960s, Preston found that only 12 per cent of the increases in life expectancy over time were related to improvements in GNPpc. The remaining 88 per cent appeared to be independent of economic growth. More recent analyses have strengthened this picture. Also, using data covering countries at all levels of development, Cutler et al. (2006) found that:

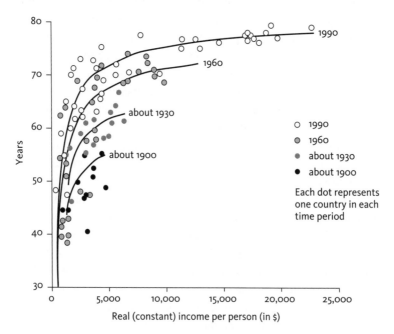

3.2 Real (constant) income per head (US$) and life expectancy (years) (*source*: Preston 1975)

Cross-country data show almost no relation between changes in life expectancy and economic growth over 10, 20, or 40-year time periods between 1960 and 2000. Many countries have shown remarkable improvements in health with little or no economic growth.

As part of his defence of aid to developing countries, Charles Kenny argues that it is wrong to measure progress primarily in terms of income growth (Kenny 2011). He shows that even in countries where increases in real incomes have been small or non-existent, there have still been transformative improvements not only in the length of life, but also in its quality.

The general picture is of rapid, historically unprecedented progress in the quality of life – progress has been faster in the developing world than in the developed. This is true for measures covering health, education, civil and political rights, [and] access to infrastructure (ibid.: 4).

Global rates of infant mortality have halved since 1960. The proportion of the world's children in primary school rose from about half in 1950 to almost 90 per cent by the end of the century. Even in sub-Saharan Africa, where income growth has been poorest, the proportion of the population who are literate doubled – from one-third to two-thirds – between 1970 and the end of the century.

There has been considerable discussion of the clear relation between life expectancy and GNIpc at any one point in time but the lack of a strong relationship in trends over time (Cutler et al. 2006). That the improvements in health are not simply a lagged effect of earlier rises in incomes is clear from the experience of several sub-Saharan African countries that had major improvements in health despite little or no increase in incomes since independence.

An obvious first thought is that the health improvements may be so weakly related to growth over time merely because health improvements resulting from immunisation, bed nets, clean water and so on are cheap and so are not closely tied to economic growth. But the explanatory problem looks more fundamental than that: many other aspects of the quality of life show the same mismatch between the international cross-sectional and time series evidence.

In an analysis of changes shown in measures of many different aspects of the quality of life (covering education, health, transport and communications, class and gender inequality, crime, violence, war, pollution, suicide, nutrition, sanitation, political stability, human rights, and the rule of law), Easterly found that only 8 out of 69 measures were significantly related to long-term economic growth. Forty-three of them were more closely related simply to the passage of time than to economic growth (Easterly 1999). This suggests that the apparently paradoxical cross-sectional and time series relationships between GNPpc and life expectancy reflect similar patterns in many other aspects of well-being.

Economic growth is largely a misnomer. Rather than being a process of quantitative accumulation, the long history of transformation from traditional agriculture to modern urban societies is primarily a process of qualitative change and innovation in the way people live and in productive methods. The qualitative changes and innovations involved spring from the worldwide development and spread of science and technology, knowledge, education, and rational thought itself. Together these have made possible a process of human empowerment and emancipation. As we have increasingly become the masters of our circumstances, innovation has served to change life for the better and has allowed us to adapt to changing circumstances. Sometimes those changes would contribute to measured increases in the value of production and economic growth, but often they would not.

Part of the problem is that innovation and change are seen as if they were the result, rather than the cause, of economic growth. This reflects the fact that new technologies often involve expensive investment in research and development and are conceptualised as substitutions of capital for labour. But that is truer at the forefront of technical and scientific advance. In contrast, the populations of less developed countries face a vast accumulated backlog of possible improvements in their way of life – the full scope of 'modernisation' from the use of nails and soap to spectacles and electric light – that may involve little more than changes in the way in which *existing* levels of income are spent, but that still bring huge benefits both to the quality of life and to productive capacity. And, as the pace of technical advance increases, that is true for most of us: we replace worn-out consumer durables with better quality and more capable goods, often at lower cost – and again, that happens even without increases in income.

However, although life expectancy is still rising even in societies where it is already high, several other measures suggest that developed countries have reached the limits of how much increases in material living standards can add to the real quality of life. While GNPpc measures the total of monetised economic activity, both the Genuine Progress Indicator and the Index of Sustainable Economic Welfare adjust GNP to provide better measures of meaningful progress. They take out the costs of 'bads' – such as car crashes – and include the cost of pollution, environmental damage and crime. They also take account of the value of unpaid labour, such as childcare. In contrast to the long-term rise in GNPpc, the results suggest that genuine progress in the material circumstances of the populations of developed countries has stalled or declined since the 1970s (Lawn 2003).

Figure 3.3 shows that the UNICEF Index of Child Well-being in Rich Countries is also unrelated to GNIpc. The same is also true of the Index of Health and Social Problems (Figure 3.4), which includes not

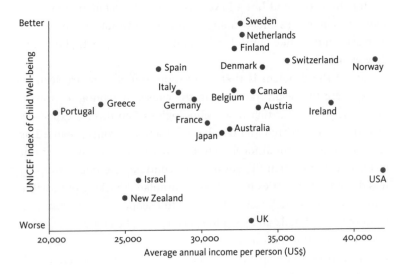

3.3 Child well-being is not related to average incomes in rich countries (*source*: Wilkinson and Pickett 2009)

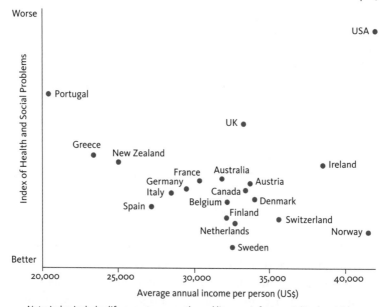

Note: Index includes life expectancy, maths and literacy, infant mortality, homicides, imprisonment, teenage births, trust, obesity, mental illness, drug and alcohol addiction, social mobility.

3.4 Health and social problems are not related to average incomes in rich countries (*source*: Wilkinson and Pickett 2009)

only physical and mental health, but a wide range of social problems including violence, drug abuse and low maths and literacy scores.

Subjective indicators of the quality of life – such as measures of happiness or 'life satisfaction' – suggest that these too have stalled in the richer countries. Although in analyses of rich and poor countries, subjective measures appear to be related *cross-sectionally* to the log of GNIpc (Stevenson and Wolfers 2008), Easterlin, looking at changes over time, has shown that, apart from the short-term ups and downs that reflect the business cycle, life satisfaction has ceased to rise in the longer term with GNIpc (Easterlin 2013). Using data spanning periods of change of between twelve and thirty-four years for fifty-five countries at different levels of development, he finds that there is no evidence of a positive relationship between economic growth and life satisfaction – neither when countries are considered together nor when grouped by region or level of development. Indeed, most of the relationships are insignificantly negative.

Given that neither subjective nor objective measures of well-being show continuing progress in the developed countries, the increases in life expectancy appear paradoxical. However, they may turn out to be lagged effects of past improvements, either in the childhood circumstances of older generations or even intergenerational – possibly epigenetic – effects on health. But whatever their source, they are – even cross-sectionally, as Figure 3.1 shows – unrelated to GNPpc (Bygren 2013; Drake and Liu 2010). Research also suggests that influences such as the obesity epidemic may mean that the rise in life expectancy comes to a halt before the middle of this century (Olshansky et al. 2005). Indeed, there are already signs of a rise in premature mortality associated with persistent disadvantage in Scotland (Norman et al. 2011).

Public recognition that economic growth now makes so little difference to the quality of life might be expected to increase support for decisive action to reduce carbon emissions. But a much more important remaining obstacle is the fact that, as individuals, almost all of us would very much rather be richer than poorer. And, of course, if everyone wants more money, that looks very like a societal desire for economic growth. But the reason why we all want more money, even though the richest of the developed societies do not do better than the others, is because money is seen as the key to social status

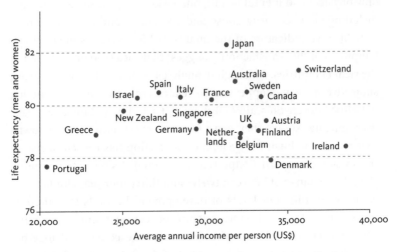

3.5 Health is not related to income differences between rich societies (*source:* Wilkinson and Pickett 2009)

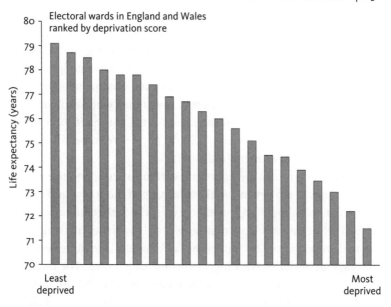

3.6 Health is related to income difference within rich societies (*source*: Wilkinson and Pickett 2009)

and self-advancement. That it is relative income (income relative to others in our society) that matters rather than the effects of absolute material standards regardless of social position can be shown quite simply. Figure 3.5 uses the same data on life expectancy and GNIpc as Figure 3.1, but confines attention to just the richest countries and shows the lack of any relation between the two. But, in contrast, Figure 3.6 shows the extraordinarily close relationship between life expectancy and levels of deprivation in electoral wards in England and Wales. Not one column is out of rank order. Although the scale of the health inequalities shown for England and Wales in Figure 3.6 varies in different countries, in almost every country there is a consistent social gradient in health across the whole society.

The paradoxical impression that income differences matter within the rich developed societies but no longer do so between them is resolved if we recognise that within societies we are dealing with the effects of relative position or social status. This interpretation is now supported by a good deal of individual-level research, which distinguishes between the effects of absolute and relative income

(Elgar et al. 2013; Kondo et al. 2008; Wood et al. 2012). There are also surveys that ask people to choose between living with lower material standards in a poorer society in order to be among the better off in that society, or being materially better off but among the less well off in a richer society. The results show that people are more concerned with relativities and social status than with absolute living standards (Solnick and Hemenway 1998). It looks as if John Stuart Mill was right when he wrote 'Men do not desire to be rich, but to be richer than other men' (Mill 1907).

Income differences are important within societies because people regard them as the key to social status. One of the surest indications that we are dealing with the effects of social differentiation is that almost all of the problems that have social gradients (making them more common at the bottom of the social ladder) are more common throughout societies with bigger income differences. For example, Figure 3.7 shows that countries score lower on the UNICEF Index of Child Well-being in more unequal societies, while Figure 3.8 shows that more unequal countries do less well on the Index of Health and Social Problems. Bigger income differences seem to increase the effects of social status differentiation.

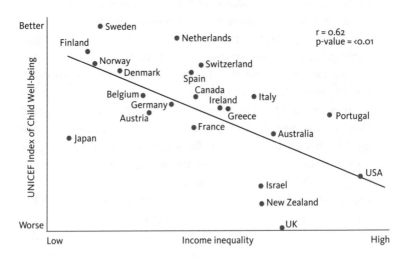

3.7 Child well-being is better in more equal rich societies (*source:* Wilkinson and Pickett 2009)

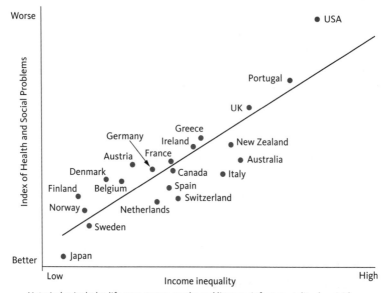

Worse

Index of Health and Social Problems

● USA

Portugal ●

UK ●

Greece
Germany
Ireland ●
Austria ─ France ● New Zealand
Denmark ● Australia
Finland Belgium Canada ● Italy
Norway ● Spain
Netherlands ● Switzerland
● Sweden

Better   ● Japan

Low   Income inequality   High

Note: Index includes life expectancy, maths and literacy, infant mortality, homicides, imprisonment, teenage births, trust, obesity, mental illness, drug and alcohol addiction, social mobility.

3.8 Health and social problems are worse in more unequal countries (*source*: Wilkinson and Pickett 2009)

It looks as if one of the effects of bigger income differences is an increase in status competition and insecurity. Because income is regarded as a key to, or marker of, status, money becomes even more important in more unequal societies. As a result, people work longer hours in more unequal societies (Bowles and Park 2005). They also get into debt more and are more likely to go bankrupt (Adkisson and Saucedo 2012; Kumhof and Rancière 2010). The indications are that greater inequality increases our tendency to judge each other more by status, thereby increasing the pressure to consume. Experiments in social psychology testify to the way people use the consumption of high-status goods to try to offset the ego damage of low social status: the authors of one research report refer to status goods as 'affirmational commodities' (Sivanathan and Pettit 2010).

Consumerism is almost certainly the greatest obstacle to any attempt to make major reductions in carbon emissions. Our desire to maintain our social standing means that any threat to our purchasing power is a threat to our social existence. And because consumer-ism is driven substantially by status competition, it is a zero sum game. This seems to explain why we, as individuals, all want to be richer, even though economic growth in the developed countries appears no longer to increase the real quality of life in societies as a whole. What is a trajectory of progress for individuals within any society is not the same as the trajectory of progress for society as a whole. It is therefore no longer legitimate to treat our individual desires for more income as if they amounted to a societal demand for economic growth.

Governments are unable to respond adequately to the evidence of global warming and climate change because whole societies are caught in this psychological headlock: rather than risk the incomes that underpin our social standing and pursuit of status, we prefer to risk the planet.

The country that is perhaps taking the most radical approach to these problems is Bhutan – well known for its commitment to max-imising gross national happiness (GNH) rather than gross national product. Nor is GNH an empty slogan. Bhutan's constitution charges the government with pursuing happiness (by which the Bhutanese mean something more like what might be called well-being or ful-filment). They have set out the conditions for well-being in nine domains, covering not only health, education and living conditions, but also psychological well-being, time use, cultural diversity and resilience, good governance, community vitality, ecological diversity and resilience. These are broken down into thirty-three component indicators that take a very broad view of the social and environmental conditions for human flourishing.[1]

As a result, Bhutan has taken a number of unusual steps. For instance, for the sake of local socio-economic and environmental interests, it has not joined the World Trade Organization; it aims to become the first country with entirely organic agriculture, and since 2004 it has been illegal to grow, manufacture or sell tobacco in Bhutan. But, as if in recognition of the fact that it cannot insulate itself from the world's problems, it hosted a conference at the United Nations (UN) in New York in April 2012 to draw attention to the need to set out a 'new development paradigm' capable of reorienting the social, economic and environmental development of humankind to serve the sustainable well-being of the planet. Speaking at that meeting, the prime minister said:

> I hope that by 2015 the international community will have adopted a sustainability-based economic paradigm, committed to promoting true human well-being and happiness, and ensuring at the same time, the survival of all species with which we share this planet.

As a result of its initiative and at the request of the UN, the government of Bhutan established an international expert working group to advise on what a new development paradigm would look like. An interdisciplinary group of fifty people at the forefront of their various fields has now started work. Its central task is to think through how human well-being can best be combined with a sustainable low carbon economy.

The need to develop low carbon sustainable economic systems is now desperately urgent. In May 2013, CO_2 levels in the atmosphere reached 400 parts per million (ppm) for the first time. This is 40 per cent above pre-industrial levels, higher than at any time in human existence, and substantially higher than the 350 ppm that James Hansen (NASA) and an international team estimated is the safe limit if we are to keep the rise in global temperatures below 2 degrees Celsius (Hansen et al. 2008). As a result, climate scientists are increasingly abandoning the hope that global temperature rises can be kept below this limit. In 2009, the Geneva-based Global Humanitarian Forum, presided over by Kofi Annan, estimated that climate change was already causing 300,000 deaths a year and that there were already 26 million people displaced by climate – a figure thought likely to triple by the 2020s. Ninety per cent of the deaths were in developing countries rather than in the rich countries with the highest carbon emissions per head. The annual number of deaths was predicted to rise to 500,000 a year by 2030, but since then the indications are that global warming may be proceeding more rapidly than previously thought. Some of the effects already set in train by higher CO_2 levels take long periods of time to come through, so that even if we manage to prevent further increases in CO_2 emissions, sea levels (currently rising at a rate of around 3 millimetres per year) will continue rising into the distant future (Rahmstorf 2012). It is estimated that to stabilise atmospheric concentrations of CO_2, the carbon emissions caused by global human activity would have to be reduced by 80 per cent on 1990 levels (Parry et al. 2008).

The environmental crisis is, however, more than climate change. As Clive Spash points out, it is also soil erosion, deforestation, water salinisation, the systemic effects of insecticides and pesticides, particulates in the air, tropospheric ozone pollution and stratospheric ozone loss, toxic chemical waste, species loss, acidification of the oceans, decline of fish stocks, hormone discharges into the water supply, and so on (Spash 2013).

The task of the International Expert Working Group is therefore to set out the social, economic and technological structures likely to maximise human well-being and flourishing with a minimum environmental impact. Approaching sustainability is usually viewed as a matter of reducing the environmental impact of a given way of life, using a combination of more efficient technology and modifying lifestyles only where minor changes would make them less wasteful. The problem is seen as one of preserving lifestyles as far as possible within the limitations of sustainability. To many, the ideal would be a lifestyle-preserving technical fix. However, the Bhutanese aim of maximising GNH means we have to think more broadly: we need to think whether there are changes in lifestyles and social structures that would increase well-being while perhaps also reducing a society's ecological footprint.

In this context, the need for new technologies and greater fuel efficiency is the obvious part. More difficult is how we address the many dysfunctional forms of social organisation and expenditure – such as the US$1,753 billion (2.5 per cent of world GDP) that the world spent on armaments in 2012,[2] or the international inequalities that mean that the richest 20 per cent of the world's population consume 86 per cent of its goods while the poorest 20 per cent consume just 1.3 per cent, or how we can reduce the insatiable consumerism of rich societies.

Particularly since the financial crash of 2008, think tanks, charities and research groups round the world have produced a spate of publications pointing to the need for a fundamental transformation in the conduct of economic and social life – a recognition that what is now utopian is the idea that we can continue with 'business as usual' (German Advisory Council on Global Change 2011; SEI 2002; Share the World's Resources 2012). Many of these reports address not only the need to reduce carbon emissions, but also the problem of growing inequality, the need to tackle world poverty, and so on.

Asking what a sustainable economy and social system would look like if it were designed to maximise human well-being suggests five key areas of change in the way in which our societies work. The first, for the reasons already discussed, is to recognise that economic growth in the rich countries is no longer a reliable source of increases in well-being. Although we need innovation and change, partly in the service of sustainability, we need to reduce – rather than increase – the use of non-renewable resources. Useful here is Herman Daly's concept of a 'steady-state' economy in which we think of maintaining the stock of goods in use, focusing on durability and repair rather than on the flow from production to consumption to waste.

The second is a concomitant of the first. Given that we have got to the end of the most important benefits to well-being of higher material standards, we need to shift attention from an overdependence on consumption and material sources of satisfaction to social sources, rooted in community and the quality of social relationships, as the area with the greatest potential for future advances in the subjective quality of life. Research on happiness has repeatedly emphasised the importance of social relationships (Layard 2005; Ura et al. 2012). With the break-up of community, the quality of the social environment may be particularly inadequate in developed societies where the lack of friendship and poor social integration are now among the more powerful influences on population death rates (Holt-Lunstad et al. 2010).

The third major social change contributing to sustainable well-being is a reduction in inequality. Oxfam reported that the combined incomes of the richest 100 people on the planet amounted to US$240 trillion – four times what would be needed to end extreme poverty all over the world (Oxfam 2013). Reducing inequality in living standards between countries is fundamental not only because the scale of inequality between rich and poor is unacceptable or because the rich have much larger carbon footprints than the poor. Crucially, the very large international differences in living standards have been a major obstacle to reaching international agreements on reducing carbon emissions. The 'contraction and convergence' framework for reducing carbon emissions is an attempt to tackle the links between international inequality and any agreement to tackle global warming. But the gap between more and less developed societies must be dramatically reduced if agreements are to stick and economic migration is not to be substantially increased by the effects of climate change.

Inequality within societies also needs to be reduced – partly for the same reasons that make it necessary to reduce international inequalities and partly for quite separate reasons. Like inequality between societies, large differences in consumption within those societies means that the more urgent needs of the poor go unmet while productive resources are squandered on conspicuous consumption by the rich. But greater inequality within societies also has powerful social and psychological effects. Inequality is socially divisive and weakens social cohesion and community life, so more unequal societies are less conducive to meeting human social needs. The evidence shows that bigger material differences widen social class divisions and increase social distances, making societies more dysfunctional – with more violence, less good health, more mental illness, and lower levels of child well-being (Wilkinson and Pickett 2010).

However, great inequality is a particularly powerful obstacle on the path to sustainability. This is because large inequalities intensify consumerism. Consumerism is substantially driven by status competition, which is heightened by greater inequality. Money becomes more important in more unequal societies because it is how we show what we are worth: as we have seen, people work longer hours, save less, get into debt more and are more likely to go bankrupt (Adkisson and Saucedo 2012; Bowles and Park 2005; Kumhof and Rancière 2010). This means that if we are to rein in consumerism, it is crucial to reduce inequality. Lastly, if, as a former governor of the Federal Reserve Bank has suggested, rising incomes are a substitute for greater equality, a steady-state economy may need to be underpinned by greater equality (Wallich 1972).

Globalisation and the growing interdependence of humanity across the world have increased the need for international co-operation. Governments not only fail to agree action to prevent runaway global warming, they also fail to respond adequately either to world poverty or to the burden of preventable disease; they continue to spend vast sums of money on armaments; they fail to deal with tax havens despite vast losses of revenue from those who can most easily afford to pay; and the governments of wealthy countries continue to promote international trade agreements that benefit them more than poorer countries. All these problems demand international agreement and action, but all too often nations compete in what becomes a race to the bottom. They fear that they will go under if they don't, but the truth is that we will go under if we fail to develop new international co-operative structures, institutions and ways of thinking. Competition between nations is becoming increasingly counterproductive; hence, the fourth major structural change we need is stronger systems for making and enforcing international law and for fostering international co-operation.

The fifth of the changes is the need to extend economic democracy, increasing employee representation on company boards and expanding the share in the economy made up of mutual, co-operative and employee-owned companies. Over the last few decades, large international corporations have been powerful generators of inequality. From the 1970s to the early 1980s, the chief executive officers (CEOs) of the largest 350 US companies were paid twenty or thirty times as much as the average production worker. By the first decade of the twenty-first century they were getting between 200 and 400 times as much (Mishel and Sabadish 2012). Among the 100 largest UK companies (FTSE 100 companies), the average CEO received just above 400 times the minimum wage (Equality Trust 2012). These levels of pay, which are at best only very weakly related to measures of performance, are an indication that there is no effective system of accountability for people at the top (Tosi et al. 2000).

Not only have pay differentials expanded, but large companies have also avoided paying tax. In 2008, the US Government Accountability Office reported that eighty-three of the USA's biggest 100 corporations had subsidiaries in tax havens. The Tax Justice Network reported that ninety-nine of Europe's largest 100 companies also used tax havens. A substantial proportion of the largest companies manage to pay little or no tax.

The scales of top pay and of tax avoidance are just two indications of the mismatch between profit-seeking and the public interest.

Others include corporate-funded opposition to scientific evidence of harm associated with company products (including the role of fossil fuel companies opposing climate science) and the purchase of political influence on a scale that threatens the effective functioning of democratic institutions. The huge power of multinational corporations combined with a lack of effective public accountability has led to a resurgence of interest in more democratic economic institutional structures, which may be more compatible with maximising sustainable human well-being. Mutuals, co-operatives, employee-owned companies and charities all tend to have much smaller pay ratios among their staff. In the Mondragon group of companies (84,000 employees and annual sales of £13 billion), pay ratios average around 1:5. In large public sector organisations, ratios are usually between 1:10 and 1:20.

Co-operatives and employee-owned companies have other characteristics that would lend themselves to sustainable well-being. Community life has weakened substantially in rich countries over the last generation, but, as Oakeshott remarks, an employee buyout can turn a company from being a piece of property into a community (Oakeshott 2000). Perhaps a stronger sense of community at work could replace the sense of community that has declined in residential areas. It is also likely that less hierarchical structures at work could begin to change the experience of work, making it possible for more people to gain a sense of self-worth and of being valued from their work.

Co-operatives and employee-owned companies also seem to perform better than others in ethical terms. In 2012, the *Financial Times* and the International Financial Corporation (part of the World Bank Group) awarded the Co-operative Bank – on the basis of its ethical policy – the title of Europe's most sustainable bank for the third year running, and in 2008 the Co-operative Group was voted the UK's most ethical brand.

It was the American political philosopher and ecologist Murray Bookchin who said: 'Capitalism can no more be "persuaded" to limit growth than a human being can be "persuaded" to stop breathing' (Bookchin 1990). If that is true, what hope is there for a sustainable, steady-state, economy? One of the things a rich society needs to help move it towards sustainability is to develop a 'leisure preference'.

That is to say, the benefits of any improvements in productivity need to be used to reduce work time and increase leisure rather than to increase incomes and consumption. Corporations that are legally obliged to maximise shareholder income do not have a choice: improvements in productivity must, in one way or another, be used to increase profits. But employee co-operatives and employee-owned companies have both the freedom and at least some incentive to shorten working hours when they can. A society in which people preferred leisure over consumption would also be a society in which people had more time for friends, family and community – all crucial to their quality of life.

Moving towards sustainability and maximising well-being both involve changing some of the counterproductive aspects of our social and economic systems. Humanity cannot develop sustainable ways of life on the basis of huge international inequalities, unbridled consumerism or international conflict, with our economic life dominated by enormously powerful corporations that avoid any effective democratic accountability. Addressing each of these issues is not only about removing a major obstacle to sustainability, it is also about enabling important advances in well-being.

The challenge is daunting, but the problems we face are linked in such a way that solving one paves the way to solving others; similarly, each one that is unsolved exacerbates the others. Addressing world poverty will make it easier to reach international agreement on measures to check global warming. A stronger framework of international law will make it easier to reduce levels of military expenditure, and that in turn will make it easier to tackle the preventable burden of disease in poorer countries. Effective international measures to prevent the use of tax havens for avoiding national taxes would make it easier to reduce inequality, which would reduce status competition and consumerism, thereby improving the quality of life for all.

Progress will depend not only on government action, but on civic society more widely, and particularly on a worldwide alliance of concerned organisations. Many governments, international agencies and organisations round the world have been working to set out the path towards sustainability. The UN High Level Panel has set out post-2015 development goals and, at the Rio+20 Conference on Sustainable Development, UN member states agreed to put together a series of sustainable development goals. The European Environment Agency has provided the main European thrust. There are also many highly influential campaigning groups in the charitable sector: some, such as Oxfam and Save the Children, work on poverty and inequality, while others, like WWF, Friends of the Earth and Greenpeace, are focused on environmental issues. Numerous other organisations – such as Avaaz, Occupy, the Tax Justice Network, Make Poverty History – have picked up and campaigned effectively on a wide range of related issues.

To help bring together information and evidence, both on how to make the transition and on examples of what people are achieving in different parts of the world, the International Expert Working Group established by the Bhutan government at the request of the UN is setting up an alliance of all interested parties. It is intended to act as a hub and a forum for discussion, debate and exchange, helping organisations co-ordinate their efforts worldwide. The Alliance for Sustainability and Prosperity (ASAP)[3] has a website at www.asap4all. org. It aims to facilitate the global movement to craft a sustainable future by bringing together all those working to redefine the relationship between humans, economic life and nature. The need is not only to develop policy but also to win crucial public support, without which the scope for government action is severely limited. ASAP has expertise, it has vision, it lacks money, but it invites all interested governments, organisations, groups and individuals to contribute to our common project.

Notes

1 See www.grossnationalhappiness.com/docs/GNH/PDFs/GNH_Variables.xls.

2 See the 2013 figures on the Stockholm International Peace Research Institute (SIPRI) Military Expenditure Database. Available at www.sipri.org/research/armaments/milex/milex_database.

3 The ASAP Coordinating Group is Robert Costanza, Jacqueline McGlade, Steve de Bonvoisin, Petra Fagerholm, Joshua Farley, Enrico Giovannini, Ida Kubiszewski, Frances Moore Lappé, Hunter Lovins, Kate Pickett, Greg Norris, Thomas Prugh, Kristin Vala Ragnarsdottir, Debra Roberts and Richard Wilkinson.

References

Adkisson, R. V. and E. Saucedo (2012) 'Emulation and state-by-state variations in bankruptcy rates'. *Journal of Socio-Economics* 41(4): 400–7.

Bookchin, M. (1990) *Remaking Society: Pathways to a green future*. Cambridge, MA: South End Press.

Bowles, S. and Y. Park (2005) 'Emulation,

inequality, and work hours: was Thorsten Veblen right?' *Economic Journal* 115(507): F397–412.

Bygren, L. O. (2013) 'Intergenerational health responses to adverse and enriched environments'. *Annual Review of Public Health* 34: 49–60.

Cutler, D., A. Deaton and A. Lleras-Muney (2006) 'The determinants of mortality'. *Journal of Economic Perspectives* 20(3): 97–120.

Drake, A. J. and L. Liu (2010) 'Intergenerational transmission of programmed effects: public health consequences'. *Trends in Endocrinology and Metabolism: TEM* 21(4): 206–13.

Easterlin, R. A. (2013) *Happiness and Economic Growth: The evidence.* Discussion paper. Bonn: Institute for the Study of Labor (IZA).

Easterly, W. (1999) 'Life during growth'. *Journal of Economic Growth* 4(3): 239–76.

Elgar, F. J., B. De Clercq, C. W. Schnohr, P. Bird, K. E. Pickett, T. Torsheim et al. (2013) 'Absolute and relative family affluence and psychosomatic symptoms in adolescents'. *Social Science & Medicine* 91: 25–31.

Equality Trust (2012) *A Third of a Percent.* London: The Equality Trust.

German Advisory Council on Global Change (2011) *World in Transition: A social contract for sustainability.* Berlin: German Advisory Council on Global Change (WBGU).

Hansen, J., M. Sato, P. Kharecha, D. Beerling, R. Berner, V. Masson-Delmotte et al. (2008) 'Target atmospheric CO_2: where should humanity aim?' *Open Atmospheric Science Journal* 2: 217–31.

Holt-Lunstad, J., T. B. Smith and J. B. Layton (2010) 'Social relationships and mortality risk: a meta-analytic review'. *PLOS Medicine* 7(7): e1000316.

Kenny, C. (2011) *Getting Better: Why global development is succeeding – and how we can improve the world even more.* New York, NY: Basic Books.

Kondo, N., I. Kawachi, S. V. Subramanian, Y. Takeda and Z. Yamagata (2008) 'Do social comparisons explain the association between income inequality and health?: relative deprivation and perceived health among male and female Japanese individuals'. *Social Science & Medicine* 67(6): 982–7.

Kumhof, M. and R. Rancière (2010) *Inequality, Leverage and Crises.* Working paper. Washington, DC: International Monetary Fund.

Lawn, P. A. (2003) 'A theoretical foundation to support the Index of Sustainable Economic Welfare (ISEW), Genuine Progress Indicator (GPI), and other related indexes'. *Ecological Economics* 44(1): 105–18.

Layard, R. (2005) *Happiness: Lessons from a new science.* London: Allen Lane.

Mill, J. S. (1907) 'On social freedom'. Posthumous essay. *Oxford and Cambridge Review.*

Mishel, L. and N. Sabadish (2012) *CEO Pay and the Top 1%: How executive compensation and financial-sector pay have fueled income inequality.* Issue Brief No. 331. Washington, DC: Economic Policy Institute.

Norman, P., P. Boyle, D. Exeter, Z. Feng and F. Popham (2011) 'Rising premature mortality in the UK's persistently deprived areas: only a Scottish phenomenon?' *Social Science & Medicine* 73(11): 1575–84.

Oakeshott, R. (2000) *Jobs and Fairness: The logic and experience of employee ownership.* Norwich: Michael Russell.

Olshansky, S. J., D. J. Passaro, R. C. Hershow, J. Layden, B. A. Carnes, J. Brody et al. (2005) 'A potential decline in life expectancy in the United States in the 21st century'. *New England Journal of Medicine* 352(11): 1138–45.

Oxfam (2013) 'The cost of inequality:

how wealth and income extremes hurt us all'. Oxfam Media Briefing, 18 January.

Parry, M., J. Palutikof, C. Hanson and J. Lowe (2008) 'Squaring up to reality'. *Nature Reports Climate Change* 2(6): 68–70.

Preston, S. H. (1975) 'The changing relation between mortality and level of economic development'. *Population Studies* 29(2). Reprinted in: *International Journal of Epidemiology* 36(3): 484–90.

Rahmstorf, S. (2012) 'Modeling sea level rise'. *Nature Education Knowledge* 3(10): 4.

SEI (2002) *Great Transition: The promise and lure of the times ahead.* Stockholm: Stockholm Environment Institute (SEI).

Share the World's Resources (2012) *Financing the Global Sharing Economy.* London: Share the World's Resources.

Sivanathan, N. and N. C. Pettit (2010) 'Protecting the self through consumption: status goods as affirmational commodities'. *Journal of Experimental Social Psychology* 46(3): 564–70.

Solnick, S. and D. Hemenway (1998) 'Is more always better?: A survey on positional concerns'. *Journal of Economic Behavior & Organization* 37(3): 373–83.

Spash, C. L. (2013) 'The shallow or the deep ecological economics movement?' *Ecological Economics* 93 (September): 351–62.

Stevenson, B. and J. Wolfers (2008) *Economic Growth and Subjective Well-Being: Reassessing the Easterlin paradox.* Working Paper 14282. Cambridge, MA: National Bureau of Economic Research.

Tosi, H. L., S. Werner, J. P. Katz and L. R. Gomez-Mejia (2000) 'How much does performance matter? A meta-analysis of CEO pay studies'. *Journal of Management* 26(2): 301–39.

Ura, K., S. Alkire, T. Zangmo and K. Wangdi (2012) *A Short Guide to Gross National Happiness Index.* Thimphu: The Centre for Bhutan Studies.

Wallich, H. C. (1972) 'Zero growth'. *Newsweek*, 24 January.

Wilkinson, R. G. and K. Pickett (2009) *The Spirit Level: Why equality is better for everyone.* London: Allen Lane.

— (2010) *The Spirit Level: Why equality is better for everyone.* Revised edition. London: Penguin.

Wood, A. M., C. J. Boyce, S. C. Moore and G. D. Brown (2012) 'An evolutionary based social rank explanation of why low income predicts mental distress: a 17 year cohort study of 30,000 people'. *Journal of Affective Disorders* 136(3): 882–8.

4 | ARE PROSPERITY AND SUSTAINABILITY COMPATIBLE?

William E. Rees

Introduction: on the nature of prosperity and sustainability

'Prosperity' is an elusive and culture-specific concept. To most people in Western industrial societies it implies the lack of poverty, a state of possessing more than adequate monetary wealth with the promise of more to come. But if we extend the meaning to include the various intangibles that make living worthwhile, prosperity might mean material adequacy combined with a richness of family, friendships and community relationships, i.e. a wealth of 'social capital'. I recall a presentation by an Iranian academic with materially modest roots who argued that his people were unaware that they lived in poverty until so informed by international development experts. The latter did not include the villagers' traditional endowment of social and cultural wealth in their definition of prosperity. With this as the context, let us agree that 'prosperity' is a relative concept and declare that *a community is prosperous if it offers material sufficiency and spiritual well-being for all.*

'Sustainability' or 'sustainable development' is probably an even more contested concept, with many definitions that are often so vague as to be practically meaningless. The best known definition, that of the United Nations' World Commission on Environment and Development (WCED, or the Brundtland Commission) is as flexible as any. The Commission saw sustainable development as 'development that meets the needs of the present without compromising the ability of future generations to meet their own needs' (WCED 1987). While this definition popularised the concept, and was ground-breaking in recognising the obligations of the present to future generations, it can be interpreted to satisfy virtually any economic, ecological or social prejudice. Indeed, the Commission itself assumed that apparent environmental limits to economic growth are imposed not so much by nature as 'by the state of technology and social organization' (ibid.:

43) and that while future expansion would have to be qualitatively different from present forms of growth, 'a five- to tenfold increase in world industrial output can be anticipated before the population stabilizes [at about twice the present numbers] sometime in the next century' (ibid.: 213). In other words, one can interpret the WCED definition as an endorsement of the status quo – continuous growth by improved governance and more benign technology.

I prefer something marginally more concrete. For present purposes, we will assume that a system, including our global socio-economic system, is sustainable if it could continue on its current trajectory or could function in its current configuration indefinitely, without undermining the biophysical or social basis of its own existence. In terms that the more economically inclined might endorse, an economy is sustainable if prevailing levels of production and consumption do not reduce real wealth (natural, human and man-made capital) per capita. It follows that *sustainable development is a process of positive social change* (meaning qualitative 'improvement', not quantitative 'growth') *characterised by continuous investment in maintaining the ecosystems, economic structures and socio-cultural institutions upon which society depends.*

According to these definitions, it is clear that neither most national economies nor the global economy are presently sustainable. They do not provide sufficiency for all and are systematically eroding the ecological, social and even the economic foundations of their own existence. The human enterprise is therefore structurally and functionally vulnerable to collapse.

What makes us unsustainable?

This should not be a surprise. Humanity is arguably unsustainable by nature (Rees 2002; 2010). Ecologists recognise that Homo sapiens' reproductive habits mark humans as an archetypal K-strategist species. K-strategists are typically large, long-lived, slowly reproducing, competitive organisms with intensive parental care and therefore high survival rates to maturity. Such species tend to live in dense populations (relative to habitat quality) and continuously press up against local carrying capacity.[1] By these criteria, humans are clearly K-strategists, a distinction we share with other mammals ranging from tapirs through elephants to blue whales.

How does this biological reality manifest itself? There are two obvious behavioural tendencies that Homo sapiens shares with all other species. Unless or until constrained by negative feedback (disease, resource shortages, conflict or war), human populations: 1) expand to fill all accessible habitat; and 2) use all available resources. (In the case of humans, of course, 'available' is determined by contemporary technology.)

If you doubt these assertions, how do you otherwise explain that Homo sapiens has the widest geographical range of all advanced vertebrate species, that we occupy all habitable landscapes on the Earth (as well as many that are technically not habitable – such as Antarctic research stations) and that we dream of colonising the universe? Note, too, that in the scramble for resources to maintain our expansionist trajectory, we are mining ever poorer qualities of ore in ever more remote locations and drilling for oil kilometres beneath the seabed, which is itself kilometres below the surface of the sea. We are literally scraping the bottom of our planetary barrel! Consider, too, that monetary income is merely a surrogate for real resources and that ordinary people tend to spend all their income whether that income is US$20,000 or US$100,000 per year. In this light, credit cards can be seen as an example of human ingenuity in the face of limits: personal credit enables us to continue consuming after our immediately available money resources have been exhausted. One result is that household debt in North America now typically exceeds annual household income. (We need say nothing about the fiscal deficits and accumulated debts of many nations.)

To complicate matters, humanity's natural expansionist tendencies are currently being reinforced by our increasingly global cultural narrative, the double-barrelled myth of continuous progress and perpetual material growth (more on this to follow). Listen to Lawrence Summers in 1991 when he was chief economist at the World Bank:

> There are no ... limits to the carrying capacity of the earth that are likely to bind any time in the foreseeable future ... The idea that we should put limits on growth because of some natural limit, is a profound error [with] staggering social costs (cited in McQuillan and Preston 1998: 25).

Summers carried these same views to his many subsequent

influential roles, including secretary of the Treasury of the United States (1999 to 2001), the presidency of Harvard University (2001–06) and, most recently, director of the National Economic Council for the Obama administration from (2009 to 2011). An even more ebullient champion of human technological prowess was the late Professor Julian Simon of the University of Maryland: 'Technology exists now to produce in virtually inexhaustible quantities just about all the products made by nature' and 'We have in our hands now ... the technology to feed, clothe, and supply energy to an ever-growing population for the next seven billion years' (Simon 1995).

This assertion may be arithmetically challenged, but the spirit behind it unites the contemporary world in unwavering loyalty to a cultural narrative that promises ever increasing wealth for everyone, everywhere. Particularly since the 1950s, most national governments have subscribed to a common vision of global development and poverty alleviation based on continuous economic expansion fuelled by open markets, more liberalised trade and new technology. At the heart of this expansionist vision is the belief that human welfare can be all but equated with ever increasing material well-being (income growth).

The result of this marriage of nature and nurture is entirely predictable: the explosive expansion of the human enterprise. Gradually freed from natural negative feedback (disease, food and other resource shortages, and so on), the human population and aggregate economy have been growing exponentially for 200 years. Human numbers expanded fourfold in the twentieth century alone (from 1.5 to 6 billion). Meanwhile, energy consumption increased sixteen-fold, fish catches thirty-five times and industrial output by about forty-fold (Arrow et al. 2004, citing McNeill 2000), while average per capita consumption grew by a factor of ten or more.

While people today consider such trends to be the norm, the present age of explosive growth and material exuberance is, in fact, the single most anomalous period in human history. It is also worth noting that none of it would have been possible without abundant cheap energy, particularly fossil fuels. The modern human enterprise is arguably the *product* of fossil fuels, since energy is the means by which we acquire all the other resources essential to modern civilisation, from aluminium to zirconium.[2]

Our excessive ecological footprint

Unfortunately, the human explosion is unfolding on a non-growing, finite planet. Since the economy is a fully contained, dependent subsystem of the ecosphere, the material expansion of the former must ultimately be constrained by the productive output and waste assimilation capacities of the latter (Rockström et al. 2009).

Box 4.1. The human ecological footprint – in overshoot

The 'ecological footprint' (EF) of a specified population is the area of land and water ecosystems required, on a continuous basis, to produce the bio-resources that the population consumes, and to assimilate the population's carbon wastes, wherever on the Earth the relevant land/water may be located.

At present, average per capita EFs in high-income countries range between 4 and 10 global average hectares (10 to 25 acres); the world's poorest people live on a third of a global average hectare (0.74 acres). In effect, monetary wealth gives people access through markets to the biological wealth of the planet.

Problem: There are only about 12 billion hectares of adequately productive land and water on Earth or about 1.8 hectares per person. North Americans, with EFs of over 7 global average hectares, use four times their equitable share of global biocapacity while impoverished people use only a fraction of theirs.

By 2008, the aggregate EF of humanity had reached approximately 18 billion hectares (average per capita EF = 2.7 global average hectares). This means that the global community is already in 'overshoot' – using more than nature can provide sustainably – by about 50 per cent (WWF 2012).

In 2012, 'overshoot day' (the day by which humans will have consumed more of nature's goods and services than the Earth will produce in that year) occurred around 22 August. In effect, for the duration of 2012, the growth and maintenance of the human enterprise will be funded by unsustainably depleting Earth's limited 'natural capital', polluting ecosystems and otherwise degrading global life support functions.

We can illustrate this constraint using ecological footprint analysis (EFA) (Rees 2013; Wackernagel and Rees 1996). EFA estimates humanity's demand on productive ecosystems and enables comparisons with available supply. EFA studies confirm that humanity's aggregate ecological footprint already exceeds the long-term biocapacity of Earth. The human enterprise is in a state of overshoot, using 50 per cent more biocapacity than ecosystems can sustainably supply (WWF 2012). It currently takes '1.5 years for the Earth to regenerate the renewable resources that people use, and absorb the CO_2 waste they produce, in [a given] year' (ibid.; see Box 4.1).

The major biophysical consequence of overshoot is that further growth of human numbers and per capita consumption can occur only at the expense of depleting vital natural capital stocks (for example, fish stocks, tropical forests, soils and ground water), filling waste sinks to overflowing and destabilising global life support functions (such as the climate system). It is therefore no stretch to describe the present relationship of humanity with nature as parasitic. (A parasite is an organism that gains its vitality at the expense of the vitality of its host.) In a similar vein, ecological economist Herman Daly argues that we may well have entered a new era of uneconomic growth – growth that generates more costs than benefits at the margin. This is *growth that makes us poorer rather than richer* (Daly 1998; 2102), itself a sound economic definition of unsustainability. Indeed, history shows that societies that ignore the symptoms of overshoot are prone to collapse (Diamond 2005; Tainter 1988).

Human potential subverted

In theory, modern humans are uniquely positioned to solve the (un)sustainability conundrum. Of the many intellectual and emotional qualities that distinguish Homo sapiens from other advanced vertebrates, five stand out that should serve us well in present circumstances:

- an unparalleled capacity for evidence-based reasoning and logical analysis;
- a unique ability to plan ahead, to shape our own future;
- the capacity for moral judgement;
- compassion for other individuals and other species;
- a predisposition to co-operate.

In light of this potential, why has the world community – particularly rich, economically and technologically competent nations – failed utterly to reverse or even substantially slow the degradation of the ecosphere, the widening income gap, biodiversity loss, and so on? On the contrary, overshoot is worsening and the bulk of this ecological destruction can be traced to production and consumption by the richest, best-educated nations on the planet. In the words of David Orr, the depletion and pollution of the planet 'is not the work of ignorant people. Rather it is largely the result of work by people with BAs, BSs, LLBs, MBAs and PhDs' (Orr 1994).

At least part of this enigma is being revealed by evolutionary psychology and cognitive neuroscience. Homo sapiens is a conflicted species. Humans may be capable of high intelligence, but our well developed cerebral cortex evolved only relatively recently and is by no means the only governor of our thoughts and actions. We 'live' in conscious awareness (by definition) and believe that we are acting rationally most of the time. However, the evidence shows that when people perceive a threat to anything from simple comfort to safety or survival, innate behavioural tendencies that operate *beneath consciousness*, in the more 'experienced' emotional limbic system or the instinct-laden brain stem, may well override more reasoned responses.

Given a moment's reflection, most people will admit that in their responses to situations involving temptation, danger or other emotional stress, *passion and instinct often trump reason* (for a generally positive take on the relationship between emotion and intelligence, see Ridley-Duff 2010). At the societal level, climate change and ecological degradation represent threats to the socio-economic status quo, including existing hierarchies of personal wealth, social status and political power. It should be no surprise that our corporate and ruling elites downplay the problem and seem more interested in protecting their own privileged status than in exercising society's collective intelligence in the development of strategies for humanity's collective security.

There is a further complication in the way in which people's brains develop and learn. Cognitive neuroscience shows that sensory experiences and elements of social learning to which a developing individual is repeatedly exposed literally help to shape the brain's synaptic circuitry in patterns that reflect and embed those experiences. In effect, various *socially constructed* social norms (such as political ideologies, academic paradigms and religious doctrines) acquire a physical presence in the 'soft-wiring' of our brains.[3]

The critical factor in the present context is that, once a coherent, habitual neural circuit has developed, people subsequently seek out *compatible* experiences. That is, humans naturally tend to spend time with friends or in circumstances that reinforce their existing beliefs, values and assumptions. Most importantly, 'when faced with information that does not agree with their [preformed] internal structures, they deny, discredit, reinterpret or forget that information' (Wexler 2006). Think again about mainstream society's non-response to the unfolding crisis.

Whether by accident or by design, the phenomenon of cognitive soft-wiring has played into the hands of those with a vested interest in maintaining the status quo, particularly the political right. For the past several decades (and particularly since the election of Ronald Reagan to the US presidency, his first term starting in 1981), the world has seen a determined campaign to entrench the values of market capitalism and neoliberal economics in the minds of the world's citizens (who, remember, are already culturally primed to expect continuous progress and income growth).

At the heart of the neoliberal paradigm is the supremacy of the individual, free to exercise all legal rights in the pursuit of wealth and happiness as a 'self-interested (short-term) utility maximiser' (whither social responsibilities?). The assumed efficiency of free markets in maximising production and consumption has become the highest of economic ideals. Deregulation is the free-market mantra; governments are inefficient; taxes anathema. The (increasingly global) market alone should determine how much gets invested in what goods and services and where in the world that investment should be made. Nations must specialise in a few things for which they have a comparative (efficiency) advantage and trade for everything else. All other values – self-reliance, economic diversity and resilience, job-security, social equity, loyalty to place and community, ecological integrity – are swept aside in the singular pursuit of growth and that extra margin of profit. The dominance of these beliefs in political and economic discourse around the world has been so effective that millions of people now regularly vote for policies that are against their own interests. Indeed, the neoliberal right may have designed the single most successful campaign of mass social engineering in human history (see Herman and Chomsky 1988; Klein 2008). And this is increasingly problematic. Apart from their theoretical efficiency in resource allocation, markets are as dumb as a post. Market exchanges reflect only the short-term interests of participating individuals and firms as if unconstrained self-indulgence were an adequate substitute for longer-term environmental and community values. And since many ecological and social costs have been externalised, prices communicate only a diminished fraction of the true social costs of production and consumption. This makes contemporary markets inherently *inefficient*. Moreover, markets tell us nothing at all about the lags, thresholds, positive feedbacks and other non-linear behaviours of the complex ecological and social systems that the growing economy is putting under stress. The world's commitment to individual choice and markets in the pursuit of monetary wealth may well be driving critical ecosystems and life-support functions ever closer to fatally irreversible tipping points. It also sanctions a global climate of 'complacent irresponsibility' (Drèze and Sen 1989: 276) that allows us to forget our moral obligations to the present and ignore our collective duties to future generations.[4] Far from abolishing poverty, the income gap yawns ever wider even as over-consumption and pollution by the wealthy destroy ecosystems and visit violence on the poor (increasingly frequent extreme storm events, floods, drought and other dimensions of 'climate change', for example).

Clearly, the prevailing global economic narrative is woefully maladaptive in both ecological and social terms. Capitalist market economies are, in fact, inherently unsustainable. Our current precarious state is an inevitable 'emergent property' of the interaction between two fundamentally incompatible systems – the human economy as presently conceived and the ecosphere (Rees 2010). In today's world of rapid global ecological change, blind obeisance to rigid market ideology is tantamount to abandoning high intelligence and our ability to plan a better world. Humanity is cognitively addicted to a dangerous economic paradigm completely divorced from emerging biophysical reality.

Facing the new reality

We have seen that Homo sapiens, like all species, has an innate propensity to expand and to consume all available resources in the process. These natural predispositions are currently being reinforced by the myth of continuous progress and economic growth, most recently manifested in the global proliferation of capitalist values and neoliberal market economics. The result is a world in ecological overshoot, a globalised economy that is steadily degrading the biophysical and social basis of its own existence.

No amount of 'reform' (tinkering at the margins) is likely to improve this situation. To achieve sustainability will require that we replace the core beliefs, values and assumptions of the present global economic system with a new set of operational principles compatible with real-world ecosystems and human communities. The scientific evidence suggests that ecological sustainability will require *substantial absolute reductions* in aggregate energy and material consumption and waste production; at the same time, social sustainability depends on greater social equity. So far, however, the global community has proved unwilling to contemplate the policy measures necessary to achieve these ends. Mainstream voices call for improved technology and greater efficiencies to resolve our so-called 'environmental' problems, and for further income growth to address chronic poverty. This is the status quo only more so! Our leaders and much of the population are foundering in deep collective denial.

What to do? Towards a co-operative model for global sustainability

Let us assume that global change science and the evidence of resource shortages are roughly correct. (Is there any reason not to?) In these circumstances, it may well be that the anomalous two-centuries-long period of more or less assured economic growth is coming to an end.[5] Indeed, it is arguable that in coming decades the global community will experience an absolute (if geographically uneven) contraction in gross economic activity – the 'scale' of the world economy is overdue for a significant structural adjustment. In this light, a truly intelligent species would recognise that it has a stark choice – the world community can either:

1 remain on the present 'business-as-usual' course, in which case
   nature is likely to impose a chaotic, painful contraction characterised by civic unrest and resource wars; or

2 choose to exercise humanity's unique capacity for collective intelligence and co-operative social organisation to plan a controlled
   contraction that provides sufficiency for all while avoiding geopolitical chaos and ecosystemic collapse.

The potential horror of an imposed implosion (option 1) should
be sufficient motivation for intelligent co-operation, but there is also
a positive argument for option 2. The global system is intricately
interconnected – no individual or nation can achieve sustainability
on its own. Sustainability is thus a collective problem requiring
collective solutions. Perhaps for the first time in human history,
*individual and national self-interests have arguably converged with
humanity's collective interests.*

Should the world community rise to the challenge of option 2, a
reasonable plan might be to strive for 'one-planet living'. This goal
describes the average material standards that could be extended to
the entire human family without jeopardising the long-term biocapacity of the Earth. At present, this implies a per capita ecological
footprint of about 1.8 global average hectares: that is, each member
of the human family would have a right of access to the productive
and assimilative capacity (goods and life-support services) of 1.8
hectares of average productive ecosystem (Box 4.1).

Evidence suggests that with a combination of conservation, the use
of efficient technologies and appropriate lifestyle choices, a reasonable, more equitable level of material prosperity could be achieved
within the 'one-planet living' constraint (see, for example, von
Weizsäcker et al. 2009). That said, 'one planet' implies that Western
Europeans should be taking measured steps to reduce their average
ecological footprints by about 60 per cent to reach their 'fair Earth-
share' (1.8 average hectares). North Americans need a 75 to 80 per
cent reduction. And here we reveal the really inconvenient truth, the
inelegant elephant in the sustainability parlour. A just sustainability
on a crowded, finite planet requires redistribution. People must learn
to share the Earth's ecological and economic bounties. By reducing
their own consumption, wealthy people vacate the ecological space

necessary for poor people to increase theirs.[6] Altruism, particularly reciprocal altruism, is the ultimate in co-operative relationships and an essential part of the process.

In fact, global sustainability will require unprecedented forms of co-operation and myriad co-operative institutions at all spatial scales. The world needs a global framework agreement for sharing bio-capacity and resources, but for practical reasons the implementation of sustainability plans will take place at the national and local levels.

In theory, achieving these multiple levels of co-operation should be possible. While many advanced species are known for their co-operative behaviour and social structures, few can match Homo sapiens for the diversity and complexity of co-operative social structures and institutions already in place. Indeed, co-operation is an innate quality of individual human behaviour and is the foundational organising principle of civilisation. Regrettably, the co-operative instinct has been repressed at the broader community level for decades by the focus of neoliberal rhetoric on competitive individualism in the exercise of short-term self-interest in the marketplace.

The spectrum of behavioural possibilities

People are naturally capable of a great deal more. Table 4.1 lists some of the relevant 'colours' at opposite ends of the wide-ranging spectrum of human behavioural potential. The bad news is that society has spent decades stridently entrenching the darker anti-social behaviours that are anathema to co-operation and sustainability. However, the fact that cultural context determines which socio-behavioural qualities dominate social discourse is also the good news. The world must now begin to fashion a new cultural narrative from the brighter colours of behavioural possibilities. In essence,

TABLE 4.1 Elements of the human behavioural spectrum

Dominant today: the darker colours	Needed: the brighter colours
Individualism; self-centredness	Community/social orientation
Selfishness	(Mutual) altruism
Short-term gratification	Longer-term (delayed) gratification
Indifference; heartlessness	Compassion; empathy
Disengagement (even obstruction)	Co-operative engagement with community

the underpinning values of society must shift from competitive individualism, greed and narrow self-interest towards community, co-operation and other values that reflect our mutual interest in the survival of global civilisation. Fortunately, other-regarding emotions such as compassion, empathy, love and altruism are key components of the human behavioural repertoire (Manner and Gowdy 2010).

Implications for economic life

The new, more adaptive cultural narrative has major implications for the structure and function of the economy. A fundamental change is the replacement of the neoliberal policy focus on efficiency and growth (merely getting bigger) with an ecological economics emphasis on equity and development (qualitative improvement). Table 4.2 contrasts some of the key value shifts necessary to achieve a sustainable 'steady-state' economy.

TABLE 4.2 The shift in economic values and assumptions (getting better is better than getting bigger)

From neoliberal thinking	To socio-ecological thinking
Growth	Steady state (constant 'throughput' of energy/matter within the means of nature)
Efficiency	Inter- and intra-generational equity
Maximum scale	Optimal scale
Capital accumulation	Qualitative improvement
Substitution among types of capital	Complementarity among types of capital
Minimal interference in markets	Active intervention to correct for market failures
Weak sustainability (maintaining the aggregate value of natural and man-made capital)	Strong sustainability (maintaining adequate physical stocks of natural and man-made capital)

The world will also have to rethink the whole idea of 'globalisation', which currently implies the dissolution of national boundaries and integration of national economies into one. Under conditions of continuous growth, the present form of globalisation actually accelerates ecological degradation by exposing remaining pockets of resources and biocapacity to an ever increasing global market.

Critically, the global economy is an enormous system characterised by great internal diversity, multiple equilibria, various lags, unknown thresholds and other behaviours typical of complex systems. It is simply too large and too rife with irreducible uncertainty to be 'managed' at all, let alone sustainably. Certainly leaving untrammelled market forces in charge is foolish, possibly catastrophic (climate change, for example, is a symptom of gross market failure).

In this light, the new world economy should be an economy of co-operating regions or nations linked by strictly managed trade. In effect, the world must de-globalise to reduce regions' and nations' dependence on foreign sources and sinks. At the same time, in order to achieve long-term sustainability, national and regional economies should begin to:

- re-localise, i.e. re-skill domestic populations and diversify local economies through import displacement where possible and practical;
- increase local and national self-reliance in food, energy and other essential resources as a buffer against climate change, rising scarcity costs and global strife;
- invest in rebuilding local and national natural capital stocks (for example, fisheries, forests, soils and biodiversity reserves) using revenues collected from carbon taxes or resource quota auctions; and
- advance *producer and consumer co-operatives* as an efficient, effective and equitable way to achieve economic stability (the Mondragon co-operatives are a good working model).

Structural change would also have an impact at the local and community level. In the best of circumstances, long-term sustainability will require that people share jobs and work.[7] A planned economic contraction with job-sharing and adequate social safety nets holds out the promise of improved general well-being through greater job security and more satisfying forms of employment. The latter will be delivered, in part, by fostering greater regional economic diversity and self-reliance (reduced trade dependence). The diversity of side benefits ranges from a reduced risk of dangerous climate change (or other eco-catastrophe), through enhanced food security, to more 'spare time' for personal development, family relationships, community engagement, or simply goofing off. Bottom line? A higher quality of life – true prosperity – is theoretically possible with sustainably less material consumption and pollution.

Epilogue

Regrettably, theoretical possibilities are not always realised. Time is short and there will undoubtedly be strenuous pushback from powerful elements of society who perceive that they have more to lose than to gain from general sustainability (and who will fight to maintain their privileged positions), from those whose soft-wired conventional neural circuitry is particularly resistant to reprogramming, and from those who are otherwise in denial about the ecological crisis. People's natural tendency to react emotionally or instinctively to perceived threats to their social status combined with decades of strident insistence on the 'rightness' of capitalist and market ideologies represent formidable barriers to modest reform, let alone the wholesale transformation of society.

Neuroscientists have understood the effect of (if not the mechanism for) cognitive dissonance in various contexts for a long time. As French psychologist Gustave Le Bon wrote in 1896:

> The masses have never thirsted after truth. They turn aside from evidence that is not to their taste, preferring to deify error, if error seduce[s] them. Whoever can supply them with illusions is easily their master; whoever attempts to destroy their illusions is always their victim (Le Bon 1896).

More than a century later, American pop philosopher Derrick Jensen described how the human mind shields itself from the prickly barbs of reality:

> For us to maintain our way of living, we must ... tell lies to each other, and especially to ourselves ... the lies act as barriers to truth. These barriers ... are necessary because without them many deplorable acts would become impossibilities (Jensen 2000).[8]

It is therefore possible – even likely, considering the lack of international progress to date – that the world community is too deeply committed to conventional myths, too fractious in outlook and too belligerent in defence of tribal territory (cognitive as well as spatial) to rise fully to the sustainability challenge. Preferred lies and familiar illusions may well hold sway over discomforting truths. Should this come to pass, it wouldn't be the first time human society risked tripping into the abyss. Indeed, as Joseph Tainter concluded: 'what is perhaps most intriguing in the evolution of human societies is the regularity with which the pattern of increasing complexity is interrupted by collapse' (Tainter 1988).

What would be unprecedented is the sheer scale of the implosion – if *global* civilisation goes down, it might mean the end of the human evolutionary experiment in high intelligence, co-operative planning and social justice. Success, on the other hand, would mark the triumph of reason and compassion over more primitive predispositions, thus opening a whole new chapter in the human evolutionary saga. Surely that is worth fighting for.

Notes

1 This was Malthus' great insight – human populations would always tend to outstrip local food or resource supplies.

2 This is a cause for concern as the era of abundant cheap energy comes to an end.

3 This is 'soft-wiring' because these patterns can be changed (although in some cases it takes considerable time and effort). The brain is a highly 'plastic' organ that can 're-wire' itself.

4 Social costs are high and rising even in developed countries. As the market tail wags the societal dog, communities are paying dearly in terms of self-reliance, economic diversity, local ownership and well-paid manufacturing jobs. Market forces have simplified regional economies, de-skilled their populations, lowered wages and expectations, and sold off – or depleted – their resources. (Remember the collapse of the North Atlantic cod fishery?) Average gross domestic product per capita may be growing, but most gains go to the already wealthy; poverty and unemployment are stagnant or increas-

ing; the middle class is eroding; and we are told we can no longer afford quality public education, adequate healthcare or decent (un)employment insurance.

5 Various analysts argue that the current prolonged 'stall' in the customary pattern of global growth is the result of increasing energy and resource scarcity and rising costs, and may be permanent.

6 Average consumption could later gradually rise – if desirable – with further technological improvements and population reductions.

7 The 'best of circumstances' assumes that we can, in fact, co-operatively engineer a smooth economic contraction; that there will be adequate engineered energy to supply people's needs without human drudgery; that people take more satisfaction from intangibles than from material possessions, and so on.

8 Even supposedly objective scientists are not immune to self-delusion: 'a new scientific truth does not triumph by convincing its opponents and making them see the light, but rather because

its opponents eventually die, and a new generation grows up that is familiar with it' (Planck 1949).

References

Arrow, K., P. Dasgupta, L. Goulder et al. (2004) 'Are we consuming too much?' *Journal of Economic Perspectives* 18(3): 147–72.

Daly, H. (1998) 'Uneconomic growth in theory and in fact: the first annual Feasta lecture'. *Feasta Review* 1. www.feasta.org/documents/feastareview/daly.htm.

— (2012) 'Uneconomic growth deepens depression'. *The Daly News*. Center for the Advancement of the Steady State Economy (CASSE). http://steadystate.org/uneconomic-growth-deepens-depression/.

Diamond, J. (2005) *Collapse: How societies choose to fail or succeed*. New York, NY: Viking.

Drèze, J. and A. Sen (1989) *Hunger and Public Action*. Oxford: Clarendon.

Herman, E. S. and N. Chomsky (1988) *Manufacturing Consent: The political economy of the mass media*. New York, NY: Pantheon Books.

Jensen, D. (2000) *A Language Older than Words*. New York, NY: Context Books.

Klein, N. (2008) *The Shock Doctrine: The rise of disaster capitalism*. Toronto: Vintage Canada.

Le Bon, G. (1896) *The Crowd: A Study of the popular mind*. Kitchener, Canada: Batoche Books (2001 reprint). http://socserv.mcmaster.ca/econ/ugcm/3ll3/lebon/Crowds.pdf.

Manner, M. and J. Gowdy (2010) 'The evolution of social and moral behavior: evolutionary insights for public policy'. *Ecological Economics* 69(4): 753–61.

McNeill, J. R. (2000) *Something New Under the Sun: An environmental history of the twentieth-century world*. New York, NY: W. W. Norton.

McQuillan, A. and A. Preston (eds) (1998) *Globally and Locally: Seeking a middle path to sustainable development*. Lanham, MD: University Press of America.

Orr, D. (1991) 'What is education for?' *In Context* 27: 52. www.context.org/iclib/ic27/orr/.

— (1994) *Earth in Mind: On education, environment, and the human prospect*. Washington, DC: Island Press.

Planck, M. K. (1949) *Scientific Autobiography and Other Papers*. Translated by F. Gaynor. New York, NY: Philosophical Library.

Rees, W. E. (2002) 'Is humanity fatally successful?' *Journal of Business Administration and Policy Analysis* 30–1: 67–100. Reprinted in P. Nemetz (ed.), *Sustainable Resource Management: Reality or illusion?* Cheltenham: Edward Elgar.

— (2010) 'What's blocking sustainability? Human nature, cognition and denial'. *Sustainability: Science, Practice & Policy* 6(2): 13–25. http://sspp.proquest.com/archives/vol6iss2/1001-012.rees.html.

— (2013) 'Ecological footprint, concept of,' in S. Levin (ed.), *Encyclopedia of Biodiversity*. 2nd edition. San Diego, CA: Academic Press.

Ridley-Duff, R. (2010) *Emotion, Seduction and Intimacy*. Seattle, WA: Booktrope.

Rockström, J., W. Steffen, K. Noone et al. (2009) 'A safe operating space for humanity'. *Nature* 461: 472–5.

Simon, J. (1995) *The State of Humanity: Steadily improving*. Cato Policy Report, September/October. Washington, DC: Cato Institute. www.cato.org/policy-report/septemberoctober-1995/state-humanity-steadily-improving.

Tainter, J. (1988) *The Collapse of Complex Societies*. New York, NY: Cambridge University Press.

Von Weizsäcker, E. U., K. Hargroves, M. H. Smith et al. (2009) *Factor Five: Transforming the global economy through 80% improvements in resource productivity*. London: Earthscan.

Wackernagel, M. and W. E. Rees (1996) *Our Ecological Footprint: Reducing human impact on the earth*. Gabriola Island, Canada: New Society Publishers.

WCED (1987) *Our Common Future*.

Oxford: Oxford University Press for the UN World Commission on Environment and Development (WCED).

Wexler, B. (2006) *Brain and Culture: Neurobiology, ideology, and social change*. Cambridge, MA: The MIT Press.

WWF (2012) *Living Planet Report 2012: Biodiversity, biocapacity and better choices*. Gland, Switzerland: WWF International.

5 | LIVING WELL: EXPLORATIONS INTO THE END OF GROWTH[1]

Peter A. Victor

Introduction

Looking back over the twenty-first century, future historians may well see it as even more tumultuous than the century that preceded it. In the twentieth century the human population more than tripled, average life expectancy at birth more than doubled, and real gross domestic product (GDP) increased nearly forty times. Huge numbers of people experienced very real improvements in living standards as economic growth spread around the world, yet huge numbers were living in extreme poverty when the century ended. Political systems from Nazism to Communism rose and fell, while democracy in its various forms survived. Well over 200 million people died in wars and conflicts, and nuclear energy was unleashed with the specific purpose of annihilating many tens of thousands in a flash. Seemingly magical technologies in transportation, communication, entertainment and computation proliferated, as did enormous cities and corporations with global reach. Societies were transformed for better and worse, as was the planet itself.

Despite claims to the contrary, nature was not conquered. Instead, human societies and economies became ever more dependent on increasing quantities of materials, energy and wastes (i.e. increasing 'throughput') as well as on the transformation of land, as more and more was brought into direct use by humans. Towards the end of the twentieth century, attempts to gain a quantitative picture of these environmental changes yielded new indicators such as the ecological footprint, the human appropriation of the net products of photosynthesis (HANPP), and various measures of direct and total material throughput – all of which, with some local exceptions, point in the same threatening direction. In the second decade of the twenty-first century, humanity's impact on the rest of nature is on the rise and shows little sign of reversing. In the language of planetary boundaries, we are exceeding the safe operating capacity of the planet to sustain us (Rockström et al. 2009).

At the same time as we are being constrained by what earth systems can tolerate, incomes and wealth are becoming more unequally distributed, the global financial system is faltering, economies are struggling, and confidence in political systems to address these problems is in decline. These trends are more than disturbing; they portend catastrophe. But their continuation is not a given. A brighter and genuinely more prosperous future may still be possible: one in which everyone lives well without depleting or degrading natural systems and where all humans and all nature flourish. However, such a future will come to pass only if we think hard about our predicament, examine a wide range of possibilities, and strive for what we want rather than just accepting what comes our way.

Among these possibilities, there needs to be a reconsideration of the priority given to the pursuit of economic growth, especially in developed countries, where, arguably, the costs of economic growth have begun to outweigh the benefits (Victor 2012b). Biophysical constraints to continued growth are becoming more apparent. There is mounting evidence indicating that higher incomes do not make people happier beyond a level of per capita incomes far surpassed by many in developed countries, and, despite decades of substantial economic growth, many social and environmental problems remain. If adopted, a thoughtful strategy in which economic growth became merely a by-product of other, more focused objectives would set a very different example for other countries to follow.

Not that economic growth itself is directly and inextricably related to increased throughput, although, historically, the connection has been strong (Kraussman et al. 2009). But as long as economic growth remains, it will be the most important measure of economic success, either for its own sake or for the benefits it is presumed to bring, and efforts to reverse the rising impacts of humans on the biosphere will always take second place. This raises the question of whether it is possible for people to live well in a society in which economic stability rather than economic growth is the norm, where all its members flourish, and social justice is served. Such a circumstance should not be confused with economic stagnation and societal decline, but should stand in sharp contrast to that dismal scenario so often touted as the only alternative to endless economic growth.

In *Prosperity without Growth*, Tim Jackson argues that developed economies require economic growth if they are to avoid the downward spiral of deflation, recession and depression (Jackson 2009). He also argues that such growth cannot be sustained because of its resource requirements and the unacceptably high burden it places on the environment. He refers to this as the dilemma of growth. We can't live with it and we can't live without it, or so it appears, unless we open our minds to a broader range of alternative futures than is normally contemplated. The essence of my recent work and the main theme of both this chapter and my collaborative work with Tim Jackson is to investigate how achieving the ecological benefits of lower growth is compatible with social justice and social welfare or equality objectives.

Exploring alternatives to economic growth

There are many ways of thinking about alternative futures. One that I have found fruitful is to develop empirically based simulations of national economies so that we can examine key trends and identify ways of strengthening desirable ones and of turning undesirable ones around. My work has been focused on national economies because most of the necessary data for analysing economies is most readily available at that level. Having said that, it is clear that we also need to understand likely and possible futures at the sub- and super-national levels, a demanding agenda indeed.

The purpose of scenario analysis is not to develop a specific prescription for the future. Rather, it is to see if the future – which will be very different from the past, whether we decide to make it that way or not – could be attractive even in the absence of continued economic growth. Not that zero economic growth should replace continuous economic growth as the overarching objective of economic policy. But the prospect of reduced, zero or even negative economic growth should not stand in the way of the increasingly urgent measures required to reduce the burden of our economies on nature. If we fail to reduce this burden, then the possibility of a good life for all will disappear.

The LowGrow model

When I was a PhD student at the University of British Columbia in the 1960s, I was most fortunate to be supervised by the distinguished progressive economist Gideon Rosenbluth. Under his guidance, I developed and applied a methodology for estimating the material 'throughput' of an economy based on the law of conservation of matter. The fundamental principle, which applies to all monetised economies, is that, associated with each expenditure in the economy, there is a direct and indirect flow of material inputs, and ultimately a disposal of an equal amount of wastes (Victor 1972). This is true for all expenditures, whether they be on goods or services or for current consumption or investment, although the difference between throughputs for equal expenditures varies tremendously according to what is purchased. For example, energy-intensive products such as transportation result in much greater emissions of greenhouse gases than the services provided by hairdressers.

Over the years, I kept in touch with Gideon. Still, I was pleasantly surprised when, about ten years ago, he suggested that we collaborate on the 'growth question'. I had just completed my term as dean of the Faculty of Environmental Studies at York University in Toronto, having resumed my academic career in the mid-1990s, and I was ready to embark on a substantive research project. It was an opportunity and a privilege to work with Gideon again. Even in his eighties he was an intellectual force to be reckoned with.

Although it was not our original intention to build a macro-economic simulation model, we found a common interest in doing so. We were sceptical of the mainstream view that endless economic growth was feasible, desirable, and essential for full employment, eradication of poverty and significantly reduced impacts on the environment. We were also unsatisfied by critiques of such a view that did not also provide an account of how an economy might function in a radically different way. So we set ourselves the task of answering the following question: is it possible to have full employment, no poverty, fiscal balance and reduced greenhouse gas emissions without relying on economic growth? We developed LowGrow, a simulation model of the Canadian economy specifically designed to answer this question. Our results suggested the possibility that an attractive set of social, economic and environmental objectives could be met in the absence of economic growth. This led us to the conclusion that economic growth could and should be relegated to its proper secondary place as a policy objective.

All models are simplifications of whatever they represent. This is as true of computer models as it is of model aeroplanes and model villages. Whether they are satisfactory simplifications depends on their intended uses. A model plane may be designed to closely resemble a particular commercial or military jet but rest on a stand, unable to fly. Another model might be designed to fly, powered by hand, an elastic band or an on-board engine. Yet it may only vaguely resemble a full-size aircraft. Which of these two model planes is better depends on whether you want a visual replica of a real plane or something that flies. Building simulation models of an economy is not that different.

The overview of LowGrow that follows may appear tedious, but it is necessary to give some idea of what lies behind the scenarios that it generates.[2] Figure 5.1 shows the simplified structure of Low-Grow. Macro demand is determined in the normal way as the sum of consumption expenditure, investment expenditure, government expenditure, and the difference between exports and imports. Their sum total is GDP, measured as expenditure. There are separate equations for each of these components in the model, estimated using Canadian data from about 1981 to 2005, depending on the variable. Production in the economy depends on employed labour and employed capital (i.e. buildings, equipment, software and infrastructure). Changes in productivity from improvements in technology, labour skills and organisation are captured depending on time. Macro supply is shown at the bottom of Figure 5.1, and it determines and is determined by employment and capacity utilisation, as shown in the centre of the figure.

There is a second important link between macro demand and production. Investment expenditures (net of depreciation), which are part of macro demand, add to the economy's stock of capital, increasing its productive capacity. Also, capital and labour tend to become more productive over time. It follows that, other things being equal, without an increase in macro demand, these increases in capital and productivity reduce employment: as labour becomes more productive over time, less is required to produce any given

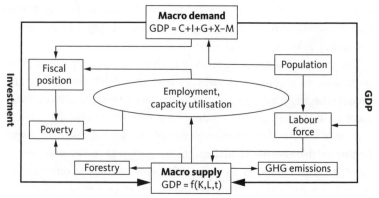

Note: C = consumption, I = investment, G = government, X = exports, M = imports
K = capital, L = labour, t = time

5.1 The high-level structure of LowGrow (*source*: Victor 2008)

level of output. On this basis, economic growth (i.e. an increase in GDP) is needed to prevent unemployment rising as capacity and productivity increase.

Population is determined exogenously in LowGrow, which offers a choice of three projections from Statistics Canada. Population is also one of the variables that determines consumption expenditures in the economy. The labour force is estimated in LowGrow as a function of GDP and of population.

There is no monetary sector in LowGrow. For simplicity, we assumed that the Bank of Canada, Canada's central bank, regulates the money supply to keep inflation at or near the target level of 2 per cent per year. LowGrow includes an exogenously set rate of interest that remains unchanged throughout each run of the model. A higher cost of borrowing discourages investment, which reduces macro demand. It also raises the cost to the government of servicing its debt. The price level is not included as a variable in LowGrow, although the model warns of inflationary pressures when the rate of unemployment falls below 4 per cent (effectively full employment in Canada).

LowGrow includes features that are particularly relevant for exploring the possibilities for an economy that is not growing. It includes emissions of carbon dioxide and other greenhouse gases, a carbon tax, a forestry sub-model, and provision for redistributing incomes.

It measures poverty using the United Nations' (UN's) Human Poverty Index (i.e. HPI-2 for selected Organisation for Economic Co-operation and Development, or OECD, countries) (UNDP 2006). LowGrow allows additional funds to be spent on healthcare and on programmes for reducing adult illiteracy (both included in HPI-2) and estimates their impacts on longevity and adult literacy with equations from the literature.

Expenditures on anti-poverty and environmental programmes are automatically added to government expenditures in LowGrow. Other changes in the level of government expenditures can also be simulated in LowGrow through a variety of fiscal policies, such as an annual percentage change in government expenditures that can vary over time and a balanced budget. LowGrow keeps track of the overall fiscal position of all three levels of government combined (federal, provincial and municipal) by calculating total revenues and expenditures and by estimating debt repayments based on the historical record. As the level of government indebtedness declines, the rates of taxes on personal incomes and profits in LowGrow are reduced endogenously, which is broadly consistent with government policy in Canada.

In LowGrow, as in the economy that it represents, economic growth is driven by: net investment, which adds to productive assets; growth in the labour force; increases in productivity; growth in the net trade balance; growth in government expenditures; and growth in population. Low- and no-growth scenarios can be examined by reducing the rates of increase of each of these factors either singly or in combination.

A business-as-usual scenario It is convenient to start analysing low- and no-growth scenarios by establishing a base case with no new policy interventions. This is the 'business-as-usual' case illustrated in Figure 5.2 and describes what would happen in the Canadian economy if the trends in the years before 2005 were to continue for another thirty years. It is not a prediction of the future, but rather a benchmark against which to compare alternative scenarios.

In the business-as-usual scenario, between the start of 2005 and 2035, real GDP per capita more than doubles; the unemployment rate rises, then falls, ending above its starting value; the ratio of

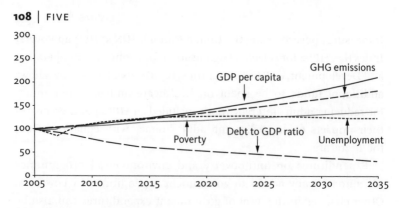

5.2 Business as usual (*source*: Victor 2008)

government debt to GDP declines by nearly 40 per cent as Canadian governments continue to run budget surpluses; the poverty index rises, largely due to the projected increase in the absolute number of unemployed people; and greenhouse gas emissions increase by nearly 80 per cent.

A low- or no-growth scenario A wide range of low- and no-growth scenarios can be examined with LowGrow. One promising scenario is shown in Figure 5.3. Compared with the business-as-usual scenario, GDP per capita grows more slowly, levelling off around 2028, at which time the rate of unemployment is 5.7 per cent. The unemployment rate continues to decline to 4.0 per cent by 2035. By 2020 the poverty index declines from 10.7 to an internationally unprecedented level of 4.9, where it remains, and the debt-to-GDP ratio declines to about

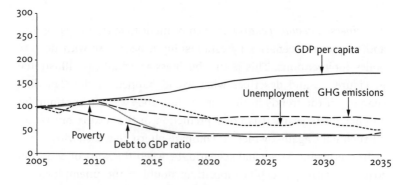

5.3 A low- or no-growth scenario (*source*: Victor 2008)

30 per cent, to be maintained at that level to 2035. Greenhouse gas emissions are 31 per cent lower at the start of 2035 than in 2005, and 41 per cent lower than at their high point in 2010.

Policy directions for a low- or no-growth scenario

What does it take to achieve the kind of outcomes illustrated in Figure 5.3? One advantage of a simulation model such as LowGrow is that it helps answer this question. The scenario is based on a number of key changes in the model that could come about through the cumulative changes in autonomous behaviour of individuals and organisations, by policy measures introduced by government, or, most likely, by some combination of the two.

The scenario in Figure 5.3 results from a variety of changes, some more controversial than others, that would be required to transform the business-as-usual scenario in Figure 5.2 into an attractive scenario in which economic growth is not required to meet economic, social and environmental objectives. These changes include the following:

- *Consumption*: Consumption is one of the main driving forces of the economy. In a successful economy not geared to growth, we would expect the pattern and level of consumption to be very different from those in a growing economy. For example, well-being would be enhanced with a greater emphasis on public goods, which includes the environment; on shared provision of private goods, as we are already seeing with cars and bicycles in many cities; and on services, rather than commodities. More controls on the content and placement of advertising would be helpful.
- *Investment*: In economic terms, investment refers to the purchase of new infrastructure, buildings and equipment. Some of this investment replaces what has been worn out. The rest adds to the stock of built capital and is a major source of economic growth since it increases the productive capacity of the economy. A viable low- or no-growth scenario requires major changes in the quantity and type of investment. These changes will transform the capital stock so that environmental impacts are reduced, degraded ecosystems are restored, renewable materials and energy are substituted for non-renewables, and people are better served

in terms of housing, transportation, education, healthcare and other social services.

- *Employment*: One aspect of the dilemma of growth is that, with an expansion of the capital stock, labour becomes more productive. Unless there is economic growth, an inevitable consequence is unemployment, since fewer and fewer people are required to produce any given level of output. A complicating factor is that, in most economies, paid employment is the primary source of income for most adults, so higher rates of unemployment threaten an increase in poverty. This aspect of the dilemma can be overcome by several changes. First, in a more socially just economy – especially one with an ageing population – there would be more jobs in the human services sector where increases in labour productivity are likely to be less than those in the production of goods. Second, by strengthening the social safety net and establishing a guaranteed minimum income, we would rely less on income from employment for distributing the output of the economy via wages. Any concern that this might reduce the incentive to work is less problematic in an economy in which growth is no longer regarded as an imperative. Third, a reduction in average hours spent in paid employment provides a means by which people can benefit from increases in labour productivity other than through an expansion of economic output. Beyond some level of material well-being – different for each person, but likely within the range already surpassed on average in developed economies – more leisure makes a greater contribution to well-being than a higher income.

- *Population*: The scenario in Figure 5.3 is based on an assumption that the population and labour force will stabilise over the next twenty years or so. In Canada, as in many developed countries, the fertility rate (i.e. the average number of children born to a woman over her lifetime) is below the replacement rate of about 2.1. Under these circumstances, net immigration becomes the source of population growth. Stabilisation of the Canadian population would require a reduction in net immigration to about 200,000 people per year. This would still allow Canada to maintain a level of about 100,000 immigrants in its family unification and refugee categories and would require a reduction only in immigrants admitted to Canada to promote economic growth.

- *Poverty*: The idea that poverty can be eradicated through the trickle-down effects of economic growth has been shown wanting. Poverty is more than a matter of inadequate income. It is also about social exclusion, which is closely related to the distribution of income and wealth and not just their amount. Recent experience in many developed countries has shown little or no increase in real living standards for the majority of people despite economic growth, and that the gains from that growth have been enjoyed by a relatively small proportion of the population. It is clear that more focused anti-poverty programmes that address the social determinants of illness and provide more direct income support are required to eliminate poverty. Such measures are included in the scenario shown in Figure 5.3.

- *Technological change*: Technological change has been an important aspect of human progress ever since the Stone Age. Today's seemingly magical technologies in areas such as communications, entertainment, medicine and transportation represent a rapid acceleration of trends that have been in play for millennia. To say that new technologies are often a double-edged sword is a cliché, itself a metaphor based on a technology that in previous times had considerable military significance. Our contemporary environmental problems are evidence of the second edge. The way forward will require novel technologies that reflect an approach to life in which social and ecological as well as economic consequences are considered in advance of their widespread adoption. This can be achieved through technology assessment, changes in the education of scientists and engineers, and the adoption of a broader range of objectives (not just financial gain) by those engaged in technology development.

- *Government expenditures*: The scenario in Figure 5.3 allows for some increase in total government expenditures followed by an eventual levelling off as the size of the economy stabilises. The precise level at which this levelling should take place will be determined by the respective roles for the public, private and not-for-profit sectors. The scenario in Figure 5.3 corresponds to a level quite similar to the traditional role of the public sector in Canada.

- *Trade*: International trade can be mutually beneficial, but it can become destabilising if a country's imports and exports move significantly out of balance. The scenario in Figure 5.3 is based on a small but positive trade balance in which Canada earns slightly more from its exports than it spends on imports. Eventually, if the economy is not growing, we should expect imports and exports to balance.

- *Greenhouse gases*: The emission of greenhouse gases would very likely diminish as the rate of growth slowed, and this effect is captured in Figure 5.3. In addition, the scenario assumes the imposition of a substantial revenue-neutral carbon tax in which there is a tax on energy use based on the carbon content of that energy. In the scenario, revenues from the carbon tax are exactly matched by a reduction in personal and corporate income taxes, so that there is no increase in overall government revenues from the carbon tax.

The scenario in Figure 5.3 is based on all of these changes. In addition, there are other changes that would usefully complement those included in the LowGrow simulation but that are not directly provided for in the model. Among these is the adoption of better measures of success than growth in GDP to drive policy. There are several candidates, such as the UN's Human Development Index and the Genuine Progress Indicator, both of which show that prosperity and economic growth are only loosely related. Climate change is only one of several environmental problems facing humanity in the twenty-first century. A comprehensive approach will require limits on throughput and comprehensive ecological fiscal reform in which, for example, taxes are shifted from labour to activities that cause environmental damage and space is used less aggressively through better land-use planning and habitat protection.

LowGrow is a modest first step in the development of tools grounded in economics for describing alternative futures in which economic growth is not given priority. Numerous other models have been created with the clear intention of showing how economic growth can be sustained, or even accelerated, while the burden on nature is reduced (UNDP 2011). And yet other models – such as World 3, which was used to develop the famous scenarios in *The Limits to Growth* – provide interesting, even inspirational scenarios without economic growth, but they were not designed according to established principles of economics (Meadows et al. 1972). Furthermore, LowGrow was built using data for Canada and, while the broad conclusions that emerge from it apply to other developed economies, national differences would no doubt yield rather different numerical results. Since its publication a few years ago, there has been considerable interest in LowGrow in many parts of the world, and a few researchers in other countries (Sweden, New Zealand, Germany) have adapted LowGrow with mixed results.

During the past two years, Tim Jackson and I have been collaborating on GEMMA (Green Economy Macro-model and Accounts), a new macro-economic model of a national economy designed to address the following questions (Victor and Jackson 2012):

• Is growth in real economic output still required in advanced economies in order to simultaneously maintain high levels of employment, reduce poverty and meet ambitious ecological and resource targets?
• Does stability of the financial system require growth in the real economy?
• Will restraints on demand and supply – for example, in anticipation of or in response to ecological and resource constraints – cause instability in the real economy and/or the financial system?

These important questions require better answers than are currently available, but credible answers are needed if we are to make the thoughtful, deliberate transformation of our economy that the mounting evidence of environmental degradation, financial instability and increasing social and economic inequality indicates is necessary. We hope that GEMMA will provide insights into these problems and will produce more comprehensive and detailed scenarios showing that we can live well in an economy that does not depend on economic growth. Most important of all, we will be able to free ourselves to think more broadly and more imaginatively as we contemplate the end of growth.

Notes

1 This chapter is reprinted from Victor (2012a), with sections adapted from Victor (2008).

2 Gideon and I collaborated on an early version of LowGrow (Victor and Rosenbluth 2007). My book *Managing without Growth* was an extensive elaboration of the modelling and arguments

we had begun to develop together (Victor 2008). Gideon passed away in 2011.

References

Jackson, T. (2009) *Prosperity without Growth: Economics for a finite planet*. London: Earthscan.

Kraussman, F., S. Gingrich, N. Eisenmenger et al. (2009) 'Growth in global materials use, GDP and population in the twentieth century'. *Ecological Economics* 68(10): 2696–705.

Meadows, D. H., D. L. Meadows, J. Randers and W. W. Behrens, III (1972) *The Limits to Growth: A report for the Club of Rome's project on the predicament on mankind*. London: Earth Island.

Rockström, J., W. Steffen, K. Noone et al. (2009) 'Planetary boundaries: exploring the safe operating space for humanity'. *Ecology and Society* 14(2): 32. www.ecologyandsociety. org/vol14/iss2/art32/.

UNDP (2006) *Human Development Report 2006. Beyond scarcity: Power, poverty, and the global water crisis*. New York, NY: United Nations Development Programme (UNDP). www.undp.org/content/undp/en/ home/librarypage/hdr/human-development-report-2006/.

— (2011) *Modelling Global Green Investment Scenarios: Supporting the transition to a global green economy*. New York, NY: United Nations Development Programme (UNDP). www. unep.org/greeneconomy/Portals/88/ documents/ger/GER_13_Modelling. pdf.

Victor, P. A. (1972) *Pollution: Economy and environment*. Toronto: University of Toronto.

— (2008) *Managing without Growth: Slower by design, not disaster*. Cheltenham: Edward Elgar.

— (2012a) 'Living well: explorations into the end of growth'. *Minding Nature* 5(2): 24–31. www.humansandnature. org/living-well--explorations-into-the-end-of-growth--article-111.php.

— (2012b) 'Uneconomic growth'. *Canadian Dimension* 46(2): 25–30.

— and T. Jackson (2012) 'Towards an ecological macroeconomics'. Paper presented at the Institute for New Economic Thinking, Annual Plenary Conference, Berlin, 12–14 April.

— and G. Rosenbluth (2007) 'Managing without growth'. *Ecological Economics* 61: 492–504.

6 | COMPLEXITY: SHOCK, INNOVATION AND RESILIENCE

Thomas Homer-Dixon

Introduction

I largely endorse the arguments and evidence offered in the last two chapters. In this chapter, I will extend these chapters' arguments but offer somewhat more optimistic conclusions. I will focus on emerging turbulence in our global systems, economies, critical systems, food systems and other areas that could influence our capacity to build prosperous economies and societies in the future.

First, though, I wish to highlight a link between what we have learned in the previous chapters and my comments here. Bill Rees and Peter Victor both suggested that we are starting to approach the biophysical limits of economic prosperity on this planet. When approaching such limits, complex systems often start to behave in somewhat bizarre ways. Specialists call this behaviour 'chattering': the system in question starts to exhibit wide amplitude swings in its key properties and variables. These are what I call here 'shocks'.

Some of the events we're seeing in our world today are evidence – you might say leading indicators – that we're approaching system boundaries, a process that could ultimately lead key social-ecological systems to flip from one state or equilibrium to another.

In this chapter, I will tell two stories. One story will be about shock, about increasing turbulence, about crisis that arises from rising stress on our global systems combined with these systems' rising complexity. Another will be about innovation and especially about the role of innovation in societal resilience.

Examples of shock

Let's begin with shock. Figure 6.1 is a photograph of the Deepwater Horizon oil platform in the Gulf of Mexico before the platform sank. We were told that this kind of event was virtually impossible. For

6.1 Deepwater Horizon (*source*: 'US Coast Guard – 100421-G-XXXXL– Deepwater Horizon fire': http://commons.wikimedia.org/wiki/File:Deepwater_Horizon_offshore_drilling_unit_on_fire_2010.jpg)

instance, specialists and engineers who developed and installed the blow-out preventers on the seabed under this platform told us that the chances of a disaster of this magnitude were vanishingly small.

But as we have learned from Rees and Victor, we also know that human beings are venturing into more extreme natural environments to drill deeper for smaller pools of lower-quality oil. Cheap oil is getting harder to find, so we have to develop more complex technologies to drill in more extreme environments. And with more complex technologies, often things happen that one doesn't expect, such as shocks like the one in the photograph here.

Figure 6.2 shows another example of shock. Same summer, same year. The figure shows a frequency distribution of average July temperatures in Moscow over the last sixty-odd years in terms of their deviation from the mean July temperature in Moscow between 1970 and 2000. Each vertical line represents a single July temperature since 1950. The lines cluster around the mean, but 2010 is clearly an extraordinary anomaly: it is a four-sigma event, which is statistical jargon for an event four standard deviations from the mean. If there

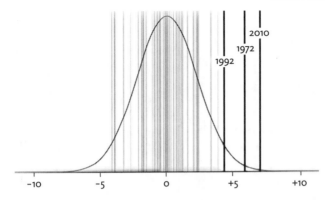

6.2 July temperature anomalies in Moscow since 1950 (degrees Fahrenheit) (*sources*: NOAA, NCEP, CPC and CAMS data from IRI/LDEO online data library)

is no underlying causal factor driving such a deviation – in other words, if the event in question is purely a random occurrence – then its odds are around 16,000 to one. But in July in 2010 in Moscow, something was happening to drive the deviation.

The Earth's climate is changing, and this change is producing more extreme weather events. The consequences can be dire. The heatwave in Russia in the summer of 2010 caused a sharp drop in the country's grain yields, so it closed its borders to grain exports. This action in turn drove up grain prices around the world. And one of the consequences of that food-price spike, it is now widely believed, was the outbreak of violence and protests against regimes in the Middle East and North Africa during the autumn of 2010. Analysts now widely agree that the proximate stimulus for those revolutions of violence was the global rise in food prices.

Figure 6.3 illustrates the granddaddy of all recent shocks we have experienced: the global economic crisis starting in 2008 and continuing to 2010 – even into the present by some analyses. The vertical bands represent recessions going back to the Second World War. The left axis represents the magnitude of the drop in US national income in terms of billions of nominal dollars. This representation does not, however, control for growth in the economy. Figure 6.4, which represents percentage changes in US national income, does control for this factor.

We can see that the economic crisis that took place from 2008

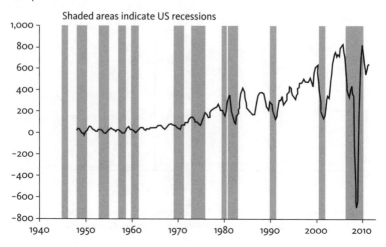

6.3 National income (NICUR): change from the previous year (US$ billion)
(*source*: US Department of Commerce, Bureau of Economic Analysis)

until late 2009 was larger in percentage terms than all other recessions going back to the Second World War, except for the recession
immediately after that war in the late 1940s.

Figure 6.4 reveals an interesting story. During the 1950s and early
1960s, the amplitude of recession-induced swings in the economy
declined. Although a recession occurred every five years or so, the

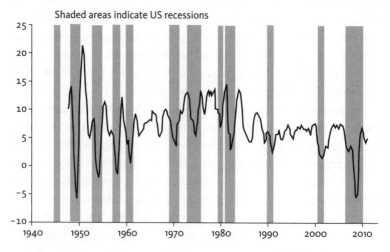

6.4 National income (NICUR): percentage change from the previous year
(*source*: US Department of Commerce, Bureau of Economic Analysis)

magnitude of its percentage impact on the US economy fell. The institutions managing the US economy – federal and state governments and the Federal Reserve – appear to have been learning to do a better job. They drew on the new Keynesian economics to apply fiscal and monetary tools to stabilise the American economy, and they succeeded for almost a decade.

Then the late 1960s arrived. The Johnson administration responded to the fiscal strain arising from the Vietnam War by pumping enormous amounts of liquidity into the economy, which contributed to rising inflation. Partly in response, Nixon decoupled the US dollar from gold in the early 1970s. This event occurred just before the first of two major exogenous energy shocks – the 1973 Yom Kippur War and the OPEC oil embargo, each of which quadrupled real oil prices. The second shock occurred in 1979, and both were marked by recessions.

Throughout the 1970s, the US economy experienced a pernicious combination of inflation and low growth labelled 'stagflation'. During the early 1980s, Federal Reserve chairman Paul Volcker used harsh monetary tools to squeeze inflation out of the economy, precipitating the worst recession in two decades. By this point, policy-makers had decisively abandoned Keynesian economics, turning to the monetary policies advocated by Milton Friedman in their stead.

So the chart tells a story about how policy-makers learned to manage the economy and respond to shocks such as wars and oil crises over a period of forty years, from the 1950s to the 1980s. These policy-makers continued to use monetary tools during the 1990s, a period called the 'Great Moderation'. That label now seems astonishing and deeply ironic. We were told during that period that recessions were a thing of the past, because economic managers had discovered how to stabilise or even eliminate the business cycle. Our economic managers, it was claimed, could now keep the economy from cycling back and forth between periods of growth and recession.

In the early 1990s, a brief recession occurred in the wake of the Gulf War, an event that again caused a sharp jump in real oil prices; but the recession was short and shallow. At the end of the 1990s and into the first years of the new millennium, we saw the Asian financial crisis and the dot-com implosion, but economic elites assured us that these events were anomalous. The US economy subsequently returned to a period of stability and reasonably good growth for over half a decade.

Then, in 2008, something almost entirely unexpected happened – the biggest economic crisis since the 1930s. Although unexpected, the foundation for the crisis had been laid over the previous twenty years. During the Great Moderation, securitisation of debt, the development of complex derivatives from securitised debt, and the increased interdependence of balance sheets of firms holding these derivatives around the world produced an enormous but largely unseen and unremarked increase in financial connectivity. This connectivity enabled a shock in a relatively small part of the global financial system – specifically in the US subprime housing market – to cascade very quickly far and wide.

In the wake of the Lehman collapse in the autumn of 2008, securitised assets such as collateralised debt obligations and credit default swaps suddenly had indeterminate value. Firms found that they could not accurately assess their counterparties' financial health, so trade and lending came to a virtual halt worldwide. Every major economy in the world tipped into recession simultaneously, something never before seen in history, not even in the 1930s. The subsequent recession exceeded in length any since the Second World War and was almost as severe in percentage terms as the recession that followed the war.

The causes of shock

The three examples above suggest that we are experiencing a rising frequency of shocks in our complex global systems and that these shocks are becoming increasingly severe. What might be causing these changes? I could offer a long and elaborate answer, but given space constraints here I will focus briefly on three principal drivers: the convergence of simultaneous stresses, overuse of natural systems and resources, and finally the rising complexity of social, technological and human-ecological systems.

Converging stresses First, compared with the middle of the last century, the systems our societies use to manage change – our governments, public and private organisations, and individual leaders – are increasingly overwhelmed by multiple converging stresses. Figure

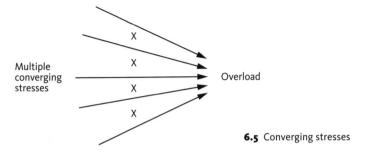

6.5 Converging stresses

6.5 represents this situation. The multiplication signs between each arrow show that the stresses together are more than the sum of their individual effects. They have a greater impact together, because of the interactions between them, than they would have if they were considered only in sum.

This convergence of stresses is producing a phenomenon I call 'overload' in which governments, organisations or leaders perceive that things are simply out of control – that they are facing too many challenges coming at them at the same time from too many directions. They really don't know how to respond effectively to this incessant, constantly changing load of interacting problems. Any contemporary manager recognises this phenomenon.

In my book *The Upside of Down*, first published in 2006, I identified five such challenges. I called them tectonic stresses, because they are operating under the surface of humankind's global civilisation. Just like the real stresses arising from the Earth's shifting tectonic plates that sometimes cause geological earthquakes, the pressures arising from these five challenges are slowly building and could ultimately cause enormous social earthquakes. The five stresses I identified are: population growth, environmental damage, energy scarcity, climate change, and economic instability and inequality.

The chapters in this book provide details of several of these challenges, so I won't dwell on most of them further. But I do want to emphasise that we're seeing, in the current conversation in elite circles about the state of the world, a rising recognition of the importance of simultaneous complex stresses.

Figure 6.6 reproduces a chart from the 2012 *Global Risks Report* of the World Economic Forum, released in Davos, Switzerland. Looking at that chart, you can see many of the same factors I highlighted in

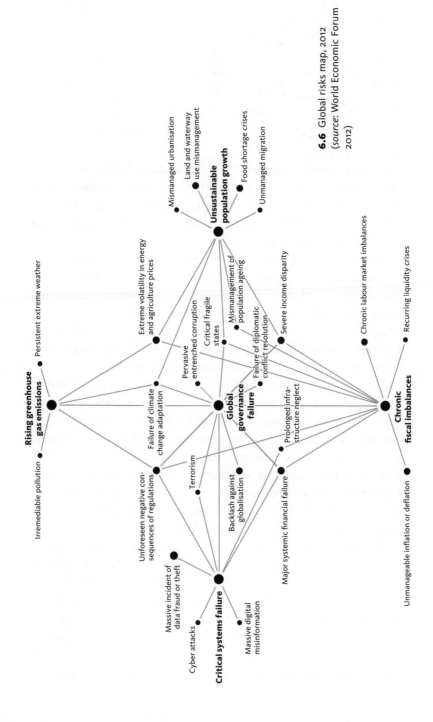

6.6 Global risks map, 2012 (*source*: World Economic Forum 2012)

Rising greenhouse gas emissions

Persistent extreme weather

Irremediable pollution

Unsustainable population growth

Mismanaged urbanisation

Land and waterway use mismanagement

Food shortage crises

Unmanaged migration

Extreme volatility in energy and agriculture prices

Pervasive entrenched corruption

Critical fragile states

Mismanagement of population ageing

Severe income disparity

Failure of diplomatic conflict resolution

Failure of climate change adaptation

Global governance failure

Chronic labour market imbalances

Recurring liquidity crises

Chronic fiscal imbalances

Prolonged infrastructure neglect

Unforeseen negative consequences of regulations

Terrorism

Backlash against globalisation

Major systemic financial failure

Unmanageable inflation or deflation

Massive incident of data fraud or theft.

Critical systems failure

Cyber attacks

Massive digital misinformation

my 2006 book. It identifies as key risk factors unsustainable population growth, climate change, energy issues and economic inequality. These factors, and some others, all stress global governance and thus produce, at the chart's centre, global-governance failure. This outcome is roughly equivalent to system overload.

The World Economic Forum's representation takes complexity seriously. The chart shows dozens of background connections between the major risk factors. Most of our world's policy-makers and elite system managers don't like to acknowledge these connections, because they want to believe that the systems around us can be simplified, fully understood and managed (by them) largely in isolation from each other. But increasingly, as the Forum's analysis shows, some of these elites are reluctantly accepting that the very complexity arising from today's simultaneity of risk factors is a big part of the problem humanity faces.

Overuse of natural resources The second principal driver of the rising frequency and severity of shock in our global systems is overuse of natural systems and resources. I will focus here on human-induced climate change, which is a function of the overuse of the atmosphere's sink capacity for carbon dioxide and other greenhouse gases. This problem is representative of humanity's challenges with regards to many different natural systems, but it is also probably the most threatening environmental challenge of all.

Studies of decadal surface temperature anomalies for the period from the 1970s to the 2000s show a remarkable change in the last four decades (Hansen et al. 1999). Warming has been more pronounced in the northern part of the planet, largely because of the loss of sea ice in the Arctic, a process that amplifies the underlying warming trend. Researchers are just now beginning to understand one of the most interesting parts of this story. A major step forward was an analysis by James Hansen and his co-authors published in 2012 in the *Proceedings of the National Academy of Sciences* that identified the change in the frequency of extreme heat events around the planet.

Figure 6.7 shows changes in the proportion of the Earth's surface experiencing extreme heat events. Hansen and his colleagues placed a grid over the world, thus dividing its surface into boxes. For every year going back to 1951, they identified each box's average June–August

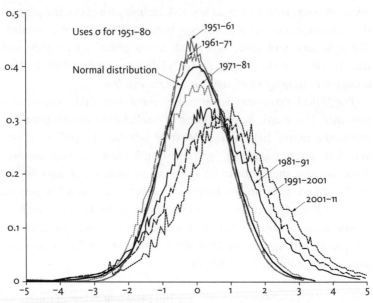

6.7 June–July–August temperature anomaly distribution, 1951–2011 (*source*: Hansen et al. 2011)

surface air temperature. Then they determined that temperature's difference in standard deviations from the box's average June–August temperature between 1951 and 1980.

Each wiggly curve shows the frequency distribution of all the boxes' June–August temperatures over a decade. The units on the x-axis are standard deviations and the smooth black line in the background is a normal distribution or Gaussian distribution – what we commonly refer to as a bell curve. Note that the 1951 to 1961 distribution maps very closely on to this curve: for that decade, some 95 per cent of local June–August temperatures fell within two standard deviations of the 1951–80 average for that locality. Events more than three standard deviations above the 1951–80 average made up less than 0.2 per cent of the total.

You can see that as the decades have passed, the distributions have moved to the right and have become flatter and broader. These changes have had a remarkable effect on the frequency of extreme heat events, defined as June–August temperatures at least three standard deviations – or three sigmas – above the local average. Between

1951 and 1961, such events affected about 0.3 per cent of the surface area of the planet. But in the most recent decade, they affected 10 per cent of the planet's land area. In other words, the frequency of extreme heat events has increased about thirty-fold in six decades. Hansen and his co-authors say that this trend is likely to continue. They write: 'If global warming is not slowed from its current pace, by mid-century 3σ events will be the new norm and 5σ events will be common.'

Rising complexity Rising complexity is the third driver of the rising incidence and severity of shock in our global systems.

We need to shift from seeing the world as being composed mainly of simple machines to seeing it as composed largely of complex systems. When I explain this idea to my students I show them an early twentieth-century wind-up mantelpiece clock – the kind that chimes every fifteen minutes and gongs every hour. I note to my students that I can take the thing apart and break it down into its bits and pieces – its springs, bushings, cog wheels, screws and the like. I can understand precisely the relationships between all of these bits and how each bit works in the larger machine. And when I put the clock back together, if it doesn't work properly – and, by the way, it means something to say the clock doesn't work properly – I can almost always attribute the problem to a piece that is out of place, broken or missing.

Because of these properties, I can have a very precise understanding of the entire machine. This is what philosophers call a reductionist understanding, because it is the understanding one arrives at by reducing the machine to its parts. The machine is ultimately nothing more than the sum of its parts.

Such simple machines generally show proportionality between cause and effect. In other words, small causes in the machine lead to small effects, while big causes lead to big effects. Complex system theorists call proportional causation linear causation, and they say that this kind of causation leads to linear behaviour. Largely because of proportional causation, the behaviour of simple machines tends to migrate towards equilibrium, which we often call normal behaviour. When the clock is working properly, it is in a form of dynamic equilibrium, and we say it is working normally.

As a result of these characteristics, we can usually predict the behaviour of simple machines, which makes them easier to manage.

But the situation is very different with complex systems. They are more than the sum of their parts; they have what philosophers call 'emergent' properties. When we put all their bits and pieces together, they often do things that we couldn't have anticipated solely from knowledge of the properties of their constituent components.

Imagine that you're putting the wind-up clock back together and, as you turn the last screw, it sprouts a couple of legs, stands up on its feet, looks at you, and says, 'Hi, I'm out of here' – and then walks out of the room. You would gasp in astonishment. Complex systems behave in astonishing ways all the time.

A big part of the reason for such behaviour is disproportional causation. In complex systems, small causes sometimes cause really big effects, while big changes sometimes don't produce much effect at all. And partly because of this disproportionality, complex systems can flip from one pattern of behaviour to another. They have what system theorists called multiple equilibria.

Figure 6.8 represents a complex system as a ball in a valley. If the ball is pushed hard enough, it will pop over the hill and roll into another valley. This new valley is another equilibrium or stability point for the system. If the system is pushed even harder, it will roll further away into a more distant valley. With complex systems, we usually can't see the surrounding behavioural landscape well, so we don't know its full topography – where the valleys are, how deep they are, and what kind of system behaviour they sustain. We also don't know how close the system might be to flipping into another equilibrium.

We have seen flips in complex systems many times recently in the world around us. Off Canada's east coast, the cod fishery flipped from a highly productive state to a far less productive state, and it now seems to have stabilised in that new low-productivity equilibrium. In 2008, the global economy flipped from an equilibrium characterised

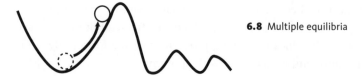

6.8 Multiple equilibria

by growth and price inflation to a different equilibrium characterised by stagnation – or even contraction – with episodes of price deflation.

Together, the three factors I have mentioned – emergence, disproportional causation and multiple equilibria – make complex systems hard to manage, because their behaviour is often unpredictable.

The sources and consequences of complexity If this is the nature of complexity, what is causing our societies and economies to become more complex? A number of factors play a role, but I will emphasise here improvement in the performance of the component parts of our social systems – that is, of the bits and pieces inside our economies, technological systems, organisations and firms. As these components get better at doing what they are supposed to do, which is a natural process in competitive environments, our societies' overall complexity rises. In recent decades, advances in information technology have particularly contributed to this performance improvement.

Partly as a consequence of performance improvement, especially of information technologies, the networks within our societies and economies have more nodes – in the form of organisations, firms and individual technologies – denser networks of links among these nodes, and faster movements of material, energy and especially information along these links.

Faster movement means, in turn, that our technological, economic and social systems are more tightly coupled than previously: events happen in more rapid succession within these systems, and system managers have less opportunity to intervene if things start going awry. A tightly coupled system that is perturbed or shocked may experience a cascading failure, a phenomenon that is like a row of dominoes falling over. When the system is shocked in one location, the disturbance propagates far away in the blink of an eye.[1]

Again, we have seen many recent examples. One week after SARS erupted in Hong Kong, it arrived in Toronto and shut down the city's medical system. A perturbation in a relatively small part of the global economy, the subprime mortgage housing market in the United States, contributed to the failure of Lehman Brothers in September 2008, and almost immediately every single major economy in the world tipped into recession.

I don't want to give the impression that complexity is always a bad thing. Complexity can be a good thing in a variety of ways. First, it can be a source of innovation: by bringing ideas, institutions and technologies together in unexpected ways, it increases the likelihood that novel combinations will occur. Novel combinations are a fundamental source of innovation in our economies. Second, because complexity increases both the diversity of problem-solvers and the networked distribution of problem-solving, it increases the ability of our economies to adapt to a rapidly changing environment.

At the same time, though, complexity can be a bad thing. First, by making systems more opaque, complexity makes it harder for managers to see what is happening inside the systems they are responsible for managing.

We can get a sense of this problem by comparing the engine of a car from the 1950s with the engine in a late-model car today. When I was a teenager, I restored a 1952 Oldsmobile. Just as we can take a mechanical clock apart, I took the car's engine apart and put it back together again. Looking under the Oldsmobile's hood, I could see many of the engine's major components, and I came to understand what they did. I challenge you to identify the major components of a modern car's engine when looking under the hood. The machine is a mass of modules, each of which is manufactured and serviced by highly specialised industries. The engine performs much better than the 1952 Oldsmobile by many measures, but it is opaque to anybody except an expert, which means we can't repair our own cars any more.

Second, complexity can be a bad thing because it can make systems more likely to flip between equilibria. Third, to the extent that complexity generates multiple simultaneous stresses, it can overload managers with tasks and problems. And fourth, certain kinds of complexity make systems more brittle, especially when those systems become mature.

From risk to uncertainty

The three factors that I have identified as drivers of the increasing frequency and severity of shock – simultaneous stresses, overuse of natural systems and rising complexity – are propelling us from a world of risk to a world of uncertainty.

This distinction goes back to the work of the American economist

Frank Knight in the 1920s. Knight was one of the world's pre-eminent economists at the time, but his work was later overshadowed by that of John Maynard Keynes. Keynes himself, though, drew on Knight's distinction between risk and uncertainty, and more recently – especially with the latest economic crisis – the distinction has been resurrected.

In a world of risk, one can identify the pathways a given system might follow, and one can estimate the costs and benefits of following a particular path. In a world of uncertainty, one simply doesn't have enough evidence to arrive at such judgements. It is impossible to gauge which pathway the system might move along, and it becomes impossible to estimate the costs and benefits of moving along a particular path.

A world of uncertainty is a world of unknown unknowns. The erstwhile US Secretary of Defense, Donald Rumsfeld, popularised this phrase when he spoke about the challenges US forces faced in Iraq. He was ridiculed at the time, but the phrase had actually been in use for years, especially in military circles. Military folks understand unknown unknowns very well, and this understanding has its roots in historical analysis. The great nineteenth-century Prussian military theorist Carl von Clausewitz, in his treatise *On War*, spoke about 'friction' on the battlefield and the 'fog of war'. People who have experienced combat know that surprises happen regularly in war.

In a world of unknown unknowns, we are ignorant of our own ignorance, and we don't even know what questions to ask about the situation we face. In such circumstances, we need to be resilient and flexible in response to surprises. In the last part of this chapter, therefore, I will discuss resilience, innovation and creativity.

Resilience

Previous chapters have discussed the relationship between crisis – or what I have called here 'shock' – and the opportunity for innovation; they have considered whether we need a big shock to create the possibility for things to change. Scholars of innovation debate the extent to which shock is necessary for innovation. It seems clear, though, that to the extent to which shock can facilitate innovation, a society will fare better if its people prepare themselves in advance to take advantage of shock, if and when it happens.

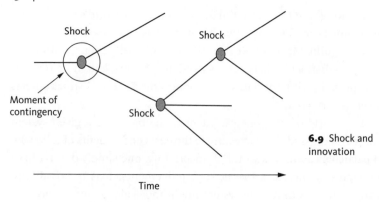

6.9 Shock and innovation

Figure 6.9 is a simple schematic of a possibility space of societal innovation over time. Shocks create what I call 'moments of contingency': at these moments people are scared and angry, and prepared to challenge conventional arrangements. This situation creates opportunities for deep change. But once a society selects a path – however that selection process happens – it is locked into those particular arrangements for a period of time before the next shock. This is what complexity theorists call 'path dependency'.

What happens between shocks is critically important. It is during these periods that societies can develop the new ideas they might implement during the next moment of contingency. Implementing them immediately isn't possible, because between shocks social systems tend to be too rigid. Nevertheless, during these periods people can develop new ideas and experiment with new forms of economic and social arrangement. Then, when the next shock happens and society is casting around for answers, these people will have ideas to put forward, and society as a whole will have some well-grounded responses to try. I call this approach 'complex adaptation', and it is at the core of my notion of resilience.

In my definition of resilience, resilient people, institutions and societies have the capacity to withstand shock without catastrophic failure. They have the capacity for self-reliance and are highly innovative in their response to novel challenges. Such resilience will be extraordinarily important if we are entering a world of more frequent and severe shock.

However, we need to distinguish between two notions of resilience that people often conflate: engineering resilience and ecological resilience. If a system exhibits engineering resilience, as I define the concept, it can absorb a shock and bounce back to where it was beforehand. This is a conservative notion of resilience, because the system doesn't change fundamentally.

On the other hand, if a system exhibits ecological resilience, according to my definition, it adapts to the shock through a process of creative destruction. The shock causes the system to give up some core properties and features while introducing new ones, and the process involves deep and fundamental system change. I believe that it is ecological resilience we should promote in our societies today.

What we can do

The co-operative movement can play a very important role in introducing the ideas and practice of resilience to our national and global communities. For instance, it can help communicate the vital truth that greater connectivity doesn't always make life better and that sometimes it actually makes our societies more brittle. Loosening coupling between the components in our economies – making them less tightly coupled – can reduce our vulnerability to cascading failures.

The co-operative movement can also boost our societies' innovation capacity by supporting a greater diversity of firms, communities, ideas and institutional forms. It can encourage decentralised problem-solving by getting more heads engaged in solving problems and a greater range of different groups experimenting with new ideas for generating energy, growing food and sustaining our healthcare.

The co-operative movement should encourage, in particular, what the renowned Canadian ecologist and pioneer of resilience thinking Buzz Holling has called 'safe-fail' experimentation. Safe-fail experiments, if and when they do fail, don't damage the larger system they are part of. Instead, failure stimulates learning and guides further experimentation.

Promoting resilience isn't a failure-averse approach to innovation. If one really wants to innovate, one has to fail over and over again. We all know that the biggest lessons we have learned in our personal lives have come from our failures. The same is true of societies, so we should aim to create societies where failure produces knowledge that can ultimately be shared across the entire social system for the collective benefit.

The probability is perhaps low that humankind will successfully address its future challenges. But if our societies do address these challenges through resilience and innovation, they will undergo what some economists call a 'general-purpose technology' (GPT) transition. We have seen GPT transitions in the past: the introduction of railroads and electricity in the nineteenth century, of the internal combustion engine in the early part of the twentieth century, and of the personal computer in the 1970s and 1980s. In each case, a wave of creative destruction swept across the affected economies. New industries formed and old ones disappeared, and the technological transition created enormous opportunities for profit and innovation.

The next GPT transition – a green-energy transition that moves us towards a zero-carbon economy – will probably be as big as all of the others combined, because it will implicate every facet of our economies.

This prospect sounds daunting, even scary, but we are actually entering an enormously exciting time that is replete with immense possibility. My wife and I have two small children, Kate and Ben – currently four and seven years old respectively. All parents know exactly what I mean when I say that looking at one's young children is like looking through a window out fifty, sixty, seventy or eighty years into the future. It's an astonishingly intimate connection to the future.

We know enough to be deeply worried about what that future might hold for our children. But I also know that when Ben and Kate come to me in a few years and ask, 'Dad what have we done to the planet, and what are we going to do to make things right?,' I'll answer that this is quite possibly the most exciting time in human history. It's a moment of staggering opportunity for creativity, entrepreneurship and, frankly, bravery. There will be great turbulence and many shocks. But those crises will offer us opportunities to make the deep changes we need to ensure prosperity for centuries to come.

Note

1 For a persuasive case in support of the arguments in this and the previous paragraph, see Helbing (2013).

References

Hansen, J., M. Sato and R. Ruedy (2011) 'Climate variability and climate change: the new climate dice'. www.

columbia.edu/~jeh1/mailings/
2011/20111110_NewClimateDice.pdf.
— (2012) 'Perception of climate change'.
*Proceedings of the National Academy
of Sciences* 109(37): 14726–7.
Hansen, J., R. Ruedy, J. Glascoe and
M. Sato (1999) 'GISS analysis of
surface temperature change'. *Journal
of Geophysical Research* 104(D24):
30997–1022.

Helbing, D. (2013) 'Globally networked
risks and how to respond'. *Nature*
497: 51–9.
Homer-Dixon, T. (2007) *The Upside of
Down: Catastrophe, creativity and
the renewal of civilisation*. London:
Souvenir Press.
World Economic Forum (2012) *Global
Risks 2012: Seventh edition*. Geneva:
World Economic Forum.

7 | FINANCE FOR THE ANTHROPOCENE[1]

John Fullerton

Introduction

> The true nature of the international (economic) system under
> which we were living was not realized until it failed. (Karl Polanyi,
> *The Great Transformation* 1944)

The recent near-collapse of the financial system has raised fundamental questions about its viability, its ethics, and the ideology that guides it. The ethical challenges facing finance are clear to most thoughtful observers on and off Wall Street. However, what we should be addressing are the far more pernicious defects that reside at the core of our finance-driven economic system.

Finance, ultimately an abstraction, is two steps removed and therefore to a large degree disconnected from the physical life-sustaining systems of the biosphere upon which the real economy and all life on Earth depend. Irresponsible behaviour and speculative financial bubbles that inevitably collapse have real and long-lasting effects on Main Street. Discouragingly, this is a lesson we appear to need to learn again and again, as our memory tends to fade in the exuberance that accompanies the next bull market. But few mainstream economists go on to connect the dots to the biosphere, despite overwhelming evidence that the real economy, at its present scale, is embedded in, and not separate from, the environment. Therefore, by extension, the financial system, too, is inextricably linked to the biosphere. Once we make this connection, a fundamental rethinking of finance, both theory and practice, is required of us.

This conflict can no longer be ignored in the Anthropocene. There is a limit to how far we can expand the stock of financial capital at the expense of natural capital. Said crudely, we enter the Anthropocene with too much money and not enough Earth!

In the face of this emerging reality, not yet perceived by most policy-makers and practitioners, we continue to operate a financial system that by its very design ensures that this imbalance only gets worse, making the inevitable future adjustment exponentially harder. As we shall see, finance is designed to manage and optimise for financial value, treating values such as social and environmental objectives as constraints. This is not a value judgement about finance or financiers. Rather, it is an objective description of what mainstream financial theory and practice are currently designed to do.

The central premise of capitalism is that by optimising for financial capital formation, resources will be most efficiently allocated for the greatest good of society – the magic of Adam Smith's 'invisible hand' at work. Much has been written to dispel this simplistic myth when applied to a highly complex global economy (Nadeau 2008), but it is important to focus on the fundamental differences in terms of scale and impact that have developed over the past 250 years.

Today's global economy measured by gross domestic product (GDP) in constant 1990 US dollars is 465 times larger than the global economy Adam Smith observed (DeLong 2013). Furthermore, Adam Smith's economy supported less than a billion people, ran on renewable resources, and disbursed its non-toxic wastes locally. Financial capital was scarce, while natural capital appeared to be endless.

Today, the opposite is true. We have a surplus of financial capital, run on non-renewable energy, natural capital – from forests to oceans to the atmosphere – is deteriorating, population exceeds 7 billion, and wastes are toxic and increasingly problematic. There is a corollary to ecological overshoot, what we call 'financial overshoot' (Fullerton 2012). There is no easy retreat from overshoot, but what we do know is that, if we continue on this path, the inevitable result is collapse. Only the timing is in doubt.

The art of finance

Finance can be understood as applied economics that drives public and private decision-makers. It defines the core operating system of our mainstream, global corporation-dominant capitalist economy, modified with rules and regulations. Yet, nothing in mainstream finance acknowledges the profound change in the macro circumstances regarding scale and impact that we outline above. As a result, financial overshoot continues to reinforce ecological overshoot, making our path to sustainability immeasurably more problematic than currently thought.

Finance erroneously equates money with wealth. It values only financial capital (financial assets and built capital that can be converted into financial assets via the market), not human capital (education, friendship, community, health, freedom, etc.) nor natural capital (soils, forests, rivers, oceans, the climate system, scenery and so on, and the ecosystem services they provide). Finance is very useful in quantifying and manipulating financial capital, but incapable of valuing the dimensions of the human economy that cannot be monetised, such as the love that bonds families together, and the fresh air we breathe.

The transition from the Holocene to the Anthropocene demands a fundamental rethinking of financial and monetary theory and practice. This time *is* different, for reasons unrelated to the historical business cycles or the financial booms and busts. A finance suitable for the Anthropocene must take a holistic approach to value – financial, human and ecological. If financial capital increases at the expense of human or ecological capital, then we have not really created wealth.

Important work has been done in recent years in quantifying the economic value of social capital, such as the care a stay-at-home parent gives to his or her child. Parallel research led by Robert Costanza in 1997 estimated that the contribution of ecosystem services to the global economy should be valued at approximately US$33 trillion, nearly twice the global GDP of US$18 trillion in that year (Costanza cited in Pannozzo and Colman 1997: 59).

It is important to measure ecosystem services to appreciate their relative scale in relation to the monetised economy. But since both human and financial capital are dependent upon healthy ecosystem *function*, preserving our ecosystem and the services it provides is foundational to both human and financial wealth. Indeed, at some critical level, *ecosystem function* is therefore priceless, rendering efforts to put an economic value on it meaningless. This simple truth creates a profound challenge for financial analytics, which have no means to deal with value that cannot be quantified or substituted.

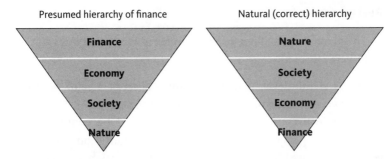

7.1 Interdependent embedded hierarchies

In his ground-breaking and still critical *Holism and Evolution*, Jan Smuts described holism as 'the universal life principle that explains matter, life, and spirit' (Smuts 1927). It is a principle of holism that natural systems – including the human-created economic system – exist in an interdependent embedded hierarchy. Finance, it would appear, inverts the natural (and therefore real) hierarchy, which understands that the economy is embedded in our social systems, which in turn are embedded in the biosphere, while finance is embedded in the economy, not master of it (Figure 7.1). Financial theories and tools seek to optimise for financial outcomes while holding environmental and social factors (often defined by laws) as constraints. Such an approach is inconsistent with this natural hierarchy, and therefore wholly inadequate for the unprecedented challenges we face.

In this chapter, our purpose is first and foremost to describe and illuminate this reality in order to provide the foundation for solutions upon which to build consensus. Only with such a shared understanding can a clear path forward emerge. Too often, debate degenerates across ideological fault lines quite detached from our latest scientific understanding of the relevant facts. We will then go on to contribute our preliminary ideas on the uncertain way forward towards a holistic finance that supports the economic transition we seek.

To accomplish this task, we have organised this paper into four sections: real investment; monetary system; financialisation; and a conclusion.

Real investment

The most powerful force in the universe is compound interest.

(Albert Einstein)

At a systemic level, real investment – described below – is the link between the financial system and the biosphere. The objective of investment as understood by contemporary finance is to generate compound financial returns on capital invested. What we discover upon careful examination is that such compound returns extended exponentially – compound interest inclusive – appears to be in conflict with the entropy law, the second law of thermodynamics, in the following sense: the entropy law states that energy and matter move from order to disorder in our closed thermodynamic system. To the extent that compound financial returns necessitate the use of non-renewable raw materials and the release of waste into the closed system, they accelerate this entropic 'winding down' of the system, undermining the permanent viability of life itself. Einstein evidently had a subtle wit.

The logic of this conclusion is quite straightforward: capital investment is a vital fuel source for economic activity, which in turn places an associated demand on material throughput – resource use and waste. Such economic activity accelerates the rate of entropy, or the conversion of available energy (and materials) into used energy and waste, thereby reducing the available stock of natural capital while increasing the stock of financial capital. When this process is repeated indefinitely, the inevitable result is a diminishing of natural capital with a corresponding expansion of the stock of financial capital. However, this process is inherently self-limiting: the ongoing stability of financial capital is dependent upon a healthy ecosystem function that only natural capital can provide.

This self-limiting quality has begun to reveal itself only as the scale of the economy and the scale of accumulated financial capital have expanded. As we contemplate finance in the Anthropocene, we must first understand that, after hundreds of years of 'success' (notwithstanding many shortcomings), our finance-driven capitalism has left us with too much (inequitably distributed) financial capital, inadequate social capital, and declining life-sustaining natural capital.

We have lost the distinction between financial investment and financial speculation in our short-term financialised economy. But even more critically for our purposes, our casual use of the word 'investment' fails to appreciate the vital distinction between financial investment and real investment.

By talking about 'real investment', we are distinguishing between investments made in the real economy – such as in factories, buildings and technology – from investments made in existing financial instruments, most notably publicly traded equities and bonds. Financial investment has an impact on the real economy through feedback loops caused by changes in the cost of capital and in access to financing; however, these are second-order effects. Relatively little equity investment from financial investors goes into new real investment in the economy. Instead, it represents the trading of equity interests of existing corporations among different shareholders.

Our primary concern for the transition to a sustainable economy must be a focus on the real investment choices of the primary actors in the global economy: corporations, governments, and institutional-scale private investors and investment funds that invest in the development of real assets such as infrastructure and real estate, and in hiring the real people who do the work (although we tend not to capitalise this on balance sheets). These choices include the choice between coal plants and wind farms; between pipelines that connect the dirty oil production of Alberta's tar sands to the market and smart grids to connect remote solar farms to markets; between roads for cars or trucks and railroads.

Real investment decisions define the path to the economic system of the future in multiple ways. Since such capital investments have often multi-decade lifespans, sponsors, whether corporations, governments or financial investors, have a huge incentive to ensure that they are utilised rather than abandoned. For example, corporations use the power of advertising to promote demand for products built in their factories, and public utility commissions guarantee an economic return to utility companies through the commitment of the consumer rate basis when they approve capital expenditures. Furthermore, qualitatively distinct economic activity is generated from research and development expenditures made in both the private and the public sectors, an example of real investment in human capital.

While consumer choice and public policy provide avenues for positively influencing investment decision-making, socially responsible investment ('SRI') may also play a role. The responsible investor movement has generated a lot of attention, although the impact on corporate decision-making has been questionable (Hawken 2004). More recently, 'impact investment' – a lousy term for a good intention, because all investment has impact – is beginning to scale up, and crowd-sourcing has become a viable 'real investment' method; in both cases, the investment is aimed at starting up socially focused enterprises.

Data on aggregate real investment are difficult to assess; however, we know the numbers are immense and highly concentrated. The oil and gas industry alone now invests in excess of US$1 trillion per year in real capital expenditures (drilling new wells), half coming from national oil companies and half coming from the private sector (Global Data 2012). Just focusing on energy for a moment, unless this flow of real investment is somehow redirected into genuinely renewable sources of energy, it will be virtually impossible, as a practical matter, to transition away from a fossil fuel-based global economy. The International Energy Agency estimates that we will need to invest US$30 trillion in clean energy infrastructure by 2050 (IEA 2012), an extraordinary sum to contemplate.

The energy transition will be driven by the following dilemma. The energy reserves on the books of public and private energy companies exceed by five times what can be burned without breaching the 2 degree warming threshold that the best scientific consensus believes is the tipping point to catastrophic climate change effects. The Capital Institute estimates that the reserves that must be left in the ground have a market value of over US$20 trillion, divided between public company assets and much larger state-owned assets (Fullerton 2011). This puts a dollar figure on what Nobel economist Joseph Stiglitz calls the largest market failure in the history of capitalism.

The important point is as simple as it is critical: real investment decisions we are making today will determine the quality of the future economy. *Our financial system is inexorably linked to our ecosystem through the investment function of finance.*

We are left with another inevitable conclusion, albeit one that is radical to consider and hard to contemplate: limits to growth imply qualitative and quantitative limits to investment (Fullerton 2014). There is a relationship between the stock of natural capital (which we know is fixed in scale) and a sustainable stock of financial capital. It would appear that the presumed exponential returns on financial capital, a core operating assumption of modern capitalism, which we can prolong for a certain period of time through material productively grown, will at some point be a physical impossibility. Does the ecological overshoot now well documented in peer-reviewed science automatically suggest a corollary of *financial overshoot* (Fullerton 2012)?

I believe the answer is yes. It would appear that land, labour and capital are not interchangeable and substitutable inputs as the economics textbooks suggest. We need a far more complex economic model in which finance – and in particular the real investment function and its consequences – is entirely embedded and subject to the hard boundaries of the safe operating space of the planet as determined by our best and evolving science.

But relying on financial investors alone to drive change in a system where stock ownership has largely been divorced from the responsibilities that theoretically go with long-term stewardship is a strategy for failure. Today we live in a world where 'long-term' investor can mean an investor who expects to hold a stock for a year rather than a fraction of a second. In reality, public corporations are not 'owned' in the true sense of the word by anyone. As is called for in the Generation Investment Management's 2012 report, long-term ownership or stewardship must be rewarded, and alternative ownership models (such as well-established co-operatives) and novel approaches (such as Evergreen Direct Investment partnerships) must be explored.

The Anthropocene demands new rules and regulations that define a safe operating space for the global economy while providing the private sector with the scope to do what it does best. Governments also need to choose their investments well, balancing social and environmental needs amid competing priorities. For example, investments in military budgets to enhance national security may be directly in conflict with the need to drastically reduce the carbon intensity of the economy, which will soon be understood as the single largest threat to that very same national security objective. In the

Anthropocene, the realisation that compounding financial returns on investment are inherently in conflict with the laws of entropy demand a new ethic of thrift.

The monetary system

> It is well enough that people of the nation do not understand our banking and monetary system, for if they did, I believe there would be a revolution before tomorrow morning. (Henry Ford, cited in Maguire 1957)

Many proponents of a sustainable economy, such as David Korten, Bernard Lietaer, Margrit Kennedy, Hazel Henderson, Herman Daly, Lester Brown and the New Economics Foundation, among others, have focused on the debt-based monetary system as the root cause of the growth-obsessed economic system. The logic is sound: with a private banking system charged with the credit creation function for the economy, and this credit created 'at interest', meaning with interest-bearing debt, the monetary system has compound interest embedded in its structure, demanding exponential economic growth to service that compounding interest (Kennedy et al. 2012). This logic suggests that in order to shift to a sustainable, or what Herman Daly calls a 'steady-state' economy, one that does not require ever expanding material throughput despite the essential ongoing dynamism of the economy, we need to control the expansion of credit and find alternatives, or, as Lietaer argues, complements to the debt-based money system.

While we agree with the need to redesign the monetary system as outlined below, no modifications can be expected to shift the critical flow of real investment in the real economy to the degree needed. Monetary system reform can facilitate, but not effect, the changes in investment that are required. A proper monetary system should be constructed to serve the purpose of human well-being: an economic system that respects the safe operating space of the planet.

Let us now turn to the two key questions regarding the proper design of a monetary system suitable for the unique challenges of the Anthropocene. Who should create the money supply? And should money supply creation be segregated from the credit allocation function of the financial system?

Who should create the money supply? In the modern global monetary system, managed by the world's central banks under the coordination of the Bank for International Settlements (BIS), money is created by the banks through the credit creation function. Money is literally lent into existence as loans, which create deposits in the process. Credit is money, typically accounting for upwards of 97 per cent of the money supply, with government-created script, the physical money in our wallets, accounting for only a small fraction of the money supply. Since most (but not all) banks are privately owned, the system relies primarily on the private sector to create money.

The principal role of the central bank, under ordinary circumstances, is to manage inflation expectations by regulating the price of credit, influencing the ebb and flow of the credit creation function together with the credit allocation function with one blunt instrument: price. As interest rates go higher, individuals and firms in need of credit respond by reducing their demand for credit, just like they do when the price of anything else rises (or so the theory goes).

In response to the financial crisis, central banks around the world have embarked on a non-conventional practice known as quantitative easing (QE). The central banks' balance sheet expansion via QE is a tool to fight the recession that also adds to the money supply. QE is essentially 'printing money' (electronically) to purchase bonds (typically government bonds, but now mortgage-backed securities as well) in order to bid up prices while lowering interest rates. This policy plays a dual role of supporting private sector bank balance sheets and stimulating the economy with lower interest rates.

In the United States, there is growing interest in public banking as an alternative response to the banking crisis, as well as in the credit union system. A public bank, such as the Bank of North Dakota (ILSR 2011), is a bank owned by the state and generally uses state funds as its deposit base, rather than the state placing these deposits in the private banking system. Public banks, by definition and by legal charter, have a purely public purpose rather than a profit maximisation purpose, as assumed by most private banks. Credit unions, on the other hand, are owned and controlled by consumers (bank account holders), but their purpose, too, is different from profit-maximisation.

In the case of the Bank of North Dakota, execution of its public purpose appears to be quite strong, even through the recent financial crisis. Credit unions have also demonstrated remarkable resilience in the crisis (Birchall 2013). However, public ownership and mandate certainly do not guarantee success, as the Sparkassen system of state-owned banks in Germany demonstrated. Sloppy credit judgements have consequences, and the ownership models of banks provide little protection if speculative activities are allowed to generate boom–bust cycles.

In light of our experience of the recent financial crisis, a public debate over the right balance between private, public and hybrid banking systems and the credit creation function is long overdue.

Should money supply be separated from credit allocation? Rarely, if ever, do we consider whether the credit creation function of banks should necessarily be integrated seamlessly with the credit allocation function of the banking system. Instead, policy-makers leave it to the private banking sector to make allocation decisions (who gets loans and on what terms).

This private sector allocation mechanism at the heart of the monetary system is totally in line with the free market principles of our modern economy. According to these free market principles, private actors, widely distributed and close to their markets, are in a much better position to intelligently provide this credit allocation and credit creation function in a manner in line with economic efficiency, which in theory should lead to full employment. In managed economies such as China, where the central government either owns the banks or has tremendous influence over their behaviour, you have a much more centrally planned credit allocation and credit creation function. While such central planning of credit can go horribly wrong, it also has the potential to have a profound impact on the direction of economic activity, with far-reaching consequences.

Arguments in favour of moving either the credit creation function or the credit allocation function under more influence of policy-makers rest on an acknowledgement of the private sector's repeated failure to perform these functions in accordance with the public interest. Instead, history is rife with examples of extreme boom–bust cycles with associated real economy consequences that have been catastrophic to the public interest. This difficult question is reasonable in the context of the mainstream debate about how to improve the functioning of the banking system following recent experience.

The notion that fractional reserve banking should be replaced by 100 per cent reserve banking was first put forward (but not implemented) during the Great Depression in a series of papers known as the 'Chicago Plan' (Phillips 1992) by University of Chicago economists. The idea received support from noted economist Irving Fisher, and has been raised again in the wake of the financial crisis by economists such as Lawrence Kotlikoff (Kotlikoff 2010). The motivation for proposing it has been to make the banking system safer by taking back the credit creation function from the banks, while leaving them with the credit allocation function. Economists arguing against 100 per cent reserve banking point to the lost economic efficiency and the likely impact on economic growth. In other words, the remedy would be worse than the disease. This is a legitimate and valuable debate that should be heard, in light of the monumental costs and ongoing risks of the current banking system.

The new realities of the Anthropocene cast the debate around 100 per cent reserve requirements in a new light. Herman Daly and Joshua Farley, advocates of a steady-state economy, have called for a return to 100 per cent reserve banking precisely because of the likelihood that it will constrain exponential economic growth, the root cause of the ecological overshoot threatening not only our economy, but all life on Earth (Daly and Farley 2011). This is a welcome and provocative idea.

We propose that private sector banks be permitted to exercise the credit creation function based on the purpose and the qualitative factors of their lending. This practice has been successfully implemented by Triodos Bank and the members of the Global Alliance for Banking on Values for years, and in some cases for decades. We acknowledge that managing such a system presents significant practical challenges we are unable to address here. But suffice it to say, we need a system that distinguishes between, on the one hand, lending to local small businesses likely to be linked directly to job creation, job sustainment, healthy local economies and economic well-being, and, on the other hand, lending to leveraged buyouts of manufacturing businesses that will inevitably lead to the offshoring of jobs and manufacturing plants, often to nations with lower labour and environmental standards, just to illustrate the point. No one-size-fits-all system of reserve requirements will allow such qualitative prioritisation.

One alternative that needs further exploration is a significant expansion of co-operative financial institutions and their potential impact. Co-operative financial institutions did not produce any of the toxic financial instruments that precipitated the 2008 crisis and they were less likely to foreclose on mortgages than their 'for profit' counterparts. The dynamics of such democratically owned, user-based financial service providers have the potential to impact positively on credit creation and allocation. Co-operative financial institutions have tended to be more cautious in terms of the ratio between savings and credit creation. They are also more likely to limit loans to meeting human need and are much less likely to engage in speculative activity unless pushed by regulators to behave more like banks (see Chapter 14).

Where they have played a strong role in financing worker-owned co-operatives, as with the Mondragon co-operatives in the Basque country of Spain and in northern Italy, they have stimulated stable work places that have withstood the impacts of the 2008 Great Recession to a significant degree.[2] With more than 100 million people globally working in co-operatives, it is a scalable business model that offers significant potential. Ownership and democratic control of co-operatives by the people whose needs they meet link them to the 'real economy', root them in communities and focus them on meeting member and community need, including the need for a healthy environment. At present, co-operatives are enmeshed in the dominant investor-owned economy, but with strong expansion and with more co-operative-friendly regulation, they would have more potential to behave in ways that are much more in line with the needs of humanity for the Anthropocene.

The financialisation of the economy

> Our economy has become an anti-economy, a financial system without a sound economic basis and without economic virtues. (Wendell Berry 2009)

The four principal functions of finance are:

1   the credit creation process of the private banking system and the conversion of savings into investment (capital allocation);
2   resource allocation via finance analytics;
3   economic risk management; and
4   the provision of supporting infrastructure and related services including market exchanges and market liquidity, and the payment, settlement and safekeeping of financial transactions.

Nowhere in our discussion of the four principal functions of finance is there a claim that finance should expand the paper claims on the real economy, or do so at an exponential rate. Yet this is exactly what finance has done. As Figure 7.2 shows, something changed in the 1980s, causing global financial assets as a percentage of GDP to grow from roughly 200 to 400 per cent, after it took about 100 years for financial assets to double from 100 per cent of GDP to 200 per cent.

Trends in the US are instructive as a leading indicator of the global financial system. There have been three spikes in financial asset growth: one caused by the boom that led to the Great Depression; the second caused by the massive public funding required to mobilise for the Second World War; and the third triggered around

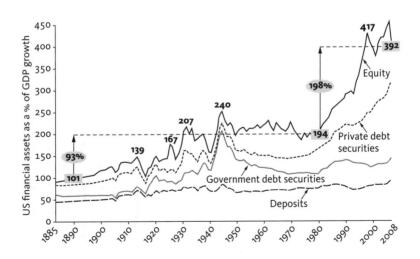

7.2 After 1980, financial asset growth accelerated (*sources*: Federal Reserve; National Bureau of Economic Research; Robert Shiller; McKinsey Global Institute)

1980, a spike that overwhelms the previous spikes, both in absolute terms and as a percentage of GDP.

Three important shifts all occurred around 1980. First and most fundamental was the introduction of the personal computer. Second was the innovation of the cross-currency swap, which, when combined with the relaxation of capital controls, linked national capital markets into one interconnected global capital market. The third critical development to occur in the mid-1980s was innovation in the securitisation market, which bundled portfolios of individual loans into securities containing pools of highly diversified risks (at least in theory) that could be sold directly into the capital markets. While residential mortgages were first securitised back in the early 1970s, Fannie Mae issued the first collateralised mortgage obligation (CMO) in 1983, addressing the structural complexity of the market and enabling rapid expansion.

By the end of the 1990s, Wall Street innovators began to combine securitisation technologies with derivatives technologies, compounding the complexity that would lead directly to the financial crisis of 2008. The adoption of capital-efficient derivatives with their embedded leverage by a broad group of speculative traders, prim-

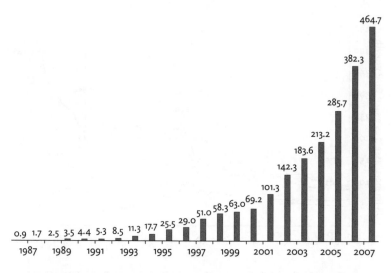

7.3 Interest rate derivatives, 1987–2008 (notional amounts in US$ trillion) (*source*: International Swaps and Derivatives Association [ISDA] market survey)

arily inside global banks and in hedge funds, drove the volumes of these products through the roof (Figure 7.3.), with total outstanding derivatives now at an incomprehensible US$700 trillion. While that number is misleading in many ways, the growth of this trading activity and the retention of long-lived (typically up to ten years) derivative contracts on the books of global financial firms have driven contagion risk among participants in the system exponentially higher in the process.

As Wall Street financial engineering moved to greater and greater abstraction, the capital markets, whose intended purpose is to facilitate the efficient flow of capital to productive use in the real economy, became an end unto themselves, a game of trading abstract risk, largely disconnected from the real economy. Add irresponsible and incompetent industry leadership, competitive egos, arrogance, human greed, inept regulatory oversight, and, at times, outright fraud, and collapse was inevitable.

Wall Street managed to 'financialise' the economy into liquid tradable capital market instruments to such a degree that we have lost the distinction between investment and speculation. We confuse what risk-taking entrepreneurs do with their own money and lives with what financial risk-taking banks and other institutional speculators do with other people's money. In the process, finance has grown to represent an astounding 40 per cent of the US economy, enabling compensation practices on Wall Street to similarly lose their connection with reality, contributing significantly to a widening wealth gap in the United States not seen since the Gilded Age near the end of the nineteenth century.

Monetising the real economy through the financialisation process has another, far more pernicious, effect when looked at through the holistic ethical lens. Once financial assets are created and distributed, there is a further separation between the investor and the investment. It should be clear that the misguided pursuit of capital market efficiency at all costs through excessive and ever more complex financialisation has been a profound mistake. Liquid and 'efficient' markets are simply a means, not the end of a healthy financial system. They certainly do not represent the entire spectrum of means. Trust, integrity and relationships are more important means. We accept a system where the tail wags the dog at our peril.

Conclusion: a challenge to our belief system and implications for reform

> The wise and virtuous man is at all times willing that his own private interest should be sacrificed to the public interest of his own particular order or society. (Adam Smith, *The Theory of Moral Sentiments*)

We will close with some preliminary policy implications that are derived from the analysis above. Such a list is, of course, inadequate and should be considered as only a starting point for the difficult policy deliberations that must be undertaken if we are to transform our theory and practice of finance to support an economy that serves the needs of people while respecting the finite boundaries of the biosphere.

1 The destructive costs of wasteful speculation in our casino financial system, amplified by the financialisation of the economy as we have described, must be forcefully curtailed with globally consistent regulation, punitive taxes on useless and destructive speculation, and thoughtfully crafted capital controls. Cries of theoretical 'lost economic efficiency' must be kept in their proper perspective.

2 The tax codes of all countries must be redesigned to encourage what we need, and to penalise what we need to curtail. A universal carbon tax is the obvious place to start. Subsidies to the fossil-fuel industries and to the fossil fuel-dependent industrial agriculture sector must be replaced with comprehensive subsidies and reinforcing policies, such as feed-in tariffs for renewable and more distributed (and therefore more resilient) energy systems. Capital gains tax can be used to encourage the capital investment we need, while discouraging entropy-accelerating investment. This, of course, is only a partial list of the critical rethinking of the tax codes, given their strong feedback loop into economic decision-making.

3 Given the scale and urgency of the transition we need, like it or not, the public sector will require bold new investment initiatives coupled with supportive policies to drive the enormous transition to renewable energy, smart electricity grids and enhanced

water infrastructure, which are estimated to require a total investment of US$100 trillion. The public sector should focus on areas where it holds comparative advantage: research and development, transition-enabling policies that create clear rules of the road for the private sector to operate within, and low-cost credit creation and allocation in partnership with private sector investment.

4 The realisation that, at a systemic level, we have excessive financial capital that has come at the expense of a declining stock of life-sustaining natural capital will force a fundamental rethinking of our attitudes towards extreme financial wealth. This new framing will not be grounded solely in the equity arguments of the past, but rather in the systemic imperative of what is possible for capitalism in the Anthropocene.

5 Public policy needs to place priority on the creation of co-operative and social economy enterprises whose core business purpose, values and principles include multiple social, economic and environmental goals. The *democratic structure* of such firms also facilitates participation in decision-making by those often most impacted by environmental and financial overshoot.

6 Government expenditures, and particularly real investment, must be re-evaluated in terms of their impact on material throughput. Prioritisation of hard choices must be demanded in the Anthropocene as never before: for example, the choice between investing in throughput-intensive new highways or military equipment on the one hand and education on the other.

7 Perhaps most daunting are the geopolitical implications of financial overshoot. Policy-makers must establish a framework for a collaborative negotiation on how to absorb the financial implications of overshoot. This must begin with a shared approach to managing stranded fossil-fuel assets. The first step towards establishing such a framework demands a new supranational institution to define and monitor the scientific foundation for the safe operating space of the economy. From that common set of facts, political and business leaders will need to negotiate equitable quotas that will determine how the sacrifice will be shared.

Any serious response to the challenges we face in the Anthropocene will need to confront head-on the conventional financial wisdom that capital must flow in such a way as to optimise financial return, considered in its conventional reductionist form. As Adam Smith himself understood well, systems and values have hierarchies. At a systemic level, financial return must be subordinated to the values we hold dear, and on which our very lives depend.

The subtle but profound shift from thinking of financial return as the objective of investment, to seeing *financial return as a constraint*, guiding some *higher purpose* – I invest to build a business that builds human well-being while respecting the safe operating space of the planet, presuming that I will earn at least some positive return over time – has the power to change capitalism as we know it.

Such a shift will allow finance to discover its role as servant to, not master of, an economy that operates within finite ecological boundaries and where wealth inequalities do not increase without limit as a consequence of the working of the system. It demands a completely new theory and practice of finance, grounded in the ethical framework. Much work lies ahead.

Notes

1 Our species' whole recorded history has taken place in the geological period called the 'Holocene' – the brief interval stretching back 10,000 years. But our collective actions have brought us into uncharted territory. A growing number of scientists think we have entered a new geological epoch that needs a new name – the 'Anthropocene'. For more information on the Anthropocene, see www.anthropocene.info/en/anthropocene.

2 In Spain, where unemployment has reached more than 25 per cent, the Basque country rate has reached only 15 per cent and in the three valleys where the Mondragon co-operative network is concentrated it has remained under 7 per cent in large measure because the co-operatives have laid off less than 1 per cent of their worker members (Burridge 2012).

References

Berry, W. (2009) 'Inverting the economic order'. *The Progressive* 73(9). www.progressive.org/mag/berry0909.html (accessed 15 April 2014).

Birchall, J. (2013) *Resilience in a Downturn: The power of financial cooperatives*. Geneva: International Labour Office (ILO). http://ilo.org/empent/Publications/WCMS_207768/lang--en/index.htm (accessed 15 April 2014).

Burridge, T. (2012) 'Basque co-operative Mondragon defies Spain slump'. *BBC News*, 14 August. www.bbc.co.uk/news/world-europe-19213425 (accessed September 2013).

Capital Institute (2013) *Evergreen Direct Investing: Co-creating the regenerative economy*. Greenwich, CT: Capital Institute. http://fieldguide.capitalinstitute.org/evergreen-direct-investing.html (accessed March 2014).

Daly, H. and J. Farley (2011) *Ecological Economics: Principles and applications*. Washington, DC: Island Press.

DeLong, B. J. (2013) 'Estimating world GDP, one million B.C.–present'. http://holtz.org/Library/Social%20 Science/Economics/Estimating%20 World%20GDP%20by%20DeLong/ Estimating%20World%20GDP.htm (accessed September 2013).

Fullerton, J. (2011) 'The big choice'. Capital Institute: The Future of Finance. http://capitalinstitute.org/blog/ big-choice-o#.UjNo7WRgb1g.

— (2012) 'Financial overshoot'. Capital Institute: The Future of Finance. http://capitalinstitute.org/blog/ financial-overshoot (accessed 15 April 2014).

— (2014) 'Limits to investment: finance in the Anthropocene'. Great Transition Initiative. http://greattransition. org/document/limits-to-investment.

Generation Investment Management (2012) *Sustainable Capitalism*. London: Generation Investment Management. www.generationim.com/ media/pdf-generation-sustainable-capitalism-v1.pdf (accessed October 2013).

Global Data (2012) 'Global oil & gas capital expenditure breaks $1 trillion barrier'. Press release, 23 August. http://energy.globaldata.com/media-center/press-releases/oil-and-gas/ global-oil-gas-capital-expenditure-breaks-1-trillion-barrier (accessed 15 April 2014).

Hawken, P. (2004) *Socially Responsible Investing*. Sausalito, CA: Natural Capital Institute. www.natural capital.org/docs/SRI%20Report% 2010-04_word.pdf (accessed 15 April 2014).

IEA (2012) *Energy Technology Perspectives 2012: Pathways to a clean energy system*. Paris: International Energy Agency (IEA).

ILSR (2011) 'Bank of North Dakota'. Institute for Local Self-reliance. www. ilsr.org/rule/bank-of-north-dakota-2 (accessed September 2013).

Kennedy, M., B. Lietaer and J. Rogers (2012) *People Money: The promise of regional currencies*. Axminster: Triarchy Press.

Kotlikoff, L. J. (2010) *Jimmy Stewart is Dead: Ending the world's financial plague with limited purpose banking*. Hoboken, NJ: John Wiley & Sons.

Maguire, R. (1957) 'In the Mercury's opinion: how internationalists gain power'. *American Mercury*, October, p. 79.

Nadeau, R. (2008) 'The economist has no clothes'. *Scientific American* 298(4): 42.

Pannozzo, L. and R. Colman (1997) *New Policy Directions for Nova Scotia*. Halifax: GPI Atlantic. www. gpiatlantic.org/pdf/integrated/ new_policy_directions.pdf (accessed 15 April 2014).

Phillips, R. J. (1992) *The 'Chicago Plan' and New Deal Banking Reform*. Working Paper No. 76. Annandale-on-Hudson, NY: Jerome Levy Economics Institute. http://ssrn.com/abstract=160989 or http://dx.doi.org/10.2139/ssrn.160989 (accessed 15 April 2014).

Smith, A. (1759) *The Theory of Moral Sentiments*. London and Edinburgh: A. Millar and A. Kincaid & J. Bell. www.adamsmith.org/moral-sentiments (accessed 15 April 2014).

Smuts, J. C. (1927) *Holism and Evolution*. London: Macmillan and Co. https://archive.org/details/holisman devolutio32439mbp (accessed 15 April 2014).

PART TWO

CO-OPERATIVES AND THE NEW ECONOMY

8 | CHOICES, INCENTIVES AND CO-OPERATIVE ORGANISATION

Stefano Zamagni

The entities whose decisions economists are engaged in analysis have not been made the subject of study and in consequence lack any substance. The firm, to an economist, as Slater has said, is 'effectively defined as a cost curve and a demand curve'. Exchange takes place without any specification of its institutional setting. We have consumers without humanity, firms without organization, and even exchange without markets (Coase 1998: 3).

Historically, co-operatives came into being after capitalist enterprises and began to expand, in various modes and at different paces, in all the advanced economies. In a way, then, co-operatives can be seen as an unexpected fruit of industrial civilisation that ripened during the 'belle époque'. Two main interpretations of this historical fact have been suggested. One explains the co-operative movement as the response to a specific 'failure' of the capitalist form of enterprise, a sort of remedy or compensation for what businesses could not provide. The other considers the phenomenon as a more advanced form of enterprise in advanced societies. That is, the movement is seen as crowning the aspirations of those who consider labour to be an opportunity for self-fulfilment and not just a productive input. This is the interpretation suggested by the great liberal thinker John Stuart Mill when he added the following passage to the third edition of *Principles of Political Economy*, published in 1852:

> The form of association, however, which if mankind continues to improve, must be expected in the end to predominate, is not that which can exist between a capitalist as chief, and work-people without a voice in the management, but the association of the labourers themselves on terms of equality, collectively owning the capital with which they carry on their operations, and working under managers elected and removable by themselves (Mill 1852: 772).

The two interpretations obviously carry different practical consequences. The first relegates co-operatives to a niche, useful and effective to be sure, but always an exception to the rule. On close inspection, the reasoning behind this interpretation is the same as one that looks to markets to compensate for government failures, and to non-profit organisations to compensate for market failures. This interpretation, albeit with significant differences of shading and nuance from author to author, fundamentally guides a whole school of thought ranging from the pioneering work of Benjamin Ward (1958) to Henry Hansmann's excellent study in 1996. The second interpretation, however, sees the co-operative as the form of enterprise into which the capitalist firm could evolve in the long term in the advanced market economies.

I concur with this latter perspective, which can be set forth succinctly as follows. The twentieth century was marked by the confrontation between two modes of production, two socio-economic models: capitalism and so-called 'real' socialism. As we know, perhaps the crucial difference was between private and public (or collective) ownership of the means of production. The century ended with the triumph of capitalism, and writers such as Francis Fukuyama (1992) too quickly announced the 'end of history'. For the fact is that ownership is not the sole relevant factor characterising economic organisation. Much more important today is the question of control – knowing who in the final instance controls the process of production. My own conjecture is that the new century will be marked by a dialectical confrontation between the two principal modes of control within the enterprise: by capital and by labour. That is, the confrontation will no longer turn on the nature of ownership, which will certainly remain largely private. (Indeed, if public enterprises do remain, they truly will be consigned to niches.) Rather, the confrontation will involve who ultimately controls the enterprise: the providers of capital, as in the business corporation, or the suppliers of labour, as in co-operatives and employee-owned firms.

If we are to conjecture as to whether the capitalistic or co-operative form will ultimately prevail, we need a theory that can take the strengths and weaknesses of each into account and explain why the capitalistic form is dominant today. Gregory Dow (2002) properly asks why the capitalistic firm is still so strongly prevalent, given that so many of the problems of contemporary society, such as worsening work alienation and inequality, the happiness paradox, or the various types of poverty traps, could be mitigated by an economic organisation such as a workers' co-operative in which workers control the enterprise where they work. A serious, credible answer must avoid a merely ideological stance – say, blaming the 'establishment' and its power in influencing government action, or the contrary position according to which the rarity of co-operatives would imply their inability to coexist with capitalistic firms. Instead, we must find persuasive arguments. On the one hand, these arguments need to properly identify the forces that can guide economic and institutional evolution towards a final equilibrium in which the co-operative form is preponderant. On the other hand, they must show how the unquestioned advantages of the capitalistic firm in accessing capital and risk diversification can be combined with the advantages of co-operatives in motivating workers (hence fostering productivity gains) and attenuating the distributive conflict.

Co-operatives and investor-owned enterprises: what is the difference?

At this point, the crucial question cannot be put off any longer. What is the ultimate discriminant between the two types of enterprise? Let us begin from the observation that any kind of economic action is always a common action, 'an action, that is, which in order to be undertaken requires the deliberate participation of two or more persons' (Viola 2004: 14). The division of labour itself makes all economic action a common action. So a market economy, necessarily based on the division of labour, is a world densely populated with common actions. According to Viola, three features define the common action. First, all participants must be aware of what they are doing: the mere presence of a number of different individuals is not sufficient. Second, each participant is responsible and accountable for what they do. This is what distinguishes common from collective action: in the latter, the individual and their identity vanish, and with them so does their personal responsibility for their action. Third, there must be a joint effort on the part of the participants to achieve the same objective. The interaction of a number of people in a given context is not, in and of itself, common action if they are pursuing different, not to say conflicting, ends. Thus the economic enterprise, which possesses all three attributes, definitely reflects common action.

There are various types of common action depending on what is held in common, which may be the means or the end. If it is the means, the enterprise will be seen as a capitalistic type, itself a commodity that can be bought and sold to the highest bidder, and interpersonal relationships will typically take the form of a contract. In a contract, of course, the parties work 'in common' (together) for its realisation, but each pursues their own ends, which may perfectly well conflict. Think, for instance, of the contract between vendor and purchaser, or the labour contract itself.

On the other hand, when what is in common is the end, the enterprise is co-operative. The essential difference is between a situation in which it is agreed that each party is to pursue their own ends (as in the capitalist firm) and one in which a common end is shared. This is the same difference as that between a common good and a local public good: in one case the benefit that each person draws from its use cannot be separated from that drawn by others. In other words, the interest of each one is realised *together* with that of each other, not *against*, as is the case with private goods, or *regardless*, as is the case with public goods. Essentially, while public is opposed to private, common is opposed to self. What is common is not *solely* one's own nor indistinctly *everyone's*.

What is the consequence of this distinction, from the economic point of view? That when 'common' action is limited to means alone, the basic problem to be solved is the *co-ordination* of the actions of many agents. This is what management science has done, at least since the pioneering work of F. W. Taylor (*The Principles of Scientific Management*, 1911) and, after the Second World War, of Herbert Simon. But when 'common' also covers the ends, the problem is how to achieve *co-operation* among the people involved.

To avoid misunderstanding, let us specify that our concept of co-operation here must not be confused with the concept employed in game theory. A game is defined as 'co-operative' when there is some enforcement mechanism to ensure that players do not renege on their commitments, but obviously each player has their own aim, which typically differs from those of the others. In formal terms, a problem of co-ordination arises from the strategic interdependence of a number of people; one of co-operation arises from interdependence of their values. This is tantamount to saying that, according to our concept of co-operation, inter-subjectivity is a value, whereas in game theory it is a mere circumstance.

How to facilitate co-operation?

What can be done to encourage co-operation? A convincing answer, in my mind, is that suggested by Bratman (1999), setting forth three conditions. First is the condition of mutual responsiveness: every participant in the common action believes that the intentions of the others are important and that they deserve respect, and knows that this belief is reciprocated. That is, it is not enough that the members intend to undertake the same action; they must also want to do it together. Second is a commitment to the joint activity, which means that it is impossible, in practice, to measure the specific contribution of each participant to the joint product. Third is a commitment to mutual support, whereby each engages to help the others in their efforts to attain the best possible final result.

Note that this mutual support must come in the course of the joint activity, not separate from or after it. So this commitment is not to be confused either with self-interest or with disinterested altruism. Since there is a joining of interests, each person, in helping the others, is also pursuing their own self-interest. In other words, it is precisely because of the person's concern for their own welfare that the co-operative member is concerned for that of the other members (Dworkin 1992). This is the co-operative enterprise's particular interpretation of the principle of reciprocity. Let me recall that the principle runs like this: I do something for you (or give something to you) under the expectation that you in turn can do something for others or, possibly, for me. By contrast, the principle of exchange of equivalents that underlies capitalistic action is as follows: I give something to you under the condition that you will give me something of equivalent value. While the exchange relation is premised upon the principle of equivalence, the reciprocity relation postulates proportionality.

What does a co-operative have to do to satisfy these conditions? First, it must facilitate communication among members. At the same time it must practise *equity*, avoiding both subjection and exploitation. Let me explain. Communication is not the same thing as information. While full information is all that is needed for the co-ordination of decisions, co-operation presupposes the practice of a special form of *deliberative democracy*: the exercise between members of the 'voice' option.

For the key distinction between 'voice' and 'exit' options,[1] we are indebted to A. O. Hirschman, who went on to say that, while the ideal typical field of application of the latter is the economy, that of the former is politics. Well, the true significance of co-operative action is that of extending the 'voice' option to the sphere of economic relations. As we know, the process of deliberation posits the possibility of self-correction – hence each person admits, at the outset, the possibility of changing their own preference in light of the arguments of others. This means that the deliberative method excludes all those who declare, in the name of hierarchy, that they are impermeable to the reasons of others. With this in mind, then, deliberation necessarily presupposes communication. According to Joshua Cohen (1989), co-operation is based on 'deliberation focusing on the common good', in which all participants are willing to question their initial preferences, because 'the relevant preferences and beliefs are those that emerge from or are confirmed by the deliberation' (ibid.: 69). Co-ops are quite a bit better equipped than their capitalist sisters to exploit the potential of the network as an endogenous form of organisation that allows its users to benefit from dynamic externalities, strategic complementarities and cumulative gains. A co-operative that ignored this specific trait and, in the name of efficiency, applied the modus operandi of the capitalist firm – where by definition there is no place for a deliberative process – would be suicidal. True enough, constructing a network requires co-ordination, but it is equally true that network structures provide their greatest benefits when Bratman's three conditions are satisfied (Bratman 1999).

The other prerequisite mentioned is the commitment to internal equity. The prime reason that motivates the members to come together freely to form the co-op is to banish subjection and exploitation. The precept of co-operation is set apart from co-ordination by the fact that it posits not hierarchy but the equal dignity of people and of the areas in which they work. As John Rawls observes, co-operation is much more demanding than co-ordination, as it is based on rules and procedures that have to be agreed to by all participants. To be sure, every common action, hence every enterprise, needs someone to exercise the command function in order to get the wills of the different individuals to converge. But whereas in a capitalist firm command flows from the power hierarchy, which may be more or less authoritarian as a matter of personal style, command in the co-operative depends on authority in a way that makes it impossible for anyone to impose their own concept of the common action on the others.

In short, a co-operative whose governance followed the hierarchical model rather than that of 'co-operative authority' would deprive itself of its best chance to capitalise on its own specific identity. Let me explain. Besley and Ghatak (2004) define a 'mission' as a set of attributes of a project such that the people involved value its success more highly than the monetary income they earn from it. In this sense a co-operative is a mission-oriented organisation whose strength springs from the motivation[2] of the agents. A motivated agent is one who pursues a given end because they know that doing a certain thing or acting in a certain way carries an intrinsic benefit. Clearly, if having a mission reduces the need to negotiate pecuniary incentive schemes, it increases the importance of the non-monetary features of organisation in optimising the agents' efforts.

As intrinsic motivations differ from person to person, a mission-oriented enterprise such as a co-operative succeeds in organising this diversity and consequently achieving substantial gains in productivity, or it fails and is paralysed by internal conflict. That is why the co-operative manager must be as 'capable' as his capitalist counterpart and must also be capable of something else, namely getting the right mix of material and relational incentives. If the co-op manager is seized by the mania for emulation and a sense of inferiority and stresses monetary incentives only, in the end they will provoke the crowding-out effect discussed by Frey and Jegen (1997), in which the intrinsic motivations are 'narcotised' by the extrinsic.

In a historical era like the present, with the end of Taylorism and when capitalist corporations themselves are induced to introduce organisational schemes and principles typical of the co-operative enterprise, co-operatives continue to imitate the capitalist firms' style of governance and demonstrate a lack of consciousness of what they are and what they do. 'A worrying possibility is that management practices based on [traditional] economic models may reduce or destroy non-economic facts like intrinsic motivations and social relations' (Gibbons 1998: 130). What an irony it would be if just now, when the most authoritative studies of capitalist corporate organisation are beginning to discover that economic sustainability cannot be ensured by controls and monetary incentives alone, the leaders of the co-operative movement let slip the chance to use their specific form of enterprise to attain objectives that mere co-ordination cannot achieve.

This is why we need a new, a *different*, economic theory of the co-operative form of enterprise, a theory that can suggest a societal governance based on the symbolic medium of the commitment to value: that is, the internalisation of the enterprise's ends by all the members, to which the means – capital and power – must be subordinated. As has been acutely observed by Putterman (1988), the basic distinction that helps us grasp the argument developed here is between seeing the firm as an association or community whose members aim to pursue democracy in governance, and conceiving the firm as a commodity that can be sold and bought in the market like any other commodity. According to the latter view, labour is merely a hired factor, hence a commodity itself. On the contrary, the former view – which is endorsed by those who see the co-operative form as superior – visualises labour as the master of production.

Two propositions

I advance two basic propositions. First, people desire to develop co-operatives not only to pursue their self-interest, but also because they are genuinely concerned about values such as democracy, justice and freedom in and of themselves. Second, a co-operative firm will not be sustainable and it will not progress over time if all its members behave according to a strict self-interested code of conduct – that is, if they do not exhibit social preferences. Simply put, since co-operation implies engagement with others in a mutually beneficial activity, co-operative behaviour typically confers net benefits on the individual co-operator. However, it may sometimes also impose net economic costs upon individuals in the sense that not co-operating in particular circumstances would increase their material pay-offs. In such cases, unless there is a hard core of members endowed with social preferences who can resist the temptation of behaving opportunistically, the co-operative will start declining and will eventually collapse.[3]

My task on this occasion is not to explain why people co-operate despite living in a capitalist environment. Rather, I seek to explain what determines the range of situations in which individuals opt to co-operate by joining a co-operative firm. The traditional approach in economics poses this question in terms of a calculation of current and future costs and benefits by the individual agent. Such an approach has been proved to be factually fallacious. The existence of social preferences has now been documented in numerous studies using laboratory evidence. The fact is that there are many people who have internalised a social norm of conduct. What makes these norms of 'good conduct' emerge and spread in a society? How do values and moral rules that sustain co-operation evolve endogenously over time? How do virtues interact with economic incentives?

I posit that a society that provides opportunities for virtuous behaviour is one that is more conducive to virtuous individuals. Furthermore, the practice of effective virtuous behaviour may lead to more people adopting virtues on their own. The central thesis of this chapter is that market economies that are pluralistic, i.e. in which the co-operative sector plays an important role, not only offer a remarkable medium of production for various kinds of goods and services, but also serve as a context for positive character formation, and therefore for a more civilised society. In other words, I suggest that a substantive diffusion of co-operative firms in our societies offers an opportunity for more people to engage in practices that permit them to experience virtuous behaviour. In this way, co-operation becomes a most effective vehicle for humanising the economy.

Indeed, it is widely known that, in our day and age, the market and the 'contract culture' underneath it have become increasingly important in our lives. It is sometimes held that the market will regenerate social obligations and redefine human relationships: it is demanded that social, political and cultural life be aimed at making mechanisms efficient and procedures effective. In recent years, competition and globalisation, or a somewhat uniform mindset, appear to have become the true ideology of post-Fordist societies. However, I believe that a new 'human dimension' must be injected into the integration process of economies through the market. The value of a development model cannot be defined in terms of efficiency of its results only, but also in terms of its ability to encompass the individual in their entirety, thus taking into account certainly the material but also the social-relational and spiritual dimensions, as well as every individual's right to realise their potential and fulfil their aspirations.

What are the challenges for the co-operative movement today?

The first delicate challenge comes from the spread of the model of market economy known as 'shared capitalism' in Western economies. Kruse et al. (2012) define shared capitalism as an organisational incentive system that seeks to align the interests of the employee with the owner by sharing participation in decisions and the residual return. So, employees will seek to increase their residual return by working to achieve organisational objectives. Today, more employees than ever before have ownership stakes in their firms through employee stock ownership plans (ESOPs) and firm-based stock ownership plans, receive stock options once limited to top executives, and are covered by profit-sharing plans. By adopting indicators such as supervision, training, pay, job security and job satisfaction, one can conjecture that shared capitalism would have a positive effect on these indicators. As shown by Kruse et al. (ibid.), the actual results stemming from the National Bureau of Economic Research's Shared Capitalism Research Project confirm the expectations. A substantial proportion of private sector workers participate in some form of shared rewards, and there is evidence that shared capitalism is spreading (see Kruse et al. 2010).

This begs the question: would shared capitalism represent a viable – not to say superior – alternative to co-operation? In other words, can enterprises adopting the rules of behaviour of shared capitalism constitute a credible threat to the very raison d'être of co-operative firms? If so, what would be the best response of co-operatives operating within a shared capitalism set-up? If it is true that capitalism smoothly evolved (not without contradictions) during the last three centuries, can we say the same with respect to the co-operative type of firm?

These, and similar, questions cannot be ignored by superficially considering them to be irrelevant or of scarce value. Indeed, many features of the co-operative mode of production have been internalised by present-day capitalist firms. Consider, for example, norms of reciprocity and equity. They are applied in many places where some form of shared capitalism is adopted (for example, the John Lewis Partnership in the UK). In situations of this nature, what would constitute the value added – so to speak – of co-operation? Looking into the near future, can one say that shared capitalism will eventually crowd out co-operation? Is 'shared capitalism' a misnomer? What is not shared is control.[4]

A second major challenge facing the co-operative movement today has to do with the question of membership. The question can be put in the following terms. It is known that the organisation design, in general, depends very much on the assumptions one makes about the nature of employees, so much so that mismatch between organisation design and employee inclinations results in losses in performance. As Sumantra Ghosal wrote (Birkinshaw and Piramal 2005), theories of organisation design that are anchored in bad theories about human nature lead to bad management theories and practice. Under these circumstances, the crucial problem for a co-operative is how to choose its members. How can it find the right members and motivate them? How should the co-operative select an incentive structure that will attract the people it wants to have?

Heterogeneity of preferences among employees will generally drive organisation design towards the more self-interested and less value-driven employees, with the result that organisation design will become unstable (Putnam et al. 1993). If this is the case in general, it is even more pronounced within a co-operative firm. In fact, the democratic rule that is typical of the co-operative enterprise is such that great heterogeneity of preferences across the members will bring the median to diverge too much from the mean of the preference distribution. The result is obvious: the co-operative will eventually collapse – as abundant historical evidence has confirmed. This is the interpretation one can give of the famous dictum by Lorsch and

Tierney (2002): 'The people you pay are more important over time than the people who pay you.'

Individuals are often willing to accept a lower expected income to join a co-operative than what mainstream economics would predict. This suggests that there is a non-monetary value to being a co-operator, as Akerlof and Kranton (2010) have indicated by introducing the concept of identity. They argue that individuals earn additional utility from an identity that matches their ideals. So identity plays an important role in explaining an individual's motivation to become a co-operator. Therefore, how can one foster such an identity within a community? Above all, how could co-operatives maintain and possibly strengthen their identity component, given that identity is a major factor in determining successful internal governance?

Internal governance is the process whereby a group of members, despite being a minority, care so much about the future of their co-operative that they are able to force a nasty CEO or the top management to act in a more co-operative-spirited way. This is frequently achieved via the construction of members' social ties in the workplace. It has been shown that a social tie such as group solidarity in the specific form of mutualism reinforces or countervails monetary incentive schemes in solving principal–agent problems. The firm benefits from the existence of social incentive, on the whole, just because people are less productive in the workplace without 'friends'.

This is easily comprehensible if one considers the notion of *connective capital* (Ichniowski and Shaw 2009), intended as the sum of the person's own knowledge capital and the knowledge capital of others that they tap into to solve a problem. What induces workers and firms to invest in connective capital? How much should each worker tap into the skill of others and how much should others be willing to share their skills? How much should the firm invest in a structure that supports workers' investment in connective capital? Given that, because of their own intrinsic characteristics, co-operative firms are actually more capable of accumulating connective capital, what should be done when they have to choose members in order to translate this potential into actual fact?

Finally, I pause to consider, although briefly, a third important challenge confronting the co-operative movement. It has to do with the phenomenon of pecuniary externalities, which can be defined as the unintended consequences of shifting market prices. Market price not only performs an allocative function, it also distributes incomes and wealth across the economy. Hence, market price changes are a de facto redistribution of burdens and benefits across the society. Economists and policy-makers, while keen on notifying technical externalities (such as pollution), about which there is a huge literature – from Pigou to Coase to Stiglitz – are much less keen on addressing pecuniary externalities[5] (Barrera 2011). Why? The reason is simple and fundamental at the same time.

Pecuniary externalities are the very instrument by which the market achieves an efficient allocation of resources. In fact, it is by means of price changes that economic agents adjust their decisions and modify their behaviour in line with what the 'invisible hand' requires. So, pecuniary externalities are the very machinery of market mechanism and, as such, there is no reason to intervene to ameliorate them. Is there a moral case for mitigating the negative consequence of market-set price levels (and by extension a role for co-operatives to engage in this type of corrective justice)? The answer that is typically given by economists is that, since people know that pecuniary externalities are inherent to the market process, they should have prepared themselves for them. This argument is quite weak. Let us see why.

If one could take for granted that in a market set-up the mere act of choice would *always* imply consent on the part of the agent, then it would be possible to conclude that to choose is to consent to the consequences stemming from the choices made. Unfortunately, this assumption is a very weak one, since there exist many cases of significantly constrained volition in economic life, which prompt the intuition that the constraints under which the agent makes a choice may matter in the analysis of individual consent. The point is that the notion of freedom of choice does not include the structure of constraints the agent faces. Only if the agent could also choose (or contribute to choosing) the set of constraints would it be true that 'to choose is to consent to'. Scitovsky (1976: 97) draws attention to the gap between being free to choose among alternatives in a *given* set and being free to choose between sets of alternatives.

People exercise freedom of choice whenever they use money to pay for goods and services and are free to decide what to pay and in what quantities. That freedom must not be confused with consumer sovereignty. The consumer is sovereign insofar as his choices influence the nature and quantity of the goods and services produced (ibid.).

It follows that I might certainly choose freely without consenting to the consequences of my choice.

The fact that people choose to sell their organs does not imply that they have consented to the institutional arrangements that confront them with such alternatives. Or that a woman who gets married may not have consented to the gender relations on which the institution of marriage is based (Peter 2004: 196).

The tendency in economic theory to put the focus on people's choices and to leave the analysis of constraints in the dark elevates the freedom to choose between given alternatives to freedom *tout court*. Yet, as Amartya Sen has repeatedly noted in his capability approach to defining personal freedom, the opportunity set an individual is presented with is as important in evaluating their freedom as is their autonomy in decision-making. Sen incorporates freedom into social choice theory by assessing individuals' opportunity sets. Preferences over outcomes (commodity bundles) miss what is of key importance to Sen: that individuals are deeply concerned with what substantive opportunities are available to them. Thus far, economics has not been able to develop a differentiation between an agent's access to concrete achievements instead of merely to goods.

In view of the above argument, one can understand (and possibly accept) why mitigating pecuniary externalities is a matter of corrective justice that is necessary to assure long-term economic efficiency. This is the case because long-term economic efficiency also depends on distributive justice, and the latter has to be realised in the short run. I believe that the presence of a vast and robust co-operative sector within the economy is much more effective in obtaining corrective justice – hence long-run efficiency – than a reliance on an intrusive welfare state. This is a fascinating challenge that I hope the co-operative movement will accept to take on, and possibly win.

A paradigm shift

Market economies are consistent with many cultures, conceived as tractable patterns of behaviour or, more generally, as organised systems of values. In turn, the type and degree of congruence of market systems with cultures are not without their effects on the overall performance of the systems themselves. Thus one should expect that a culture of extreme individualism will produce different results from a culture where individuals, although also motivated by self-interest, entertain a sense of reciprocity. In the same way, a culture of peace and harmony will certainly produce different results, on the economic front, from a culture of confrontational competition.

But cultures are not to be taken for granted. Cultures respond to the investment of resources in cultural patterns, and in many circumstances it may be socially beneficial to engage in cultural engineering. Indeed, how good the performance is of an economic system also depends on whether certain conceptions and ways of life have achieved dominance, even if that dominance is precarious. Contrary to what many economists continue to believe, economic phenomena have a primary interpersonal dimension. Individual behaviours are embedded in a pre-existing network of social relations, which cannot be thought of as a mere constraint; rather, they are one of the driving factors that prompt individual goals and motivations. People's aspirations are deeply conditioned by the conventional wisdom about what makes life worth living.

What we urgently need is a new anthropological orientation within economics, capable of enlarging the scope of economic research in order to make it more relevant for the analysis of both policy means and policy ends. In fact, what is called for today is a theoretical set-up that can explain how cultural factors and economic choices interact and how this interaction feeds back into ongoing social relations. The key notion in this respect is that of co-evolutionary dynamics: individual behaviours and social norms evolve jointly when micro and macro changes in the latter prompt adjustments in the former, and vice versa. This is clearly a very complex and far-reaching scientific endeavour, which the most recent economic literature has just begun to explore. The various attempts to demonstrate the self-sufficiency of the categories of economic discourse do not help to expand its grip on reality.

During the last century, mainstream economic theory argued for the divorce of economic judgement from moral and political philosophy. This divorce was supported by the NOMA (Non-Overlapping Magisteria) principle, which can trace its origins back to Richard Whately in 1829, according to which economics should be concerned only with means and not with ends; this has rendered the discipline of little use for the understanding of social processes and for the analysis of structural change. It may be of interest to report the following passage from an old interview given by Peter Drucker:

> Above all, we are learning very fast that the belief that the free market is all it takes to have a functioning society – or even a functioning economy – is pure delusion. Unless there's first a functioning civil society, the market can produce economic results for a very short time, maybe three or five years. For anything beyond these five years a functioning civil society based on organisations like churches, independent universities, or peasant cooperatives is needed for the market to function in its economic role, let alone its social role (quoted in Schwartz and Kelly 1996).

I do not wish to hide the difficulties lurking in the practical implementation of a cultural project targeted at nothing less than a 'paradigm shift' in economic analysis. As in all human endeavours, it would be naive to imagine that certain changes do not create conflict. The differences of vision and the interests at stake are enormous. It is no accident that a kind of widespread anguish about the future is running through society today.

Many are profoundly concerned by economic activity that is often characterised by Machiavellian cunning and deceit. Some people and certain pressure groups are exploiting this anguish as a political tool, deriving from it, depending on the circumstances, either a market-centred Machiavellianism or a state-centred Machiavellianism. It is precisely against this neo-Machiavellian culture and its underlying ethical relativism that those who are ready for the civil economy research programme should put up a fight.

In lieu of a conclusion

How can we summarise the meaning of the considerations set forth here? That in the long run the sustainability and the potential of the co-operative enterprise basically depend on two factors: the 'relative price' that workers decide to assign to freedom as against security – let me repeat Walter Benjamin's representative declaration that 'The pain that accompanies submission is preferable to the pain that always accompanies freedom' – and the ability of the co-operative movement to realise the organisational differentiation that alone can bring out the specificity of common action when 'commonness' embraces ends as well as means.

I certainly do not intend to deny or downplay the difficulties, above all that of procuring capital on market terms. But I do not think that these are the decisive problems that could lead co-operatives to adapt to the prevailing organisational model, which, within a few years, would result in them being essentially undifferentiated from the capitalist corporation, save for some additional constraints to which the latter is not subject.

In a historic phase like the present – with the end of Taylorism, and when capitalistic corporations themselves are induced to introduce organisational schemes and principles typical of the co-operative enterprise – co-operatives continue to try to imitate the capitalist firm's style of governance, with a lack of consciousness of what they are and what they do. This is why we need a new, a *different*, economic theory of co-operative forms of enterprise, a theory that can suggest societal governance based on the symbolic medium of the commitment to value, on the internalisation of objectives by all the members, to which the media of capital and power are subordinated.

In *The Baron in the Trees*, Italo Calvino told us that there are human needs that cannot be made into civil or political rights. The protagonist, finally:

> understood this: that associations make man stronger and throw the best qualities of individuals into relief and give joy – seeing how many good, honest capable people there are, for whom it is worth the trouble to wish the best – that one rarely attains living on one's own account; the opposite occurs more often, to see people's other side, for which you need to keep your hand on the haft of the sword (Calvino 2002: 129).

If we got to the point of understanding what the Baron finally saw, we would at last grasp why our societies, now more than ever, need a massive injection of co-operative culture and co-operative practice.

Notes

1 The 'voice' option refers to the actual possibility of protesting; the 'exit' option means that any member of the organisation should have the possibility of leaving in cases of fundamental disagreements.

2 An agent has extrinsic motivations when they act according to the material rewards stemming from the execution of the action. Intrinsic motivations refer to the intentions of the agent, who derives a 'warm glow' from executing the action.

3 As an example, think of the members of a fishing co-op who sell their catch to a non-co-operative buyer to gain a few cents a pound.

4 In many ESOPs, the worker has not only their job at risk without effective say but their capital as well.

5 These are externalities that operate through prices.

References

Aghion, P. and J. Tirole (1997) 'Formal and real authority in organizations'. *Journal of Political Economy* 105: 1–29.

Akerlof, G. A. and R. Kranton (2010) *Identity Economics: How our identities shape our work, wages and wellbeing.* Princeton, NJ: Princeton University Press.

Alchian, A. and H. Demsetz (1972) 'Production, information costs and economic organizations'. *American Economic Review* 62: 770–96.

Barrera, A. (2011) *Market Complicity and Christian Ethics.* Cambridge: Cambridge University Press.

Besley, T. and M. Ghatak (2004) *Competition and Incentives with Motivated Agents.* CEPR Discussion Paper No. 4641. London: Centre for Economic Policy Research (CEPR). http://econpapers.repec.org/paper/cprceprdp/4641.htm.

Birkinshaw, J. and G. Piramal (eds) (2005) *Sumantra Ghosal on Management: A force for good.* Harlow: Prentice Hall.

Bratman, M. (1999) 'Shared cooperative activity'. In M. Bratman, *Faces of Intention: Selected essays on intention and agency.* Cambridge: Cambridge University Press.

Bruni, L. and S. Zamagni (2007) *Civil Economy.* Oxford: Peter Lang.

Calvino, I. (2002) *Il Barone Rampante.* Milan: Mondadori.

Coase, R. (1998) *The Firm, the Market and the Law.* Chicago, IL: Chicago University Press.

Cohen, J. (1989) 'Deliberation and democratic legitimacy'. In A. Hamlin and P. Pettit (eds), *The Good Polity.* Oxford: Blackwell.

Dassein, W. and T. Santos (2003) *The Demand for Coordination.* CEPR Discussion Paper No. 4096. London: Centre for Economic Policy Research (CEPR).

Dow, G. (2002) *Governing the Firm.* Cambridge: Cambridge University Press.

Dworkin, R. (1992) 'Liberal community'. In S. Avineri and A. De Shalit (eds), *Communitarianism and Individualism.* Oxford: Oxford University Press.

Ellingsen, T. and M. Johannesson (2006) *Pride and Prejudice: The human side of incentive theory.* CEPR Discussion Paper No. 5768. London: Centre for Economic Policy Research (CEPR).

Falk, A. and M. Kosfeld (2004) *Distrust: The hidden cost of control.* CEPR Discussion Paper No. 4512. London:

Centre for Economic Policy Research (CEPR).

Frey, B. S. and R. Jegen (1997) 'Motivation crowding theory'. *Journal of Economic Surveys* 15(5): 589–611.

Fukuyama, F. (1992) *The End of History and the Last Man*. New York, NY: Avon Books.

Gibbons, R. (1998) 'Incentives in organizations'. *Journal of Economic Perspectives* 12(4): 115–32.

Hansmann, H. (1996) *The Ownership of Enterprise*. Cambridge, MA: The Belknap Press, Harvard University Press.

Ichniowski, C. and K. L. Shaw (2009) *Connective Capital as Social Capital*. Working Paper Series No. 15619. Cambridge, MA: National Bureau of Economic Research.

Kruse, D. L., J. R. Blasi and R. B. Freeman (2012) *Does Linking Worker Pay to Firm Performance Help the Best Firms Do Even Better?* NBER Working Paper 17745. Cambridge, MA: National Bureau of Economic Research (NBER).

Kruse, D. L., R. B. Freeman and J. R. Blasi (eds) (2010) *Shared Capitalism at Work: Employee ownership, profit and gain sharing, and broad-based stock options*. National Bureau of Economic Research conference report. Chicago, IL: University of Chicago Press.

Lorsch, J. and T. Tierney (2002) *Aligning the Stars: How to succeed when professionals drive results*. Boston, MA: Harvard Business School Press.

McGregor, D. (1960) *The Human Side of Enterprise*. New York, NY: McGraw Hill.

Milgrom, P. and J. Roberts (1990) 'The economics of modern manufacturing: technology, strategy, and organizations'. *American Economic Review* 80: 511–28.

Mill, J. S. (1852) *Principles of Political Economy*. Reprinted 1987. Fairfield, NJ: A. M. Kelley.

Peter, F. (2004) 'Choice, consent and the legitimacy of market transactions'. *Economics and Philosophy* 20(1): 1–18.

Putnam, R. D., R. Leonardi and R. Nanetti (1993) *Making Democracy Work: Civic traditions in modern Italy*. Princeton, NJ: Princeton University Press.

Putterman, L. (1988) 'The firm as association versus the firm as commodity'. *Economics and Philosophy* 4(2): 243–66.

Rawls, J. (1971) *A Theory of Justice*. Cambridge, MA: Harvard University Press.

Sacco, P., P. Vanin and S. Zamagni (2006) 'The economics of human relationships'. In S. C. Kolm and J. M. Ythier (eds), *Handbook of the Economics of Giving, Altruism and Reciprocity*. Amsterdam: Elsevier.

Schlicht, E. (2003) *Consistency in Organizations*. IZA Discussion Paper No. 718. Bonn: Institute for the Study of Labor (IZA).

Schwartz, P. and K. Kelly (1996) 'Relentless contrarian'. *The Ottawa Citizen*, 31 December, p. A11.

Scitovsky, T. (1976) *The Joyless Economy*. Oxford: Oxford University Press.

Sen, A. (1999) *Development as Freedom*. New York, NY: Random House.

Taylor, F. W. (1911) *The Principles of Scientific Management*. New York, NY and London: Harper & Brothers.

Viola, F. (ed.) (2004) *Forme della cooperazione*. Bologna: Il Mulino.

Ward, B. (1958) 'The firm in Illyria: market syndicalism'. *American Economic Review* 48: 566–89.

Zamagni, S. (2013) 'Cooperative enterprise'. In L. Bruni and S. Zamagni (eds), *Handbook on the Economics of Reciprocity and Social Enterprise*. Cheltenham: Edward Elgar.

Zamagni, S. and V. Zamagni (2010) *Cooperation*. Cheltenham: Edward Elgar.

9 | ARE CO-OPERATIVES A VIABLE BUSINESS FORM? LESSONS FROM BEHAVIOURAL ECONOMICS

Morris Altman

Introduction

Behavioural economics can contribute to a better understanding of the relative success of co-operative businesses and point to the necessary conditions for success. Of particular importance to the co-operative advantage is the incentive environment in co-operative organisations that encourages relatively high levels of productivity and reduces the transaction costs of doing business. Conventional economic theory predicts that co-operatives should not prove as successful as the traditional hierarchically structured, investor-owned, profit-maximising firms because of the perverse incentives embedded in their organisational form. But the conventional economic modelling of the firm makes simplifying assumptions that assume away the importance of particular incentives and characteristics within the co-operative that can make co-operatives competitive and even more productive than investor-owned firms (Pérotin and Robinson 2004).

Behavioural economics pays particular attention to effort variability, the importance of trust and fairness in determining productivity, the ability to punish non-co-operators, altruistic punishment, the power relationship within the firm (who makes the decisions), complex and imperfect information, identity, social capital, the preferences of co-operative members, and – related to this other-regarding behaviour – the mental models individuals use to make their decisions. In conventional economics, none of these variables is of much analytical consequence. Of particular importance to the conventional model is the assumption that the quantity and quality of effort per unit of time supplied to the firm (co-operative or traditional investor-owned) is fixed, if not maximised. Effort supply is assumed to be unaffected by work environment, market structure or power relationships.

The significance of the contribution of behavioural economics to an understanding of the economic efficiency (in simple terms, output per unit of input) of different organisational forms is that conventional economic theory is inconsistent with the relative economic success of co-operative organisations, even in competitive markets. Although co-operatives don't dominate the market, they are important, especially in some sectors. This relative success needs to be explained and modelled. Indeed, the co-operative model for organising business is adopted by individuals because it is deemed to be a pathway for economic success. From the perspective of the conventional economic model, this worldview is irrational or at least misplaced, based on a serious misconception on the economic viability of co-operative organisations. But the conventional model remains dominant. Either implicitly or explicitly, how economic efficiency is modelled plays a vital role in how laypeople, scholars and government understand whether co-operatives are a viable organisational form. And this can inform whether the co-operative is pursued as a viable and dynamic business model by potential stakeholders and whether government facilitates the development of co-operatives – treating them at least on an equal footing with investor-owned firms.

Although current estimates are far from precise, the evidence suggests that co-operatives are of importance in both developed and less developed economies, spread across 100 countries. As of the first decade of this century, there were about 800 million members in co-operatives and these co-operatives were responsible for about 100 million jobs (Altman 2009a; International Co-operative Alliance 2008; Global300.coop 2007; Global300 2011; UN 2005; 2008; 2009). About half of the world's agricultural output is marketed by co-operatives. In the financial sector, there are about 120 million credit union members in eighty-seven countries. Consumer co-operatives are also significant, as are healthcare co-operatives, which service about 100 million people in over fifty countries. Electricity supply co-operatives are also quite influential, especially in rural areas. Workers' co-operatives are least important in size, with only a small percentage of the 100 million individuals employed in all co-operatives working in co-operatives controlled by the workers themselves.

The conventional model does not predict that co-operatives can't survive. However, it explains the relative importance of co-operatives in the world economy on the basis of public subsidies, protection from competition (so they can charge relatively higher prices), or the persistent acceptance of below normal rates of return on investment, such as in plant and equipment. Subsidies represent a transfer of resources from society at large to co-operative members. The ability to charge higher prices also represents a transfer of resources, in this case from one group of purchasers, such as consumers, to the co-operative's members. If low rates of return are earned, then the resources invested in co-operatives could be used more productively elsewhere, increasing the wealth of nations. In these cases co-operatives survive for the wrong reasons, creating economic inefficiencies, transferring income from one group in society to another and, overall, reducing national wealth.

The principles of co-operative organisation are what preclude co-operatives from being economically efficient and viable, according to conventional economic wisdom. It is assumed that the co-operative organisation creates particular incentives that reduce productivity and increase average costs from what they would otherwise be in an investor-owned organisation. Of particular relevance is the fact that co-operatives are democratic organisations where profits (surplus over costs) are shared equally among co-operative members; this creates the opportunity for co-operative members to 'free ride' on others and shirk their responsibilities, reducing their contribution to the co-operative and thereby reducing productivity and the firm's competitiveness.

Related to this, it is argued that the co-operative organisation has multiple goals based on its democratic decision-making framework, reducing the probability that the co-operative behaves in a manner consistent with profit maximisation. This reduces the chances that the co-operative will perform efficiently. These negative arguments assume that democratic organisation yields relatively low productivity. Also, it is maintained that the market doesn't discipline co-operatives because they typically don't issue shares on the stock market, where shareholders expect and demand that corporations will behave efficiently, thereby increasing share value at every given point in time. Thus, co-operatives have the incentive to perform inefficiently.

It is also argued that when membership is widely dispersed (within the co-operative), it is costly (agency costs) for co-operative members to discipline co-operative management and to engage in effective and efficient decision-making, another incentive for co-operatives to be inefficient. Last but not least, co-operatives have a limited source of capital for investment purposes given their reticence, on principle, to access capital markets. This limits the co-operative's capacity to invest in necessary plant, equipment, technology, and even in worker productivity enhancement (human capital formation). It also limits the capacity of the co-operative to grow, reducing its ability to take advantage of potential scale economies, all of which contributes to lower levels of productivity. These various concerns, which flow from the conventional economic model, are addressed in this chapter and we argue that they are largely misplaced.

It is important to note that official co-operative organisations are bound by principles articulated by the International Co-operative Alliance (Altman 2009a; International Co-operative Alliance 2008). For example, co-operatives are supposed to follow the rules set out below:

- they should be transparent and democratic – one vote per member, typically irrespective of the member's investment in the co-operative, such as deposits in a credit union;
- members are supposed to contribute equitably to the capital of the co-operative and to its democratic governance;
- there is limited compensation to the co-operative member – this would be based on the member's economic (capital) contribution to the co-operative and transactions with it;
- any surpluses are largely used to build up capital reserves, to invest in the co-operative, and to contribute to the larger community; and
- any agreement entered into by the co-operative with external organisations, inclusive of those to raise capital, must be consistent with the democratic control of the co-operative by its members.

A common thread running through these principles is democratic control of the co-operative by its members and fairness in economic compensation. The key question is whether democratic control and fairness impede or preclude the pursuit of economic efficiency and competitive organisational forms.

It is important to note that there are successful investor-owned organisations that have adopted relatively co-operative organisational forms (labour–management co-operation, labour participation in management, fairness in compensation and work environment) so as to increase economic efficiency. Although these private organisations are not co-operatives (owned and controlled by members), they mimic key organisational and operational features of genuine co-operatives. Indeed, these features are replicated because of their perceived positive impact on economic efficiency. This challenges the conventional economic perspective's assumptions about what contributes to or hinders economic efficiency and competitiveness, especially the assumption that less hierarchical and more democratic organisational forms reduce economic efficiency (Altman 2002; Gordon 1998; Lampel et al. 2010; Matrix Evidence 2010).

Another important point to be made is that private companies – that is, non-publicly traded companies – are quite large, are growing in importance, and, on average, are highly profitable: some of the leading corporations in the world are not publicly traded, such as Bosch, Cargill, Koch Industries, IKEA, LEGO, Mars, Pricewaterhouse-Coopers, Rolex, Victorinox and Enterprise Rent-A-Car. This challenges the view that only publicly traded companies can be economically efficient and dynamic and have access to the funds required to invest in the resources needed to remain competitive and grow (Economist 2012). Co-operative organisations tend to be very much like non-publicly traded corporations in the sense that they don't seek funds by issuing publicly traded stock and are not, therefore, subject to the 'discipline' of the interests of public shareholders.

Based on the facts available, being a publicly traded corporation is not a necessary condition for being economically efficient and competitive. Moreover, these non-publicly traded corporations are not subject to the short-term profit maximisation worldview that very often dominates the decision-making of publicly traded corporations as part of their inherent incentive system. This type of short-termism can deter decision-makers from investing in the long-term efficiency and competitiveness of the corporation, focusing instead on maximising short-term increases in share values. This can result in less efficient and less competitive firms. The longer view that often characterises non-publicly traded corporations is also typical of the co-operative organisational form. However, a key difference between the two organisational forms is that the co-operative is subject to the control of its members and therefore potentially more transparent and accountable in its decision-making processes and outcomes.

Behavioural economics and co-operative organisations

Behavioural economics provides a theoretical framework to understand why co-operative organisations can be more productive (economically efficient) than investor-owned firms, and at least as competitive as them. One important aspect of this narrative relates to how the firm is modelled. I argue that there exists a co-operative advantage in the workers' co-operative that can extend to other types of co-operatives, including credit unions, consumer co-operatives, and producers' and marketing co-operatives (these categories constitute the largest co-operatives in the world). This advantage lies in the capacity of co-operative members to increase the quantity and quality of effort that they contribute to the production process, yielding higher levels of output and a superior quality of output or greater economic or x-efficiency (Altman 2001; 2002; 2006; 2012; Leibenstein 1966; McCain 2008; see also Ben-Ner and Jones 1995; Bonin et al. 1993; Doucouliagos 1995; Sexton and Iskow 1993).

In a co-operative organisation, members have the incentive to work harder and smarter – a possibility assumed away in the traditional modelling of the firm. Conventional theory assumes that effort is fixed and unaffected by the work environment and culture. What varies is the amount of labour time supplied by firm members, workers, managers and owners. When effort is fixed, and not sensitive to the work environment or culture, any attempt to improve member benefits and quality of work must generate higher unit or average costs of production. Of course, this would make the co-operative less competitive. Moreover, since workers' co-operatives (as well as other co-operative organisations) often focus on improving the benefits and working conditions of members, this results in higher unit costs and economic fragility, according to conventional economics.

Whichever model one employs, the assumption is that co-operatives are often more costly organisations than traditional firms because of their focus on membership and even community benefits. An additional assumption made is that co-operatives necessarily disperse savings (surplus) to members; this severely limits the capacity of the co-operative to invest, thereby reducing its ability to maintain and grow its competitive capabilities by maintaining and improving its plant, equipment and technology, as well as its human capital stock.

But if effort is variable and co-operatives need to be competitive, then attempts to improve the well-being of the membership, which could include maintaining and enhancing the quality and quantity of employment, should incentivise the co-operative organisation (its members) into behaving more efficiently (working smarter and harder) as well as adopting and developing technologies that make it competitive. Although co-operatives can be more costly to operate than traditional firms, the incentive exists within this organisational form for the co-operative to become much more productive. By increasing effort inputs and adopting and developing more productive technology, the more expensive co-operatives can end up with unit costs and profits that are at least the same as those of less expensive traditional firms.

In addition, the fact that co-operatives engender a greater degree of loyalty and solidarity among employees and clients reduces the turnover of employees, managers and consumers, further reducing production costs from what they might otherwise be. Co-operative organisations can more easily resolve what economists refer to as 'agency problems' in order to foster increases in productivity. In part, this is conditional upon the positive incentive environment that can characterise the co-operative organisational form. And this relates to the culture of trust and reciprocity that often typifies co-operatives, which is partly a function of the democratic governance structure of the co-operative as well as of its related layers of transparency and accountability.

Linked to this, the governance and incentive structure of the co-operative is oriented less towards maximising short-term returns and more towards maximising the long-term returns of the firm's owners (co-operative members) than is the incentive structure of the traditional investor-owned hierarchical firm. Long-term orientation is conducive to investing in the future of the firm and the society in which the firm is embedded and located. This investment is in plant and equipment, technology, firm members and employees, and the community (Davis 2004). A focus on immediate increases in share value is no guarantee of long-term sustainable growth or productivity strategies. As discussed above, this is one critical reason why many investor-owned firms avoid going public with share offerings. Co-operatives are not responsible to shareholders, who might be more interested in short-term increases in the share value that yield capital gains. Instead, they are responsible to co-operative members who tend to have a longer-term view of economic returns, which are often also linked to the non-economic social and psychological returns connected with being a member of a co-operative.

A critical error in theorising about corporations in general is assuming that being more expensive in the first instance generates higher unit costs of production. In this way, traditional economic theory assumes that the best or easiest way to become more efficient and competitive, in terms of effort inputs and immediate investment, is to cut labour benefits and introduce negative incentives to reduce costs and increase productivity. But there are alternative ways of being competitive that involve increasing the degree of efficiency and x-efficiency and adopting more productive technologies. Both x-efficiency and technological change are prompted by the need to remain competitive while providing co-operative members and other stakeholders with higher levels of material well-being. An important facet of the co-operative advantage is its productivity advantage over what is typically possible in the traditional firm. This advantage countervails the increased costs that are typically associated with operating a co-operative organisation.

Although co-operative organisations might be more expensive to operate than their traditional investor-owned counterparts, co-operative members can be much better off materially and socially than they might be otherwise, without this causing their firm to become uncompetitive. All types of co-operative can yield competitive outcomes without being driven out of the market by traditional hierarchical firms as a result of productivity offsets to these increased costs. Such co-operatives can function and prosper in mainstream economic sectors, even in highly competitive environments. Moreover, when workers are also owners or members of the co-operative, there is much less incentive for them to leave, reducing quit and turnover rates. This lowers production costs by maintaining the most productive workers and by reducing both average training costs and search costs for replacement workers.

Overall, co-operatives can increase the size of the economic pie.

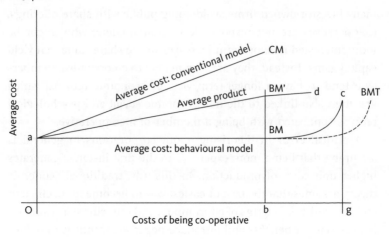

9.1 Unit production costs and the costs of being co-operative

Once one introduces x-efficiency modelling to the co-operative organisational form – and, related to this, the implication of effort variability and induced technological change – co-operatives cannot be viewed as the domain of low-productivity, economically desperate members of society. Co-operatives can be modelled and regarded as dynamic economic organisations that can lift the wealth of nations and increase the competitiveness of firms, even in increasingly competitive and globalised markets.

Aspects of this argument are illustrated in Figure 9.1 (derived from Altman 2001; 2002; 2006). In the traditional economic model, co-operatives incur higher costs, such as higher levels of labour benefits to workers in workers' co-operatives, and even in consumer and producer co-operatives, and higher incomes to members of marketing and producer co-operatives. The traditional narrative ignores the lower costs of co-operative management compared with those incurred by equivalent economic organisations in the private sector. The assumed higher costs yield higher unit or average production costs, since, in the traditional model, increasing labour benefits, for example, has no impact on labour productivity. This is shown by line segment *aCM*. More realistically, in a democratic firm exemplified by a co-operative, when labour benefits and the other costs of being a co-operative increase, labour productivity increases. Therefore, in the co-operative firm, the level of x-efficiency increases as economic and non-economic incentives improve. The co-operative firm induces its members into becoming more productive. To the extent that such productivity increases offset the increased costs associated with being a co-operative, average or unit production costs need not change as labour costs increase, illustrated by line segment *aBM*. Eventually, productivity cannot be increased sufficiently to offset the increased costs of being a co-operative, at point *b*, yielding increased average costs, shown by line segment *BMc*. Finally, the behavioural model converges with the conventional model. But this assumes no technical changes, which would result in further offsets to increasing costs when x-efficiency is at a maximum; this is illustrated by a shift in the cost curve from *BMc* to *BMT* (Altman 2009b).

This argument is further clarified by the following equation, assuming a very simple economy where labour is the only costed input (Altman 2009a):

$$AC = \frac{w}{(Q/L)}$$

where *AC* is average cost, *w* is the wage rate (our proxy for the costs of co-operation) and (*Q/L*) is the average product of labour: *Q* is total output, and *L* is labour input measured in terms of hours worked. Increasing the costs of co-operation (*w*) increases average cost in the traditional model. But in the co-operative model, the average cost need not increase if the co-operative generates sufficient cost offsets in terms of (*Q/L*). And if *w* falls in the traditional model, this reduces unit costs. But this would not be the case if lower wages resulted in sufficiently lower productivity, as workers retaliated for being treated unfairly.

Given this behavioural model, traditional hierarchical investor-owned firms, often characterised by lower wages but also by higher personnel turnover and by managerial slack (managers not working as hard or as smart as they could), need not be more competitive than co-operative firms. Co-operative firms can compete on the basis of higher productivity. However, the more productive co-operative firms need not drive out of the market the less productive traditional firms, although they have the capacity to do so on the basis of higher productivity. Co-operatives and investor-owned firms co-exist and are both competitively sustainable over time. Given the superior incentive system in the co-operative organisation, there is no good theoretical reason to presume that co-operatives cannot be both competitive and prosperous. But the superior productivity of the co-operative appears to just suffice for co-operatives, on average, to be competitive.

One indication of the potential superior productivity performance of the co-operative is that highly productive investor-owned firms mimic key aspects of the co-operative organisational form. One example of this is the investor-owned participatory firm, which allows for partial workers' ownership of firm assets, shares some of the surplus, and gives workers a considerable and effective voice. These firms are more productive than the traditional investor-owned hierarchical firms and yield higher levels of x-efficiency and induced technological change. Such participatory investor-owned firms represent another alternative to the traditional firm (Altman 2002; Erdal 2011; Gordon 1998). However, like their relatively successful co-operative counterparts, such firms do not dominate the market place. As with co-operatives, being comparatively productive does not translate into being more cost competitive. Higher productivity can only be generated by creating a superior work environment, which demands higher input costs. Given that the more participatory firms need not have a cost advantage over the more hierarchical firms and often exhibit reduced power and status of owners and managers, adopting the more participatory model either: 1) is a function of firm owners desperate to compensate for rising input costs, where increasing prices sufficiently or cutting wages, for example, are not viable options; or 2) demonstrates a preference for the participatory model, for reasons of moral sentiments for employees and other stakeholders.

Extending a behavioural model of co-operative organisations

A fundamental critique of co-operatives in economics is that they are not structured to motivate profit-maximising behaviour and thus fail to maximise the economic surplus that can be produced, limiting the capacity of the co-operative to invest in state-of-the-art technology and to maintain plant and equipment. This can undermine the competitiveness of the co-operative. In addition, it is maintained that the co-operative dispenses its surplus to members, so even if the co-operative maximised its surplus, this surplus would not be used for investment purposes, undermining the long-term viability of the co-operative organisation. Thus, a fundamental failure of the co-operative is its assumed principal obligation to distribute most, if not all, of the surplus it produces.

A key, empirically backed assumption of x-efficiency theory and efficiency wage theory (part of the behavioural economics toolbox) is that the conventional firm is prone not to maximise total economic surplus because it typically fails to maximise the level of x-efficiency or economic efficiency. The incentive environment of the traditional firm is conducive to managerial slack as well as employees not working as smart or as hard as they would under a different incentive environment, such as the one embodied by the co-operative organisational form. However, this type of behavioural model would not predict that co-operatives do not attempt to maximise profits. A profit-maximising co-operative simply does its best to maximise the difference between economic costs and benefits, given the constraints that it faces. Nothing in the 'nature' of the co-operative organisation suggests that, typically, it would fail to attempt to behave in a manner *consistent* with equating marginal costs to marginal benefits: that is, to maximise profits. Such behaviour makes more surplus available to co-operative members, given the co-operative's cost and benefit function. But a key driver of the co-operative advantage is its desire to treat members better and more fairly than they would be treated in the traditional investor-owned firm – and the realisation of this objective comes at a cost. This shifts upward the co-operative's cost function, which means that the profit-maximising co-operative generates less surplus than the traditional firm, if these additional costed inputs have no effect on productivity – the assumption of the conventional model. However, in the co-operative, these higher costs generated by treating members better and more fairly, generates higher productivity. This shifts the co-operative's benefits function upwards, and this can result in the profit-maximising outcome being a total surplus that is equal to or even greater than what is produced by the traditional profit-maximising firm.

These points are illustrated in Figure 9.2. Profit maximisation is consistent with higher or lower amounts of surplus, contingent upon the total revenue and cost functions of the firm. Also, the increased productivity in the co-operative allows it to be cost competitive with

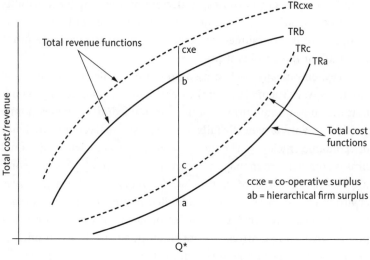

Profit maximisation: MC = MB → Q*

9.2 Surplus in profit-maximising co-operatives and hierarchical firms

the traditional firm. Furthermore, in the co-operative the surplus can increase when co-operative members decide to accept lower benefits in order to increase investments, for example. Given the nature of the co-operative, lower benefits (democratically and fairly achieved) would not have the effect of lowering productivity, as they would in the traditional firm. This flexibility in the co-operative organisation potentially provides it with a competitive edge over the traditional firm.

The concern that the co-operative organisation would simply disburse the surplus to members, based on first principles, is also misplaced. A principle of co-operative organisations is that when surpluses are distributed they must be based on members' contributions to the co-operative. This is an equity principle applied to the distribution of the surplus. But a necessary condition of being a co-operative is that not all of the surplus is dispersed. Whether any surplus is dispersed is a decision to be made by co-operative members. Some surpluses can be distributed as dividends in consumer co-operatives or as bonuses in workers' co-operatives, for example. However, the expectation is that most surpluses remain in the co-operative, where they serve to build up reserves for investment purposes or to support the larger community – this is sometimes reinforced by the tax system, such as in Italy and the United Kingdom. Members also have a vested interest in maintaining the economic viability of their co-operatives, which typically entails using surpluses to accumulate reserves, to maintain and grow plant and equipment, to invest in technological change, and to train its members and employees. Indeed, a first principle of co-operatives is their sustainability over time. The guardians of this long-term view are the co-operative members for whom the sustainability of the co-operative is of primary importance. And, given the democratic nature of co-operative governance, no one co-operative member has the ability to disperse surpluses. However, the distribution of surpluses can occur in investor-owned firms when viable firms are purchased with the objective of asset-stripping, as this maximises the short-term returns to the new investors (Jeppesen and Møller 2011). This requires a legal system tolerant of such behaviour and a worldview among policy-makers that this is an 'optimal' way of growing the economy.

There is nothing in the nature of the traditional firm that guarantees that surpluses are used optimally for investment purposes. For public corporations, dividends might be paid out of the surplus. Also, surpluses can flow to managers and to the owners as bonuses or in the form of other benefits. The latter usually does not occur in co-operatives.

Related to this, in the traditional firm, especially in the publicly listed firm, there is no clear incentive for decision-makers to focus on long-term profit maximisation or the long-term viability of the firm. There is often a focus on the maximisation of short-term returns on publicly issued shares, which need not be compatible with what is in the firm's long-term interest (its sustainability). This is a function of the importance of external stakeholder (shareholder) interest to the decision-making process. It is also related to the 'moral hazard' problem that is often ingrained in the incentive environment of the traditional firm. Corporate decision-makers are rewarded with corporate stock, so maximising short-term returns and taking high risks to do so are viewed as the optimal course of action. This happens when the costs of short-term and high-risk decisions are not internalised by decision-makers, hence moral hazard.

In contrast, in the co-operative, decision-makers are incentivised to focus on maximising the long-term returns (economic and non-economic) to the firm. This is the case when the co-operative maintains a democratic decision-making structure, where there is transparency and accountability to members, and where the costs of democratic participation and of obtaining and understanding relevant information are relatively low. The costs of democratic participation have diminished thanks to innovations in information technology (Murray 2010). Also important is the extent to which the market in which the co-operative operates is competitive, since a competitive market can result in the co-operative performing more efficiently than it might do otherwise. If there is an absence of democratic decision-making, transparency and accountability, the governance of the co-operative might collapse into that of the traditional investor-owned firm. This is a critically important point. Co-operatives do not have a co-operative advantage because of the genetic predisposition of co-operative members or leaders; rather, the incentive environment and culture (which needs to be developed, harnessed, monitored and enforced) are the critical factors. But if the correct institutional parameters are in place, there should be a co-operative advantage, so that co-operatives can compete with traditional hierarchical investor-owned firms.

The co-operative advantage takes on different forms, and the increased productivity that flows from the way in which the co-operative's members or employees are treated is only one of these forms. This productivity advantage is seen most clearly in workers' co-operatives, but it is also likely in consumer co-operatives *when and if* employees are members, or are otherwise committed to the co-operative organisation. Here, the co-operative takes the form of a multi-stakeholder co-operative, structured so that the interests of a variety of constituents are represented in the decision-making process. But this need not be the case. A co-operative can also be organised in terms of hierarchical forms of management (where employee interests are not represented) and can remain competitive on the basis of lower wages and poor working conditions. In this case, consumer co-operatives need not generate superior material welfare outcomes for their workforces. The same holds true of producer co-operatives and credit unions.

However, these and other co-operatives can generate benefits to their members even if they do not include a productivity advantage. Equally, co-operatives can be competitive and economically viable without a productivity advantage, as long as there are no serious economic (price and quality) disadvantages. There are no good theoretical reasons for a disadvantaged position. Moreover, individuals, even if they are not members of a co-operative, are willing to buy from a co-operative, or even pay a higher price (within limits) for their output, if they are sympathetic to co-operatives in general or to a particular one, because of what they believe the co-operative represents in terms of its approach to business and society. This provides the co-operative with some protection from market forces if and when necessary (Altman 2011).

Conclusion

Contrary to what is predicted in the conventional economic model, the incentive environment of the co-operative organisational form is conducive to generating relatively higher levels of productivity and economic benefits for members and for the community in which the co-operative is embedded. These benefits not only serve to increase the size of the economic pie, they also provide co-operatives with the means to remain competitive and even to become more competitive, in terms of price and quality of output, than the traditional investor-owned hierarchical firm. But the co-operative productivity advantage is most effectively achieved when all key stakeholders, including workers, are incentivised to work hard and smart. The right incentives are not entirely financial in nature. Financial incentives are typically part of a much broader incentive package where identity, trust and reciprocity are important additional features. Also, contrary to the conventional wisdom, there is no imperative in the co-operative organisational form for co-operatives not to maximise profits or surplus or to squander surpluses in the form of member benefits. Indeed, given the long-term perspective embedded in the co-operative organisational form, at least in theory, one should expect the opposite.

There is no reason to expect that co-operatives will not be competitive if they adhere to democratic, non-hierarchical forms of governance and management, accountability and transparency. This possibility, articulated through the lenses of more realistic and rigorous economic theory, allows us to better appreciate the relative success of co-operatives and the conditions necessary for their continued success as a competitive organisational form. It is important to appreciate that the competitiveness of co-operatives is largely contingent on how they are governed – their incentive systems and cultures. Also, being competitive does not imply that co-operatives will necessarily serve the interests of society at large, or even those of their employees or their immediate community. Much depends on the extent to which the interests of stakeholders are represented in the membership and governance structure of the co-operative and how empathetic co-operative decision-makers are to the preferences of stakeholders. But a co-operative has the potential to be more productive and meet the needs of its various stakeholders, while remaining competitive. This is a much less likely outcome in the traditional investor-owned hierarchical firm.

References

Altman, M. (2001) *Worker Satisfaction and Economic Performance*. Armonk, NY: M. E. Sharpe.

— (2002) 'Economic theory, public policy and the challenge of innovative work practices'. *Economic and Industrial Democracy: An International Journal* 23: 271–90.

— (2006) 'Workers co-operatives as an alternative competitive organizational form'. In P. Kalmi and M. Klinedinst (eds), *Advances in the Economic Analysis of Participatory and Labor-Managed Firms*. Vol. 9. Bingley: Emerald Group Publishing, pp. 213–35.

— (2009a) 'History and theory of co-operatives'. In H. Anheier and S. Toepler (eds), *International Encyclopedia of Civil Society*. New York, NY: Springer.

— (2009b) 'A behavioural-institutional model of endogenous growth and induced technical change'. *Journal of Economic Issues* 63: 685–713.

— (2011) 'Co-operative advantage'. *Competition and Regulation Times* 34: 8–9.

— (2012) *Behavioural Economics for Dummies*. New York, NY: John Wiley & Sons.

Ben-Ner, A. and D. Jones (1995) 'Employee participation, ownership, and productivity: a theoretical framework'. *Industrial Relations* 34: 532–54.

Bonin, J. P., D. C. Jones and L. Putterman (1993) 'Theoretical and empirical studies of producer co-operatives: will ever the twain meet?' *Journal of Economic Literature* 31: 1290–320.

Davis, P. (2004) *Human Resource Management in Co-operatives: Theory, process, and practice*. Geneva: ILO Cooperative Branch.

Doucouliagos, C. (1995) 'Worker participation and productivity in labor-managed and participatory capitalist firms: a meta-analysis'. *Industrial & Labor Relations Review* 49: 58–77.

Economist (2012) 'The endangered public corporation: the big engine that couldn't'. *The Economist*, 19 May. www.economist.com/node/21555552/print.

Erdal, D. (2011) *Beyond the Corporation: Humanity working*. London: Bodley Head.

Global300 (2011) *Global300 Report 2010: The world's major co-operatives and mutual businesses*. Geneva: International Co-operative Alliance. http://ica.coop/sites/default/files/attachments/Global300%20Report %202011.pdf (accessed 15 March 2014).

Global300.coop (2007) *International Co-operative Alliance: Global 300 list*. http://community-wealth.org/content/global-300-list-worlds-major-co-operatives-and-mutual-businesses.

Gordon, D. M. (1998) 'Conflict and cooperation: an empirical glimpse of the imperatives of efficiency and redistribution'. In E. O. Wright (ed.), *Recasting Egalitarianism: New rules for communities, states and markets*. London and New York: Verso, pp. 181–207.

International Co-operative Alliance (2008) 'What's a co-op?' International Co-operative Alliance website. http://ica.coop/en/whats-co-op.

Jeppesen, K. K. and U. G. Møller (2011) 'Asset stripping in a mature market economy'. *Journal of Financial Crime* 18: 32–46.

Lampel, J., A. Bhalla and P. Jha (2010) *Model Growth: Do employee-owned businesses deliver sustainable performance?* London: Employee Ownership Association. www.employeeownership.co.uk/publications/model-growth-do-employee-owned-businesses-deliver-sustainable-performance/ (accessed 15 March 2014).

Leibenstein, H. (1966) 'Allocative efficiency vs. "x-efficiency"'. *American Economic Review* 56: 392–415.

Matrix Evidence (2010) *The Employee Ownership Effect: A review of the evidence*. London: Employee Ownership Association. www.employeeownership.co.uk/publications/the-employee-ownership-effect-a-review-of-the-evidence (accessed 15 March 2014).

McCain, R. A. (2008) 'Co-operative games and co-operative organizations'. *Journal of Socio-Economics* 37: 2155–67.

Murray, R. (2010) *Co-operation in the Age of Google*. Manchester: Co-operatives UK. www.uk.coop/sites/storage/public/downloads/co-operation_in_the_age_of_google _for_consultation_1.pdf (accessed 15 March 2014).

Pérotin, V. and A. Robinson (eds) (2004) *Employee Participation, Firm Performance and Survival*. Advances in the Economic Analysis of Participatory and Labor-Managed Firms, Vol. 8. Amsterdam: Elsevier.

Sexton, R. J. and J. Iskow (1993) 'What do we know about the economic efficiency of co-operatives: an evaluative survey'. *Journal of Agricultural Cooperation* 8: 15–27.

UN (2005) *Co-operatives in Social Development: Report of the Secretary-General*. New York, NY: United Nations (UN). www.copac.coop/publications/un/a60138e.pdf (accessed 5 August 2013).

— (2008) *Co-operatives at Work*. New York, NY: United Nations (UN). www.un.org/esa/socdev/social/cooperatives/documents/CoopsAt Work.pdf (accessed 5 August 2013).

— (2009) *Cooperatives in Social Development*. New York, NY: United Nations (UN). ww.copac.coop/publications/un/a64132e.pdf (accessed 5 August 2013).

10 | THE CO-OPERATIVE ENTERPRISE: A VALID ALTERNATIVE FOR A BALANCED SOCIETY

Vera Negri Zamagni

Introduction

After a long span of two centuries during which self-interested individualism has been deemed the only basis for economic action, there are not many people today who can appreciate the co-operative enterprise because it is considered a utopian undertaking or a futile one, given that capitalism has already shown the way forward in furthering humanity's economic progress. Nonetheless, capitalism has given rise, and continues to give rise, to numberless problems, and is rejected by many due to the unacceptable nature of its intrinsic characteristics. Briefly, these may be considered to be as follows:

- *Inequality*: successful people are permitted to accumulate enormous wealth.
- *The instrumental nature of relations*: those who are not so successful have to work to increase the fortunes of the successful.
- *The lack of scruples*: successful people are the quickest to react, and are generally not conditioned by moral values or principles such as equality and benevolence.
- *Economic power*: anyone trying to challenge the process of capitalistic accumulation is either bought out or removed from the scene.

The underlying reasons producing these features of capitalism are widely known. Capitalism is largely based on private vices[1] rather than public virtues, to the extent to which it cannot be sustained in the long term unless accompanied by a state with two tasks: to regulate these private 'vices' in order for them to be exercised in a 'moderate' manner and to attempt to correct the effects of income polarisation. These 'vices' were to pave the way (S. Zamagni 2009) for the process of industrialisation – in itself not to be undervalued, of course – which was accomplished at the price of substantial sacrifices by billions of people that, had a different route been taken, could have been largely avoided. Given industrialisation's insatiable appetite for physical capital, the demand advanced by the holders of capital for the appropriation of all the surplus produced was justified by the aim of increasing fixed investment, since an industrialised economy improved the living standards of a vast number of people compared with what had been offered previously by an agricultural economy (or indeed by an economy based on hunting and gathering).

What are the alternatives to capitalism that have arisen over time? The greatest historical movement that ever attempted to construct an alternative to capitalism, as we all know, was the Marxist-Leninist movement, although it ultimately failed as a result of various basic theoretical flaws, the most serious of which, I believe, was the way it confused capitalism with the market as such, a misconception that the theorists of capitalism themselves had engendered when they spoke of the 'iron' laws of the market, which were in fact the laws of capitalism (rather than of the markets). The market, however, considerably pre-dates the advent of capitalism, and is an indispensable prerequisite for economic progress; but the market may be institutionalised in a number of different ways, and the capitalistic way is only one of the possible forms of its institutionalisation. The removal of the market from the communist economies came at a heavy price in terms of both the resulting loss of efficiency and the lack of encouragement to innovate, which together contributed to the failure of the so-called 'planned' economies. Nevertheless, the fact that Marxism-Leninism proved so popular, not only among the populations of the developing nations but also among many people in the developed world, including vast groups of intellectuals, says a lot about the widespread dissatisfaction with capitalism, and about the desire to create something better.

The other alternative to capitalism that has emerged over the course of history is that of co-operation, which, rather than proposing the elimination of the market as such, works for a different form of institutionalisation of the market: in co-operative undertakings, people (the members), rather than capital, constitute the focus of productive activity. This shift in priorities is based on a foundational principle of economic activity that is not individualistic but of an intrinsically relational nature, the aim of which is the maximisation of group interests, including those of large groups that may well reflect the interests of society as a whole (the *common good*). I shall never tire of reminding people that the major economists who first analysed the co-operative enterprise during the nineteenth century acknowledged its superiority over the capitalist enterprise (see Zamagni and Zamagni 2010). Besides John Stuart Mill's vision of self-management as the predominant organisational form in an improved society (see Chapter 8), Alfred Marshall placed his finger on one fundamental advantage that the co-operative undertaking has over the capitalistic undertaking, namely that:

> [in a co-operative] the worker does not produce for others but for himself, which unleashes an enormous capacity for diligent, high-quality work that capitalism suppresses. There is one ruined product, in the history of the world, so much greater in importance than all the others that it can truly be called the '*wasted product*' – the best working capacities of most of the labouring classes (Marshall 1889: 7).

It has to be said that neither of these two great economists considered co-operation as a form of enterprise to be reserved for the poorer members of society, or to be considered as of merely marginal importance, to be limited to those situations where market efficiency cannot be guaranteed (the usual market 'failures' that many scholars speak of). On the contrary, both economists underlined two main advantages of co-operation, namely self-management and creativity, both of which pertain to any social context and any moment in time.

Why, then, has such a promising form of enterprise as the co-operative failed to 'supplant' capitalism? This chapter will try to offer an answer to this question, by examining four of the joint causes of such an outcome. These four causes are: 1) the strategic importance of physical capital to industrial growth during the age of Fordism; 2) the crowding-out effect of capitalist economic power; 3) the crowding-out effect of the state-based alternative; and 4) the implications of dependent employment and of hierarchical governance. In an additional section I will set out the reasons why the current economic climate is, in my opinion, more propitious than the Fordist era for the setting up and running of co-operative undertakings. In the conclusion, I shall look at the reasons why we currently find ourselves at a crossroads: either we abandon any hope of finding an alternative to capitalist enterprise, and resign ourselves to the permanence of the abovementioned ills of capitalism; or we invest intellectual resources in a concerted effort to identify the implications and applications of the co-operative alternative, which until now have remained largely unexplored, and we focus on establishing and strengthening the co-operative alternative, in the knowledge that this may well be the way forward for society, beyond the narrow confines of capitalism.

Physical capital's strategic importance to industrial development during the age of Fordism

Co-operation was established from the bottom and did not enjoy the benefit of wealth accumulated over the centuries, which was already in the hands of the capitalists as a result of their real estate, trading and financial activities. Co-operation, which first emerged as a movement during the nineteenth century, was thus rooted in economic activities requiring relatively limited capital, at least initially (Shaffer 1999). These included retail distribution (Furlough and Strickwerda 1999; V. Zamagni et al. 2004), microcredit (Boscia et al. 2010; Fonteyne 2007), insurance, the agro-industrial sector (Chloupková 2002; Juliá Igual and Martí Meliá 2008), and craft industries. In these activities, the co-operatives have played an important role, establishing different forms of organisational network (consortiums and groups) (Menzani and Zamagni 2010) that are capable of reaching significant critical masses in various markets. Economies of networks were substituted for economies of scale, but over time it was possible to develop some large-scale undertakings and a substantial accumulation of capital. Of the 300 largest co-operatives existing today in the world, 110 operate in the agro-industrial sector, eighty in the banking and finance sector, and eighty in large-scale retail and wholesale distribution; no more than five of them are industrial enterprises, the largest of which is Mondragon.[2]

Indeed, the co-operative movement failed to find suitably fertile terrain in the manufacturing sector, with very few exceptions. High capital requirements, standardised production, assembly-line systems, unskilled employment, a vertical command chain – all characteristics of Chandler's corporation (Chandler 1976) – represent factors that effectively impeded the co-operative movement's success in the world of manufacturing, particularly during the phase of American 'Fordism'. Moreover, it is hardly surprising that the few exceptions to this rule are not to be found in the English-speaking world, but in places where the individualistic theorising was not so overwhelming.

Was the 'dehumanising' nature of the giant Fordist corporations the price to pay for the rapid increase in the quantities of industrial goods produced? This is still an open question, but the fact remains that in those countries where the Fordist model was widespread, numerous innovative institutional measures were conceived that were designed to 'temper' its dehumanising effects: the USA saw the emergence of 'philanthropic capitalism', whereby one part of the wealth accumulated by the holders of capital is returned to society, albeit at the will of the holders;[3] in Japan, the *company-as-family* model has prevailed, where companies take care of their employees for life; in Germany, 1952 marked the advent of the *Mitbestimmung* (co-determination) model, whereby trade unions participate in companies' strategic decision-making.[4] The more recent corporate social responsibility movement is another approach along similar lines; this takes it for granted that the only possible form of enterprise is that of a capitalistic nature, but tries to lend it a more human face through the consideration of other stakeholders beyond shareholders.

This latter movement owes a considerable amount to the historical presence of co-operatives: the very ideas of the firm as a community of work, of additional remuneration of employees in the form of services (as in the case, for example, of Luxottica, the large Italian spectacles company[5]) and of profit-sharing all derive from the co-operative approach, which is perceived as the very source of those principles. However, these features often struggle to survive within a capitalistic framework, the underlying tenets of which are very different from those of the co-operative.

The crowding-out effect of capitalist economic power

The fact that the industrialisation process has been governed by capitalists means that an enormous amount of political and legislative power has been concentrated in their hands (in particular, company and trade legislation, promulgated for the benefit of the capitalist cause), together with intellectual power. This explains the remarkable success of the *homo economicus* model so predominant in the English-speaking world, which has attempted to base Mandeville's original intuitions first on Bentham's utilitarianism and subsequently on mathematically founded neoclassical theories.

The underlying anthropological concept of such a paradigm is that of the self-interested individual, according to which the aim of all economic activity is the maximisation of individual utility, while economics as a science is designed to provide the means by which to achieve this objective. However, very few people are actually capable of acting as maximising subjects, and can only do so because they are able to avail themselves of thousands of employees and hundreds of economists and engineers studying the best instruments to be employed. The only restrictions on the use of the instruments proposed to maximise shareholder value are those established by the *resistance* of the labour force (physical, psychological and social resistance, through the organisation of leagues and trade unions), or those offered by ideals or precepts put forward from outside the system (by religions or philosophies recommending that people treat others 'as they would themselves wish to be treated').

Such a massive cultural investment in capitalism as the only path towards growth and development has always exalted those who identify themselves with an individualistic anthropology (we could call them the *anti-social* individuals, the world's true capitalists), and has always pushed the *asocial* individuals (those who adapt to the status quo – in other words, the majority) towards lending their support to the anti-social elements, or at the very least to be moderately belligerent (this behaviour tends to be predominant among 'dependent' employees). Even though there still are *pro-social* individuals who practise social solidarity, they have been relegated to a minority. In this way, the latter, although not giving up their ideals of solidarity, have themselves become convinced that such ideals may be expressed only outside the economic sphere, in the world of voluntary work and non-profit organisations – and sometimes even in the world of co-operatives, which are seen as marginal organisations operating in areas of little interest to capitalist corporations. This has led to the increased watering down of any real market alternative to the prevailing capitalistic model of doing business.

The crowding-out effect of the state-based alternative

On the other hand, in those countries that had rejected capitalism, and within those groups and parties that modelled themselves on the policies of such countries, the chosen alternative was the state-owned enterprise, sometimes incorrectly presented as a self-managed undertaking similar to a co-operative. It was not a completely fruitless operation, since some of the instruments employed in state planning, based on an input–output matrix and on a medium-term horizon, were widely adopted in the capitalist world as well. This happened not only in the case of the Marshall Plan, or in that of the equally famous planning approach drawn up by Jean Monnet in France (subsequently imitated by a number of other countries), but also for the purpose of managing the great multi-divisional corporations, which were to adopt 'planning and control' as their principal strategic instrument. Of course, planning was perceived by the capitalist world as an additional tool to be used to achieve the aims of the capitalist system – aims that were not questioned in any way. Furthermore, state-owned enterprises in the Western world have not all been run in a bureaucratic, inefficient manner, since they have often had to compete with domestic or international private concerns, and because governments have used them as agents of growth. However, sooner or later their unhealthy proximity to the world of politics, their nationalism and their excessively high employment levels were to emerge as limitations, pushing states to resort to privatisation, with a transformation that has invariably resulted in their becoming capitalistic enterprises.[6]

The planning approach practically eliminated any interest in a more in-depth analysis of the characteristics and practices of the co-operative enterprise, not only in the world's planned economies but also on the part of the communist parties in the West. Co-operatives therefore remained at the margins of any theoretical debate regarding the enterprise, even within left-wing circles; their existence was recognised by only a few specialists, and analysis was virtually eliminated from textbooks altogether[7] (Kalmi 2007). In fact, the major Western communist parties have for some time considered the co-operative as a mere means with which to aid the victory of the state-run enterprise, and thus as a purely transitory form of enterprise. In Italy, this view of co-operatives by left-wing parties began to change only towards the end of the 1970s, when co-operation was acknowledged as constituting a third sector, to all intents and purposes flanking the first sector, that of private enterprise, and the second sector, that of state-run undertakings. However, this attempt to raise the co-operatives' analytical profile was to prove unsuccessful (V. Zamagni and Felice 2006). When the state-run companies were eliminated, capitalism triumphed; this was also because capitalism had a comparative advantage in running by command huge companies like those it inherited from communism.

Dependent employment and hierarchical governance

For a variety of reasons, both capitalism and statism have led people to think of employment as dependent employment, where not only are no demands made on workers to be creative, but they are positively prohibited from being so (on an assembly line, for example). During the development of capitalism, the changes brought about by industrialisation occurred so fast (seen from a historical perspective) that the precarious economic conditions and low levels of schooling of the masses of urbanised peasants made it very easy to channel them into increasingly larger factories, where very few were called upon to express their creativity and the vast majority were simply ordered to carry out their tasks within time schedules and according to production methods dictated by machinery. This was even more pronounced in the planned economies, where millions of people were led to think that work was something provided and planned by others – that is, by the state. Thus work was an expression not of their own entrepreneurial capacities, but of a top-down organisation where the majority simply obeyed orders in exchange for a guaranteed wage. This is exactly the opposite of what happens in a co-operative, where work is based on entrepreneurial ability, and where risks are considered an ordinary aspect of life.

In this way, the vast majority of people became used to the idea of having work provided by other people, and this form of employment has been rightly termed 'dependent'. This has had two main consequences:

- Having rendered work monotonous and even menial, Fordism encouraged the idea that people went to work solely in order to earn a living, rather than in order to realise themselves as individuals, thus removing those 'intrinsic motivations' for working that are the only ones that render work interesting and engaging. In fact, neoclassical theory defines work as a 'disutility' to be contrasted with the 'utility' of leisure time. According to such theory, an individual only realises himself or herself during leisure time, which is considered a time for voluntary work or for switching off from the daily routine – a time when, as a reaction to the strict, unwillingly borne discipline of work, people 'party hard'.

• The pursuit of work is generally perceived as an exercise in finding a dependent job in the existing context: if a person fails to find work, then state intervention is invoked. The concept of creating work by uniting one's ideas and skills with those of others is not seen as the best way of obtaining employment, not even by university graduates.

Both of these implications regarding the generalisation of dependent employment have certainly not benefited co-operative enterprise, which, by its very nature, requires intrinsic motivation, creativity and a willingness to get involved. It is true that in many co-operatives, 'dependent' work is nevertheless a reality – especially in consumer co-operatives – and this may lead to a lack of understanding of the difference between co-operative undertakings and capitalist enterprises. An in-depth analysis of the co-operative business model could render this form of dependent employment coherent with the co-operative model. On this point, I would like to mention the retailing co-operative Eroski, associated with Mondragon, as this is based on an interesting mixed model in which the co-operative's members include not only the consumers but also the workers (numbering 50,000 to date, producing a total turnover of €8 billion). In practice, the 'true' members of this co-operative are the workers, although the consumers, as official members, are present on the board as 'independent' directors, and thus they are also parties to the decision-making process: as such, this constitutes a genuinely original model.

In order to govern the giant corporations of the Fordist age, a hierarchical system of management was developed; this has been studied by, among others, Oliver Williamson (1975; 1996), winner of the 2009 Nobel Prize for Economics. Williamson analysed the reasons behind the adoption of that particular type of governance in the cases of all the major corporations. He discovered that such a choice was basically determined by the excessively high transaction costs of the market, which led firms to opt for command chains over negotiations. His theory applies specifically to a capitalistic framework (Williamson 1985), and the anthropological assumptions he makes are no different from those set out in the third section of this chapter: this means that his conclusions would be debatable should any different assumptions be made. In practice, it is not impossible to govern a large-scale non-capitalist enterprise differently, as the other winner of the 2009 Nobel Prize for Economics, Elinor Ostrom (1990; 2005), has shown in relation to 'common' goods, if economic action is not based on pure self-interest.[8]

There are still very few examples of co-operative governance of large corporations, the most interesting being the cases of Mondragon and of the American electrical energy co-operatives. This chapter is not the right place for an in-depth analysis of their systems of governance, although a few brief observations will be of interest here. After various changes in its governance system, Mondragon now has a stable, integrated structure – the MCC (Mondragon Corporación Co-operativa) – organised in five different layers: 1) a general assembly of 650 elected members from the more than 200 co-operatives constituting the group; 2) three committees with specific tasks, including one appointed to deal with social relations; 3) the operative arm of Mondragon, consisting of a chief executive officer and an executive board; 4) a number of sectoral groups; and 5) the individual co-operatives. Any new activity deemed necessary in order to strengthen the group's capacity is set up in the form of a co-operative. MCC currently employs some 85,000 people, 88 per cent of whom are members of the co-operatives, and it boasts an overall turnover of €33 billion. It is Spain's seventh largest group (MacLeod and Reed 2009).

With reference to the American electrical power companies, I will mention the case of Florida's Seminole Electric Cooperative Inc., founded in 1948 in order to produce electricity for ten distribution co-operatives that had been in operation since the 1930s following the New Deal's rural electrification programme. Today these co-operatives serve 1,700,000 people and have a turnover of US$1.4 billion. The board of directors is composed of representatives from the ten distribution co-operatives, each of which is, in turn, governed by a board of directors formed of representatives of the member-owners.

The rise of the service economy and the emergence of new spaces for co-operation

The arguments set out in previous sections all aim to explain why the co-operative movement failed to achieve a key role in the world economic system during Fordism, and why it has had to remain in the 'peripheral' areas of the economy where the majority of co-operative enterprises are relatively small (which, incidentally, has not favoured any thoughts on how to run a large-scale co-operative). Nevertheless, it is now clear that we are coming out of the Fordist age in the West, and so we may well ask whether new spaces are opening up for the further development of co-operation. There are numerous signs that this is indeed the case, the most important of which, in my opinion, being the following:

- Today, the emerging sectors are those in the service industries, where relations are often of strategic importance for the success of economic activity (Gui and Sugden 2005), and thus greater 'intrinsic motivation' to do the work is called for. The co-ordination of teams, direct relations with customers, the interpretation of non-standard needs for which producers are called upon to put themselves 'in the customer's shoes', and the 'company' imposed by many services (many suppliers do their work in the presence of and together with their clients) are all features that were only marginally present, if at all, in the primary and secondary sectors.
- Nowadays, even industry and agriculture are required to offer an increasing variety of non-standard products, increased customisation, and greater attention to traditions and to customer service. One only has to think of the plethora of farm guest houses, of the 'slow food' movement and the increased demand for traditional foods, and of the fashion industry. Customers are now more demanding, increasingly requiring products of quality – where the term 'quality' also means the quality of the production process – and are therefore prepared to pay a premium for such goods

and services, provided they are original, ethically approvable and eco-friendly. The co-operatives could indeed champion the 'sovereignty' of the consumer, which, although very much mentioned in the past, until now has not been achieved due to the prevalence of the production side in the economic system.

- Workers are better educated, and thus more likely to be aware of their potential self-realisation through their jobs, and not just of the economic aspects of employment (Becchetti et al. 2009). The co-operative is a form of enterprise whose members may identify with its aims.

- Reaching technical and productive frontiers requires an innovative capacity to expand those frontiers, and thus calls for workers to be more actively and creatively involved (Marshall's 'wasted product' has become even more significant today). So-called *tacit knowledge* – working know-how and skills that are not transmitted in a codified manner, and that are deployed only if the worker feels involved in the enterprise – is becoming an increasingly important factor. Once again, the leading role played by co-operative members should guarantee this kind of involvement.

- A vast area of so-called 'second-level welfare' is emerging, over and above that guaranteed by the state's minimum level, and this is an area in which the co-operatives, together with non-profit enterprises, could be protagonists. This welfare is acquired by both families and companies: families, faced with a hundred and one problems (care of young children, of the mentally and physically handicapped and of the elderly; help in starting work and doing housework; supplementary healthcare provisions), must be helped in innovative ways; companies, which increasingly seem willing to offer their employees benefits in the form of welfare services, are raising the demand for quality.

- As a possible solution to the problem of the increasing need for capitalisation of co-operatives, a form of co-operative stock exchange is not entirely out of the question, while a stock exchange for non-profit-making enterprises is already in existence.

- A form of corporate governance – not of the 'classical' hierarchical kind (*managerial stakeholding*), but of the participatory variety (*democratic stakeholding*) – is emerging as a possible alternative (Tencati and Zsolnai 2010), accompanied by the political transition from representative democracy to participatory or deliberative democracy.

Co-operation has already proven its competitive credentials in some service sectors (finance and retail distribution). Today, it is also engaging in the road transport sector (Battilani et al. 2008), catering (V. Zamagni 2002), facilities management, cultural services (see the work on the Italian National Services Consortium – CNS – by Battilani and Bertagnoni 2007), computer services and social services (for social service co-operatives, see Borzaga and Ianes 2006). International research into social service co-operatives, however, has begun only recently.

Concluding remarks

The weight of history burdens the future of co-operatives with some negative elements that cannot be shaken off easily, especially in view of the fact that they have shaped people's perceptions of co-operatives, and continue to do so, through the mass media. There are several ingrained beliefs working against co-operatives: the idea that the only form of enterprise is of a capitalistic nature; the idea that the sole purpose of economic activity is the maximisation of capital holders' profits; the belief that there are 'ironclad' market laws; the perception of labour as dependent labour; the belief that a company's governance has to be hierarchical. Until efforts are made to overthrow such beliefs, co-operatives will continue to play a marginal role in the economy. It is in this post-Fordist age that new spaces for co-operation are opening up once again; however, the bearers of the co-operative heritage need to be aware of the fact that, if co-operatives are to meet the new challenges, they have to do so in a creative manner (Mazzoli and Zamagni 2005), resorting where necessary to non-traditional forms of co-operation (Battilani and Schröter 2012; Fulton 2000).

Unfortunately, too many co-operatives are stuck in the past, or try to imitate capitalistic forms of management. This type of behaviour does no justice to the founders and mentors of the co-operative movement. The founders of the co-operative movement were not afraid to throw themselves into battle, without knowing whether they would come out victorious or not, and they did this in order to improve their own conditions and those of the thousands of workers and unemployed people who, like them, led a very hard life. By taking risks, they were able to bequeath a number of substantial co-operatives to future generations. At this point we should ask ourselves the question: what exactly are *we* doing to expand the legacy we have inherited? Merely managing what we already have is far too little, as there is the risk that in an ever changing society, what exists today will be obsolete by tomorrow.

John Stuart Mill was convinced that co-operatives would prevail 'if humanity continues to improve'. I sincerely hope that the co-operatives themselves do not undermine this precondition for co-operative growth. The question here is not one of 'eliminating' capitalistic enterprise – this can continue to operate in those areas characterised by high levels of standardisation and mechanisation in capital-intensive sectors. What we should be trying to do, I believe, is to prevent capitalist enterprise from taking over those areas of economic activity where the quality of personal relations and the role played by the human factor are of key importance (Borzaga et al. 2009; Restakis 2010).

This may seem an exceedingly difficult task. However, we should always remember that there is no determinism in history: history goes in the direction that men and women take, be that towards betterment or decline. We must examine the past, before the Industrial Revolution, when thinkers developed the idea that, for society to prosper over the long term, economic activity not only has to be inspired by self-interest but must aim for 'public happiness' and the 'common good' (Bruni and Zamagni 2004; Kaswan 2007).

Notes

1 The recognition of this goes as far back as the eighteenth century – see Mandeville's famous book of 1714.

2 The other four are all Italian co-operatives – SACMI, Cmc, CCPL, together with a large consortium of construction co-operatives, the CCC (see Zamagni and Zamagni 2010).

3 See the activities of the powerful Bill and Melinda Gates Foundation.

4 They were not, however, invited to share in company profits, although one could argue that the high wages paid in Germany are indeed due to the trade unions' 'internal' control over the distribution of companies' surpluses.

5 In 2009 the company Luxottica stipulated an agreement with the unions that included a substantial packet of benefits in the form of services, especially second-level welfare services.

6 I would like to mention one interesting exception, that of Credit Agricole, the largest European bank.

Like the majority of French banks, it was run by the state, but at the time of its privatisation in 1988 it was returned to its original form as a co-operative, albeit a hybrid version.

7 A new textbook has recently been published in Italy that attempts to remedy this fact (see Becchetti et al. 2010).

8 On this issue, see the work of Shann Turnbull, for example his 2002 paper.

References

Battilani, P. and G. Bertagnoni (eds) (2007) *Competizione e valorizzazione del lavoro: la rete co-operativa del Consorzio Nazionale Servizi*. Bologna: Il Mulino. English edition: (2010) *CNS: Co-operation, Network, Service – innovation in outsourcing*. Lancaster: Crucible Books.

Battilani, P. and H. G. Schröter (eds) (2012) *The Co-operative Business Movement, 1950 to the Present*. Cambridge: Cambridge University Press.

Battilani, P., G. Bertagnoni and S. Vignini (2008) *Un'impresa di co-operatori, artigiani, camionisti: la CTA e il trasporto merci in Italia*. Bologna: Il Mulino.

Becchetti, L., L. Bruni and S. Zamagni (2010) *Microeconomia: scelte, relazioni, economia civile*. Bologna: Il Mulino.

Becchetti, L., S. Castriota and E. Tortia (2009) *Productivity, Wages and Intrinsic Motivation in Social Enterprises*. Working Paper 16. Milan: EconomEtica.

Borzaga, C. and A. Ianes (2006) *L'economia della solidarietà: storia e prospettive della co-operazione sociale*. Rome: Donzelli.

Borzaga, C., S. Depedri and E. C. Tortia (2009) *The Role of Co-operative and Social Enterprises: A multifaceted approach for an economic pluralism*. Euricse Working Paper 000/09.

Trento: European Research Institute on Cooperative and Social Enterprises (Euricse).

Boscia, V., A. Carretta and P. Schwizer (2010) *Co-operative Banking in Europe: Case studies*. Basingstoke: Palgrave Macmillan.

Bruni, L. and S. Zamagni (2004) *Economia civile*. Bologna: Il Mulino.

Casadesus-Masanell, R. and T. Khanna (2003) *Globalization and Trust: Theory and evidence from co-operatives*. William Davidson Institute Working Paper 592. Ann Arbor, MI: University of Michigan.

Chandler, A. (1976) *Strategia e struttura: storia della grande impresa americana*. Milan: Franco Angeli.

Chloupková, J. (2002) *European Co-operative Movement: Background and common denominators*. Working Paper 24204. Copenhagen: Department of Economics and Natural Resources, Royal Veterinary and Agricultural University.

Fonteyne, W. (2007) *Cooperative Banks in Europe: Policy issues*. IMF Working Paper 07/159. Washington, DC: International Monetary Fund (IMF).

Fulton, M. (2000) 'Traditional versus new generation co-operatives'. In N. Walzer and C. Merrett (eds), *A Co-operative Approach to Local Economic Development*. Westport, CT: Greenwood Publishing Group.

Furlough, E. and C. Strickwerda (eds) (1999) *Consumers Against Capitalism? Consumer co-operation in Europe, North America and Japan, 1840–1990*. Lanham, MD: Rowman & Littlefield.

Gui, B. and R. Sugden (eds) (2005) *Economics and Social Interaction: Accounting for interpersonal relations*. Cambridge, MA: Cambridge University Press.

Juliá Igual, J. F. and E. Martí Meliá (2008) 'Social economy and the co-operative movement in Europe:

contributions to a new vision of agriculture and rural development in the Europe of the 27'. *Ciriec-España* 62 (special issue): 147–72.

Kalmi, P. (2007) 'The disappearance of co-operatives from economics textbooks'. *Cambridge Journal of Economics* 31: 625–47.

Kaswan, M. (2007) 'Happiness, politics and the co-operative principles'. *Journal of Co-operative Studies* 15(1): 30–40.

MacLeod, G. and D. Reed (2009) 'Mondragon's response to the challenges of globalization: a multi-localization strategy'. In D. Reed and J. J. McMurtry (eds), *Co-operatives in a Global Economy: The challenges of co-operation across borders*. Newcastle upon Tyne: Cambridge Scholars Publishing.

Mandeville, B. (1714) *The Fable of the Bees; or Private Vices, Public Benefits*. Reprinted 1987: New York, NY: Capricorn Books.

Marshall, A. (1889) 'Co-operation', Speech at the XXI Co-operative Congress, Ipswich. Reprinted in A. C. Pigou (ed.) (1925) *Memorials of Alfred Marshall*. London: Macmillan.

Mazzoli, E. and S. Zamagni (eds) (2005) *Verso una nuova teoria economica della co-operazione*. Bologna: Il Mulino.

Menzani, T. and V. Zamagni (2010) 'Co-operative networks in the Italian economy'. *Enterprise and Society* 11(1): 98–127.

Mill, J. S. (1852) *Principles of Political Economy*. Reprinted 1987. Fairfield, NJ: A. M. Kelley.

Ostrom, E. (1990) *Governing the Commons: The evolution of institutions for collective action*. Cambridge: Cambridge University Press.

— (2005) *Understanding Institutional Diversity*. Princeton, NJ: Princeton University Press.

Restakis, J. (2010) *Humanizing the Economy: Co-operatives in the age of capital*. Gabriola Island, Canada: New Society Publishers.

Shaffer, J. (1999) *Historical Dictionary of the Co-operative Movement*. London: The Scarecrow Press.

Tencati, A. and L. Zsolnai (2010) *The Collaborative Enterprise: Creating values for a sustainable world*. Bern: Peter Lang.

Turnbull, S. (2002) *A New Way to Govern*. Working Paper 5. London: New Economics Foundation.

Williamson, O. (1975) *Markets and Hierarchies: Analysis and anti-trust implications*. Florence, MA: Free Press.

— (1985) *The Economic Institutions of Capitalism*. Florence, MA: Free Press.

— (1996) *The Mechanisms of Governance*. Oxford: Oxford University Press.

Zamagni, S. (2009) *Avarizia: la passione dell'avere*. Bologna: Il Mulino.

— and V. Zamagni (2010) *Co-operative Enterprise: Facing the challenge of globalization*. Cheltenham: Edward Elgar. Italian edition: (2008) *La co-operazione*. Bologna: Il Mulino.

Zamagni, V. (ed.) (2002) *Camst: ristorazione e socialità*. Bologna: Il Mulino.

— and E. Felice (2006) *Oltre il secolo: le trasformazioni del sistema co-operativo Legaco-op alla fine del secondo millennio*. Bologna: Il Mulino.

— P. Battilani and A. Casali (2004) *La co-operazione di consumo in Italia*. Bologna: Il Mulino.

11 | EMPLOYEE OWNERSHIP AND HEALTH: AN INITIAL STUDY

David Erdal

Introduction

Over the last three decades a particular model of human nature and of the economy has led to a small financial and corporate elite dominating the developed world both economically and politically. Since 2008, the consequences of their actions have been devastating for the vast majority of people. This result has proved a direct contradiction of their model, its analysis and its forecasts. Yet they continue to assert and act on its basic tenets – and to defend their privilege. For example, they claim, in defiance of overwhelming evidence, that human nature is almost psychotically driven by the next short-term gain, however minimal. Another pillar of their ideology is that the market governs their activities – power has nothing to do with it. According to them, the fact that the market is taking its course removes from them any obligation to consider the consequences of their actions – Adam Smith's 'invisible hand' will take care of those, making this the best of possible worlds for society as well as for the righteously selfish (Friedman 1970; Gabaix and Landler 2008). And yet Joe Stiglitz was awarded the Nobel Prize for research that he summarised as showing that in every real market, the reason why the hand is invisible is because it is not there (Stiglitz 2008).

This chapter is based on a different model of human nature, and, unlike much of the prevailing economics, it respects empirical evidence above mathematical modelling. It describes how its hypothesis, that employee ownership should be good for one's health, was generated out of the experience of introducing employee ownership into a paper-manufacturing business in Scotland. It then describes the initial test of the hypothesis, and a current effort to replicate and extend the research.

Background

Taking over as chief executive officer of a 1,500-employee paper mill in Scotland in 1985, I set out to move the management style towards participation, with five major elements: intensive communication; consultation at different levels, including a top elected body meeting quarterly with the board; improvement teams in each working area; profit-sharing; and shared ownership, the latter starting at a very low level but growing each year. The mill, Tullis Russell, was an old one, founded in 1809, and had been unionised for decades. Reinvestment had been good over the years, and the policy of specialising in difficult, top-end papers and boards had achieved prosperity for the mill.

The changes towards sharing and participation were greeted with huge suspicion, and the representatives elected to the top body were among the most hostile, chosen by their colleagues on the grounds that they were the most likely to see through what was universally perceived as a piece of management trickery. However, after about three years of fairly passive hostility, they began to understand that this change was for real – we really were telling the truth, we really were going to change the ownership so that the business was owned by everyone working in it, and we really did want everyone to participate in shaping the way things were done (Erdal 2011).

At that point, what struck me most forcibly was the power of the psychological transformation in the individuals concerned. Once they understood that their environment was changing from a top-down hierarchy, in which they were mere servants, to a shared enterprise in which they were full partners, they changed overnight from being hostile, suspicious and repressed to being energetic, positive and ready to take initiatives. A psychological response this powerful deserved to be better understood, so I signed up for a part-time PhD in the psychology of sharing.

Theory: the evolution of humanity

The theoretical approach I took was evolutionary. If we want to understand why starlings flock, we have to understand what advantage flocking gave them in evolutionary terms. When we see that chimpanzees, both male and female, sometimes band together to usurp dominant males, then we have to understand how that behaviour might have helped them as they evolved. Since, like every other living thing, we evolved, we can understand our deepest psychological responses better by understanding how those responses might have been appropriate in the social environment in which we evolved (Erdal and Whiten 1996; Whiten and Erdal 2012).

The social environment in which we evolved was that of the hunter-gatherer band – our ancestors spent perhaps hundreds of thousands or even millions of years in that social environment. On the other hand, we have had only a few thousand years in the 'civilised' social environment permitted by the domestication of animals and the development of agriculture. A few thousand years is not long enough for significant biologically driven evolution to have occurred. So the key to our positive response to sharing might lie in understanding the intensely social environment of the hunter-gatherer band.

A search of over two dozen ethnographies of early contacts with hunter-gatherers in every continent showed two universal characteristics that seemed potentially relevant (Erdal and Whiten 1994; 1996: Table 1). Firstly, meat, a resource that was absolutely key to survival but was unpredictable in supply, was universally shared. It was not shared preferentially either with kin or with those who were capable of reciprocating. It was not shared preferentially with anyone. The rule in meat-sharing was that if you had a mouth, you got fed. This was not a calculation: meat-sharing was unconditional.

Secondly, there were no institutionalised leaders, no chiefs or head men. Instead, leadership was situational: it varied from situation to situation, and in the same situation at a different time a different person might be followed. This was maintained by a universal tendency to counter any attempts at dominance. Normally, if a man was known to be a good hunter, his advice in hunting matters would be heeded more frequently than the suggestions of men less successful in hunting. But if he ever became arrogant, saying something like, 'I'm the best hunter round here, you should do what I say!', then the group would react by ridiculing him, or countering his suggestions with others, or ignoring him, or walking away. If necessary they would even ostracise him or kill him (Boehm 1999). Women were generally as important as men in the obtaining of provisions, in the discussions in camp, and in this process of countering dominance.

In this way, in every continent, the hunter-gatherer group, the social environment in which we evolved, was characterised by the sharing of key resources, and by the egalitarian control of those who sought to dominate the group, control effected through a universal counter-dominant response. This research was published in two papers where all the detailed references can be found (Erdal and Whiten 1994; 1996). It has recently been developed further into a model of a socio-cognitive niche driving human evolution (Whiten and Erdal 2012).

Hypothesis

It thus seemed likely that an egalitarian, sharing environment would be one that was deeply natural to humans, and was likely to be physiologically as well as psychologically beneficial. On the other hand, a social environment characterised by dominance hierarchies and disparities of wealth would be experienced as profoundly frustrating, even insulting to our evolved psychology. We are not designed to fit modern society, with its hierarchies, institutionalised top-down power structures and enormous disparities of wealth, any more than our bodies are designed to deal with concentrated, freely available sources of fatty, sugary foods.

There are obvious connections between this thesis and much work on health, both physical and social. The Whitehall Studies led by Michael Marmot (Marmot et al. 1978; 1991) show that people lower in a hierarchy suffer from higher mortality, even after controlling for all known relevant factors. There is a large body of work showing that the psychological locus of control is a powerful element in health (Johnston et al. 2007). And Wilkinson and Pickett (2009) show the relevance of the gap between rich and poor to a number of important social outcomes.

A testable hypothesis that arose from this research was this: if we could find a large social unit characterised by egalitarianism and a sharing culture, then we should find that the people making up that social unit thrived better psychologically than people in any similar standard social unit. The proxy for a sharing, egalitarian culture would be the proportion of people employed in businesses owned by all who worked in them. This was a relatively risky prediction, in that it assumed that the effects were not limited to those actually working in employee-owned companies, but would be detectable in the wider community.

Robert Oakeshott (1990; 2000) suggested that the town of Imola ('Cooptown') in Emilia-Romagna in northern Italy might meet that need – it had been the centre of a cluster of workers' co-operatives since the 1920s (Earle 1986). The larger nearby town of Faenza ('Midtown') (population 80,000, compared with Imola's 60,000) was reputed to have a lower proportion of workers' co-operatives, and the slightly more distant and smaller town of Sassuolo ('Normaltown', population 40,000) reputedly had no co-operatives but was equally prosperous.

Whole-population statistics were available for mortality and blood donation (a proxy for pro-social behaviour) and a postal survey produced samples of forty-four subjects matched by age and sex across all three towns and fifty-six similarly matched subjects between Cooptown and Midtown. These samples were not large enough to conduct a fine-grained analysis, but large enough to identify significant effects.

As anticipated, the research aim was met in that, in Cooptown, 26 per cent of all people working were members of workers' co-operatives; the proportion in Midtown was 13 per cent and in Normaltown zero. As is shown in Figure 11.1, quite a number of measures proved to be more positive in Cooptown than in Normaltown. The same measures for Midtown tended to fall between the two.

Some measures stand out. The most prominent difference is the perception of the gap between rich and poor (SE1). This recalls the work, in particular, of Wilkinson and Pickett (2009), which showed that, above a certain level of gross domestic product (GDP) per head, measures of social health are predicted not by further increases in GDP but by the level of equality in a society, whether in a nation or in one of the states in the USA. It seems that the effect of the co-operatives over the decades has been to even up the distribution of wealth, and this is likely to be associated with a number of beneficial effects.

The second strongest difference is in people's attitude to the authorities (SE2). For the people of Cooptown, the authorities tended to be 'on our side'. There was a high level of trust.

The third indicator of a healthy social involvement is SE3: the people in Cooptown can call on many more people to help them in times of trouble and the social networks of individuals are larger. Finally, the pro-social attitude was also seen in the total-population

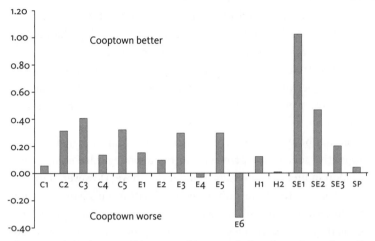

11.1 Differences between Cooptown and Normaltown (*source*: Erdal 2000)

measures of blood donation and voting: the people of Cooptown gave blood at over twice the rate of the people of Normaltown, and a significantly larger proportion of the people in Cooptown voted in elections (87.4 per cent versus 83 per cent).

The incidence of crime (C1) was extremely low in all three towns. Responding to questions on crime, the people in Cooptown were much more confident that crime was under control (C3) and, interestingly, they expected less domestic violence (C5). The question they answered was: 'How often do you think your neighbour beats his wife?' It seems that working and living in a co-operative environment creates less frustration.

In education, there were relatively small differences (in the predicted direction) in educational qualifications attained (E1), and in age at leaving school (E2). However, the children played truant less in Cooptown (E3), and to a significantly greater extent people continued to be trained and educated after leaving school (E5).

However, education also produced the only two responses that ran

counter to the predicted direction. The people of Normaltown expected their children to be playing truant marginally less than did the
people of Cooptown (E4), even while reporting that they themselves
had played truant more (E3), and the people of Normaltown placed
a high subjective value on education to a much greater extent (E6).
Yet we have seen that their children did worse, if anything, played
truant more, and studied less in later life. One possible interpretation is that because they were living in a much more individualistic,
competitive society, the people of Normaltown regarded education as
a weapon in life, one that they would like to have. However, they were
more alienated from the authorities and institutions involved in their
lives (SE2); as education is delivered in an authoritative institution, a
school, they tended to fit less easily. In Cooptown, however, education
was more of a lifelong enterprise, institutions were seen as being
'on our side', and social involvement was recognised as important.
So education was subjectively rated as being less important, but
pursued more successfully and consistently.

There were virtually no differences in participation rates in clubs
and societies (SP1). Emilia-Romagna was identified by Robert Putnam
as one of the most pro-social areas in the world, with the highest
social capital (Putnam et al. 1993). At the time the data were collected,
it was also very prosperous, with virtually full employment in all
three towns. If northern Italy declared independence, it would be
the richest country in Europe.

The self-reported differences in physical health (H1) were smaller,
and in mental health (H2) non-existent. However, the health data were
dominated by the total-population statistics on mortality (Figure 11.2).

The people of Cooptown appeared to live longer.

It was not possible to do a detailed analysis of the source of the
difference because Normaltown did not give a breakdown of the relevant statistics, but the detailed comparison of the mortality rates
of Cooptown with those of the nearby city of Ferrara highlighted
some suggestive factors. The same mortality difference was found,
the main factor being a large decrease in cardiovascular mortality.
Furthermore, the improvement was greater among men than among
women. Cardiovascular mortality is one of the main areas highlighted
by the work of Marmot as being responsive to the stress of hierarchical living, with those placed lower in a hierarchy being subject

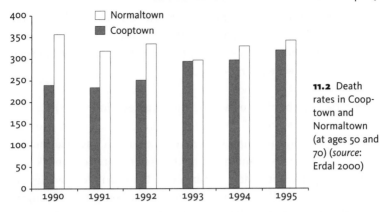

11.2 Death rates in Cooptown and Normaltown (at ages 50 and 70) (*source*: Erdal 2000)

to greater physiological stress, even after accounting for all other known factors (Marmot et al. 1978; 1991).

One possible interpretation of the difference between the sexes is that males are more sensitive than females to the humiliations of servitude, and therefore benefit more from being treated as partners in the enterprises where they work. However, another is that, since male domination is a feature of life for women in all towns, and since a lower proportion of women than men go out to work, the difference in social environment created by a difference in the workplace is less salient for females.

It is also noticeable that there was a rising trend in the mortality rates of Imola (Figure 11.2). It may be that the Roseto effect was at work (Bruhn and Wolf 1979). Roseto was a town made up of Italian immigrants in the US that showed an outstandingly low level of cardiovascular disease. This was explained in large part by the high level of social cohesion, but, over time, as the culture became more normal (by American standards), the rates of cardiovascular disease also rose to normal (high) American levels. In the same way, perhaps Imola's co-operative culture was in the process of being undermined in the 1990s.

A further test I mentioned this mortality effect to the late Ian Alexander, then the chairman of the trustees of the pension fund of the John Lewis Partnership, the UK's pre-eminent retailer, which has famously been owned by a trust for the employees since 1929. I suggested that his pension fund faced a problem: longer retirements to fund than those of his competitors. He later reported (personal communication) that he had had the actuaries check, and it was true: retirees from John Lewis lived longer than retirees from their non-employee-owned competitors.

Replication At the time of writing this chapter (summer 2012), Fred Freundlich and Monica Gago of Mondragon University were involved in a replication and improvement of the test of the relationship between co-operatives and mortality rates in the area of Gipuzkoa in northern Spain. Initial data confirm that there is indeed a relationship (Figure 11.3).[1] The solid lines across the box plots show the mean mortality for that area; the fact that the means rise as co-operative density decreases from left to right shows that there is a relationship between co-operative density and mortality – the greater the density of co-operatives, the lower the mortality.

However, the areas with more co-operatives also have low unemployment, so the co-operative effect is swamped by the unemployment effect. Further statistical analysis is under way.

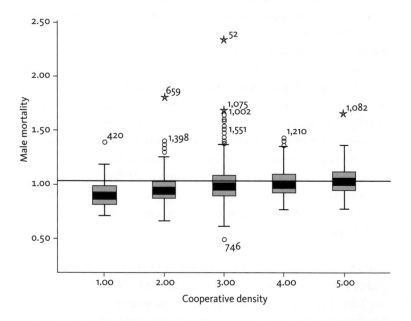

11.3 The mortality–co-operative relationship (*source*: Freundlich and Gago 2012)

Conclusion

It is early days for this research, but there are grounds for optimism. There are sound theoretical reasons for believing that a relatively egalitarian social environment, where individuals are partners rather than masters and servants, and where key resources are shared, will fit with deep aspects of human nature. Initial empirical results appear to confirm hypotheses derived from this perspective. These results, if confirmed by subsequent studies, are important. They suggest that conventionally structured firms are at odds with human nature, both in the social relationships involved and in the distribution of wealth, to the detriment of all concerned. On the other hand, workers' co-operatives and employee-owned firms suit human nature in ways that lead to widespread prosperity, healthier communities, deeper individual satisfaction and longer lives.

Note

1 The interim results were presented by Monica Gago and Fred Freundlich at Edinburgh in May 2012 (Freundlich and Gago 2012).

References

Boehm, C. (1999) *Hierarchy in the Forest: The evolution of egalitarian behavior.* Cambridge, MA: Harvard University Press.

Bruhn, J. G. and S. Wolf (1979) *The Roseto Story.* Norman, OK: University of Oklahoma Press.

Earle, J. (1986) *The Italian Co-operative Movement: A portrait of the Lega Nazionale delle Co-operative e Mutue.* London: Allen and Unwin.

Erdal, D. (2000) 'The psychology of sharing: an evolutionary approach'. PhD dissertation, University of St Andrews.

— (2011) *Beyond the Corporation: Humanity working.* London: Bodley Head.

— and A. Whiten (1994) 'On human egalitarianism: an evolutionary product of Machiavellian status escalation?' *Current Anthropology* 35: 175–8.

— (1996) 'Egalitarianism and Machiavellian intelligence in human evolution'. In P. Mellars and K. Gibson (eds), *Modelling the Ancient Human Mind.* Cambridge: McDonald Institute for Archaeological Research, pp. 139–50.

Freundlich, F. and M. Gago (2012) 'Cooperative employment density, social capital and public health: evidence from Gipuzkoa Province, the Basque country'. Paper presented at the Co-operatives and Public Health workshop, Scottish Enterprise, Edinburgh, 8 May.

Friedman, M. (1970) 'The social responsibility of business is to increase its profits'. *The New York Times Magazine,* 13 September.

Gabaix, X. and A. Landler (2008) 'Why has CEO pay increased so much?' *Quarterly Journal of Economics* 123(1): 49–100.

Johnston, M., D. L. Bonetti, S. A. Joice, B. S. Pollard, V. Morrison, J. Francis and R. MacWalter (2007) 'Recovery from disability after stroke as a target for a behavioural intervention: results of a randomised controlled trial'. *Disability & Rehabilitation* 29(14): 1117–27.

Marmot, M. G., G. Davey Smith, S. Stansfield et al. (1991) 'Health inequalities among British civil servants: the Whitehall II study'. *Lancet* 337(8754): 1387–93.

Marmot, M. G., G. Rose, M. Shipley and P. J. Hamilton (1978) 'Employment grade and coronary heart disease in British civil servants'. *Journal of Epidemiology and Community Health* 32(4): 244–9.

Oakeshott, R. (1990) *The Case for Workers' Co-ops.* 2nd edition. London: Macmillan.

— (2000) *Jobs and Fairness: The theory and practice of employee ownership.* London: Michael Russell.

Putnam, R., R. Leonardi and R. Nanetti (1993) *Making Democracy Work: Civic traditions in modern Italy.* Princeton, NJ: Princeton University Press.

Stiglitz, J. (2008) 'Presentation to the Congreso Internacional CIRIEC'. 22–24 September, Seville.

Whiten, A. and D. Erdal (2012) 'The human socio-cognitive niche and its evolutionary origins'. *Philosophical Transactions of the Royal Society: B. Biological Sciences* 367(1599): 2119–29. Theme issue: C. Heyes and U. Frith (eds), *New Thinking: The Evolution of Human Cognition.*

Wilkinson, R. and K. Pickett (2009) *The Spirit Level: Why more equal societies almost always do better.* London: Allen Lane.

12 | CO-OPERATIVES IN A GLOBAL ECONOMY: KEY ISSUES, RECENT TRENDS AND POTENTIAL FOR DEVELOPMENT

Stephen C. Smith and Jonathan Rothbaum[1]

Introduction

Since the beginning of the Great Recession, many developed countries have experienced large increases in unemployment, which have not declined in its aftermath to anywhere near the degree that they have done after previous recessions. In the United States, the Great Recession has resulted in the deepest labour market downturn in the post-war era (Elsby et al. 2010). Unemployment also rose across Europe during the same period (Arpaia and Curci 2010). Even in countries that have experienced fewer lay-offs and job losses, the rate of job growth has not been sufficient. On the other hand, in the developing world, much progress has been made through tools such as micro-finance and micro-enterprise support and formation. However, in both the developed and developing world, individuals prefer stable sources of income, generally provided through regular, stable jobs. The solution to this problem is to find ways to provide stable jobs that provide better wages and a higher quality of life for workers.

In both the developed and developing world, countries have seen increases in inequality of both income and wealth. In a recent study, inequality increased[2] in seventeen of twenty-two OECD countries between 1985 and 2008, including the United States, the UK, Italy, Japan, Canada, Germany, the Netherlands and Mexico (OECD 2011). Inequality has increased over the same period in many developing countries as well (Meschi and Vivarelli 2009). However, inequality is not limited to just income and wealth. There is also a problem of social inequality, by which we mean inequality in access to public services, political expression and social opportunities. Perhaps most importantly, this includes access to formal and informal educational opportunities. Another central issue in addressing the preceding problems is fostering innovation. Productive innovation plays an important role in firms' survival, and therefore in creating and maintaining jobs and in generating economic growth.

Within each of these areas, co-operatives can have an important role to play. In periods of crisis, co-operatives can support job creation and prevent job losses. We will discuss how co-operatives have contributed to job creation in the recent financial crisis and in other periods of economic turmoil. We will also discuss research findings on how co-operatives respond differently to changing economic circumstances compared with other businesses.

When confronting increasing inequality, the goals and outcomes that co-operatives pursue can help keep economic inequality in check. Co-operatives can be important tools for building social capital and broadening access to services. The democratic decision-making structure of co-operatives gives members skills and experience that foster social capital that can be used in other areas, such as civil society. The organisational structure of co-operatives may also be effective at harnessing the talent, ideas and insights of members and non-managerial employees. In this way, the daily experiences and observations of workers can often lead to innovations and improvements in efficiency.

However, in order to realise these benefits, there are also a number of challenges that co-operatives face. The issue of entrepreneurship and co-operative formation is one that requires attention. When potential entrepreneurs consider forming a co-operative, they are faced with the problem that if, for example, the co-operative will have 100 members, the entrepreneurs will receive only a small portion of the benefits of forming the co-operative despite incurring much of the organisational and entrepreneurial cost. Therefore, it is important to consider how co-operative entrepreneurs can be supported – with an eye to the additional non-monetary reasons that individuals could have for forming co-operatives, such as altruism and adherence to co-operative philosophy – in addition to implementing creative reward systems that remain within the spirit of co-operative ideals.

In order to achieve the other objectives of lowering inequality, fostering social capital formation and increasing innovation, effective incentives need to be in place. For example, explicit attention is needed to observe what kinds of incentives work best in a co-operative environment for encouraging innovative behaviour among members. This requires the proper institutional framework for co-operatives. Compared with conventional firms, co-operatives have very different institutional rules, and in many cases they also have different organisational structures and norms. Critics view these differences as competitive disadvantages. But, arguably, the picture is much more mixed and nuanced. To compete effectively with conventional firms, co-operatives can seek to identify and then put into practice strategies to get the greatest possible benefits from any organisational comparative advantages that these differences confer. Local and industrial variations matter a lot, and this is where a local co-operative league (federation or association) can be helpful. However, some general principles may also be identified; for example, co-operatives can leverage their advantages in gathering and adopting innovations that members think about as a result of their regular work processes.

Co-operatives can also benefit from the institutional environment in which they operate. An important fact about individual co-operatives is that they tend to be small. However, as BRAC founder Fazle Hasan Abed has said, 'Small is beautiful, but big is necessary.' Larger organisations can take advantage of economies of scale, for example in marketing and innovation, that may be difficult for smaller organisations to implement or co-ordinate. An important way in which co-operatives can capitalise on these scale economies is through co-operative leagues,[3] which can be associations or networks of many small co-operatives, including consumer, producer, worker and credit co-operatives; these are examined later in the chapter. However, despite the contributions that co-operative leagues can provide, leagues themselves can also be difficult to start. Not all regions or countries with co-operatives have effective co-operative federations.

In this chapter, we will focus primarily on how co-operatives can help address the challenges of unemployment and innovation.

Co-operatives, unemployment and economic crises

Co-operatives and unemployment Co-operatives can have an important role to play in times of economic turmoil and crisis. For example, in the late 1970s and early 1980s, another time of very slow job growth, co-operatives experienced a much faster rate of employment growth than the economy as a whole.[4] Estrin (1985) shows that, from 1976 to 1981, the percentage growth in co-operative employment in France, Italy, Spain (Mondragon co-operatives) and the UK – in fact, in the entire European Economic Community (EEC, the precursor to the European Union) – was far greater than employment growth in the economy as a whole. Table 12.2 shows just how large the differences were. In France, employment in co-operatives grew 12.1 per cent and in all firms by 1.4 per cent; in Italy, the figures were 86.2 per cent and 3.8 per cent; in Spain, 31 per cent and –8.1 per cent; in the UK, 133 per cent and –2.0 per cent; and in the EEC as a whole, 76 per cent compared with 2.0 per cent.

TABLE 12.1 Co-operatives in selected countries

Country	Year	Type	Employees	Total employment (%)
Canada	2008	Worker	8,651	0.05
		Non-financial	87,963	0.5
Chile	2005	Non-financial	34,679	0.6
Colombia	2009	Co-operative sector	137,888	0.7
France	2009	Worker	39,471	0.1
		Co-operative sector	306,596	1.1
Germany	2009	Worker	514,000	1.3
Italy	2009	Co-operative sector	1,252,378	5.5
Spain	2010	Worker	84,062	0.04
		Co-operative sector	380,286	2.1
UK	2009	Worker	2,056	0.007
US	2006	Worker	2,380	0.001
		Agricultural producer	72,930	0.05
Uruguay	2005	Worker	5,170	0.4

Sources: General employment data taken from the OECD.Stat website (http://stats. oecd.org/); Canada: Rural and Co-operatives Secretariat *Co-operatives in Canada* reports; Chile: Departamento de Cooperativas (Decoop), Ministerio de Economía, Fomento, y Turismo; Colombia: Confederación de Cooperatives de Colombia (Confecoop); France: Workers' co-operative data provided upon request by Les Scop (Sociétés coopératives et participatives); sector data from the Institut national de la statistique et des études économiques (INSEE); Germany: German Co-operative Association (DGRV) Geschäftsbericht reports; Italy: Census report on co-operatives in Italy; Spain: Spanish Co-operative Association (CEPES) social economy reports; UK: Co-operatives UK co-operative reviews and co-operative economy reports; US: University of Wisconsin Center for Cooperatives report; Uruguay: Burdín and Dean (2009)

TABLE 12.2 Co-operatives and job creation, 1976–81: increase in employment (%)

Country	Co-operatives	All firms
France	12.1	1.4
Italy	86.2	3.8
Spain (Mondragon)[1]	31	–8.1
UK	133	–2.0
EEC[2]	76	2.0

Notes: 1. 1975–80 2. 1981 EEC member countries

Sources: General employment data taken from the OECD.Stat website (http://stats. oecd.org/); co-operative data from Estrin (1985).

We have examined more recent data and research findings to see how co-operative employment growth compared with overall employment growth in recent years, including during the Great Recession. We looked at employment growth in the co-operative sector, in the economy as a whole, and in a variety of subsectors, such as agriculture, industry and services.

Figure 12.1 shows employment in Italy from 2007 to 2011 in the co-operative sector as well as for the entire economy, broken down into agriculture, industry and services. Employment in the economy as a whole has stagnated and employment in industry and agriculture

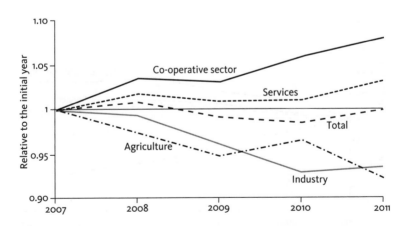

12.1 Employment in Italy in the co-operative sector and in the economy as a whole, 2007–11 (*sources:* General employment data taken from the OECD.Stat website: http://stats.oecd.org/; co-operative data from the census report on co-operatives in Italy)

declined. However, employment in the co-operative sector grew 8 per cent between 2007 and 2011 (1.9 per cent per year). Services, the only sector that increased employment over the same period, grew by 3.2 per cent (0.7 per cent per year). Since the beginning of the Great Recession, Italian co-operatives have experienced a much larger percentage increase in employment than has the economy as a whole or any subsector.

In a study on how Italian co-operatives and firms responded to shocks from 1994 to 2002, Pencavel, Pistaferri and Schivardi (2006) found that co-operative employment was less volatile, but that co-operative wages were more volatile than those of other firms. This indicates that during recessions, co-operatives are less likely to lay off workers than conventional firms and more likely to cut wages instead. This evidence is also supported by studies in Spain of the Mondragon co-operative association by Martin (2000) and Smith (2003). In their work, they discuss how employment generation is an explicit goal for Mondragon. As a result, Mondragon co-operatives are more flexible with wages and benefits than conventional firms, with the goal of preserving employment.

In France, the co-operative sector has also seen more growth in employment recently than the economy as a whole (Figure 12.2). From 2005, employment in the co-operative sector grew by 8 per cent

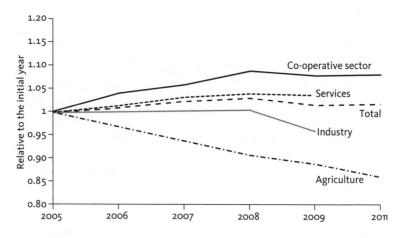

12.2 Employment in France in the co-operative sector and in the economy as a whole, 2005–11 (sources: General employment data taken from the OECD.Stat website: http://stats.oecd.org/; co-operative data from INSEE)

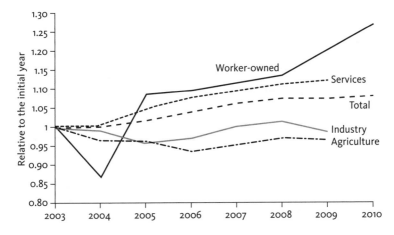

Note: 2007 co-operative data were not available in the DGRV reports

12.3 Employment in Germany in the co-operative sector and in the economy as a whole, 2003–10 (*sources*: General employment data taken from the OECD.Stat website: http://stats.oecd.org/; co-operative data from the DGRV)

(1.6 per cent per year), compared with 1.5 per cent in the economy as a whole (0.3 per cent per year). From 2008 to 2010, employment in the economy declined by 1.3 per cent and by 0.7 per cent in the co-operative sector. Pérotin (2006) studied the entry and exit of co-operative firms into the market in France. She found that a 1 per cent increase in unemployment increases co-operative creation by 10 per cent. The formation of co-operatives during times of economic hardship may help explain the employment performance of co-operatives in France (and Italy) over the last few years. Pérotin also found that the exit of firms is similar between co-operatives and capitalist firms across the business cycle.

Germany (Figure 12.3), like Italy, has also experienced fast employment growth in the co-operative sector, especially since the beginning of the Great Recession. Since 2003, worker-owned co-operative employment has increased by 26 per cent (3.4 per cent per year), while total employment increased 8.2 per cent (1.1 per cent per year). From 2008 to 2010, worker-owned co-operatives increased employment 4.9 per cent compared with 0.5 per cent for the economy as a whole. The employment growth in worker-owned co-operatives in Germany also exceeded the growth rate in industry over both periods.

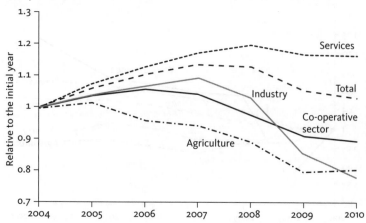

12.4 Employment in Spain in the co-operative sector and in the economy as a whole, 2004–10 (*sources*: General employment data taken from the OECD.Stat website: http://stats.oecd.org/; co-operative data from CEPES social economy reports)

The picture for Spain (Figure 12.4) differs slightly from that of the countries already mentioned. In Spain, employment in co-operatives declined 10.7 per cent (1.9 per cent per year) between 2004 and 2010, compared with a 2.6 per cent (0.4 per cent per year) increase in total employment. From 2007 to 2010, co-operative employment declined 8 per cent and total employment declined 9 per cent. However, co-operative employment has not declined at the same rate as industrial employment. From 2007 to 2010, industrial employment declined 28.5 per cent compared with a 9.5 per cent decline in co-operative employment and a 17.4 per cent decline in employment at worker-owned co-operatives (not shown).

Canadian co-operative data are available to 2008. In the pre-recession period from 2000 to 2008 (Figure 12.5), co-operative employment was relatively stable, growing by 2 per cent (0.2 per cent per year) compared with a growth in total employment of 17 per cent (1.8 per cent per year).

Within Canada, Quebec is well known for having a relatively large co-operative sector: in 2008, 49 per cent of all employees of Canadian non-financial co-operatives worked in Quebec. Figure 12.6 shows non-financial co-operative employment over time in Quebec. From 2001 to 2009, employment in co-operatives grew 17.8 per cent (2.1 per

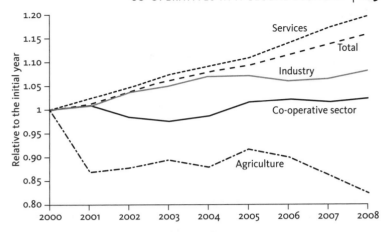

12.5 Employment in Canada in the co-operative sector and in the economy as a whole, 2000–08 (*sources*: General employment data taken from the OECD. Stat website: http://stats.oecd.org/; co-operative data from the Rural and Co-operatives Secretariat *Co-operatives in Canada* reports)

cent per year) while total employment grew 14.9 per cent (1.4 per cent per year).

The Ministère du Développement Économique, Innovation et Exportation (MDEIE, Ministry of Economic Development, Innovation and Export) conducted a study on the survival of co-operative

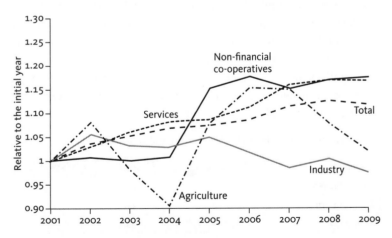

12.6 Employment in Quebec in the co-operative sector and in the economy as a whole, 2001–09 (*sources*: General employment data taken from the Institut de la Statistique Québec; co-operative data from the Ministère du Développement Économique, Innovation et Exportation Québec)

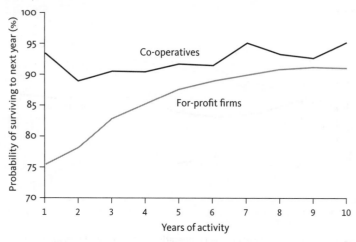

12.7 Survival of co-operatives and for-profit firms in Quebec (*sources*: General employment data taken from the Institut de la Statistique Québec; co-operative data from MDEIE)

and for-profit firms in Quebec from 1985 to 2002 (Clément and Bouchard 2008), which included 1,950 co-operatives formed during the period. They found that newly formed co-operatives were more likely to survive in any given year than for-profit businesses (Figure 12.7). They also broke down their analysis by firm size and showed that the results hold for very small enterprises (fewer than five employees surviving for ten years) and for larger enterprises (five or more employees, for all lengths of survival), as shown in Table 12.3. Table 12.4 shows similar information on the survival of new co-operatives in the province of Alberta from 2000 to 2009. Although the number of new co-operatives is very small, they have very high survival rates as well.

TABLE 12.3 Co-operative survival in Quebec: survival probability (%)

<5 employees	3 years	5 years	10 years
Co-operatives	73.9	62.4	52.4
For-profit firms	74.3	63.0	38.2
≥5 employees	3 years	5 years	10 years
Co-operatives	74.3	63.0	38.2
For-profit firms	60.2	50.6	33.8

Source: Clément and Bouchard 2008.

TABLE 12.4 Co-operative survival in Alberta

Year incorporated	Survival probability (%): 5 years			No. of firms
2000	90.9			11
2001	90.9			11
2002	89.5			19
2003	90.0			10
2004	91.7			12
	1 year	2 years	3 years	
2005	100	84.6	84.6	13
2006	85.7	78.6	78.6	14
2007	93.8	87.5	–	16
2008	100	–	–	7

Source: Stringham and Lee 2011.

We also look at co-operative data from Latin America to understand how employment in co-operatives has changed in a subset of developing countries in recent years. Employment in the co-operative sector in Colombia has grown much faster than overall employment in recent years (Figure 12.8). Colombian co-operatives in 2010 had more than 2.6 times as many employees as they did in 2000 (10.6 per cent growth per year). Overall employment grew by 35 per cent over the same period (3.1 per cent per year).

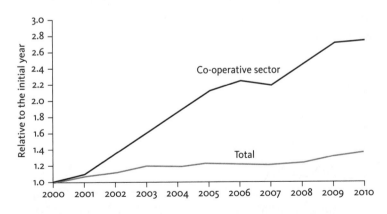

12.8 Employment in Colombia in the co-operative sector and in the economy as a whole, 2000–10 (*sources*: General employment data taken from World Bank World Development Indicators; co-operative data from Confecoop)

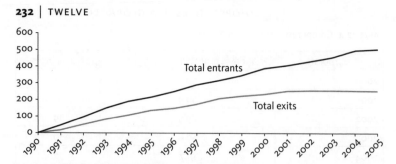

12.9 Total co-operative entries and exits in Chile, 1990–2005 (*source*: Decoop)

In Chile, the co-operative sector has been expanding over time as well, in terms of the number of co-operatives (Figure 12.9). However, Figure 12.10 highlights an important point about the co-operative sector and the institutional environment in which it operates. In Chile, the entry of new co-operatives, especially agricultural co-operatives, has varied considerably over time as the government changed from democracy to dictatorship and back.

In a study of co-operatives in Uruguay, Burdín and Dean (2009) show that during the 2002 Argentine financial crisis, workers' co-operatives decreased employment less than conventional firms. They argue that conventional firms produce a socially inefficient level of lay-offs during recessionary periods due to their 'inability to establish credible commitments between owners and workers'. In contrast, co-operatives are more able to adjust wages rather than employment during crises, which Burdín and Dean call a more egalitarian adjustment method. Burdín (2012), looking at co-operative and conventional

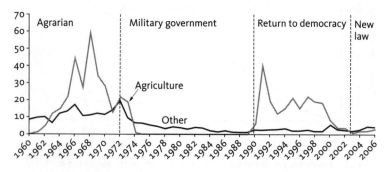

12.10 Co-operative entries and the institutional environment in Chile, 1960–2006 (*source*: Decoop)

firm survival in Uruguay, found that co-operatives had a 24 to 38 per cent lower risk of exit than conventional firms when one controlled for other organisational characteristics.

Co-operatives and economic crises Financial co-operatives may also offer advantages over conventional financial firms. Birchall and Hammond Ketilson (2009) discuss some of the advantages of financial co-operatives in light of the recent financial crisis. They discuss how the different incentive structure in financial co-operatives – for example, not being driven by profits or shareholder interests but instead by more risk-averse members – makes co-operatives less likely to engage in risky behaviour such as subprime lending. Because financial co-operatives operate in the retail banking market, which is dependent on deposits rather than financial markets for funding, they offer more stable returns and less risky investments. Birchall and Hammond Ketilson cite evidence that, after the 2008 crisis, financial co-operatives experienced growth in a number of dimensions while the larger financial markets were in turmoil. Data from the United States, Canada, the Netherlands, the UK and Taiwan reflect this pattern of financial co-operatives increasing their deposits and loan portfolios in the midst of the banking crisis and lending freeze in 2008 and 2009. Finally, financial co-operatives may also have a comparative advantage in developing and marketing new financial instruments that are specially tailored to the needs of other co-operatives, including workers' co-operatives (Waldmann and Smith 1999).

Worker and producer co-operatives can also have benefits during times of economic crisis. Birchall and Hammond Ketilson (2009) discuss how farming co-operatives grew during the Great Depression: farm supply co-operative purchases grew from US$76 million in 1924 to US$250 million in 1934. We have also discussed work by Estrin (1985) on how co-operative employment has grown during periods of high unemployment. In that paper, Estrin discusses how, during periods of economic crisis, co-operative rescues of bankrupt or declining firms can be an important avenue for co-operative formation. He studied rescues in a number of high-unemployment periods, including France in the late 1970s and early 1980s, when 63 per cent of jobs created by new co-operatives were due to rescues. He also draws attention to work by Jones (1984) on waves of co-operative formation in the US, which peaked during crises in the 1880s and 1930s. Jones found that, for those co-operative formations for which data were available, 82 per cent were rescues or buyouts.[5] Further evidence on the benefits of the co-operative sector during times of crisis comes from Argentina. Howarth (2007) studied the *empresas recuperadas* co-operative rescue phenomenon in the aftermath of the 2001 Argentine crisis. She estimated that between 130 and 200 workers' co-operatives formed from failing businesses in the post-crisis period, and that 150 of the rescued co-operatives were still in operation in 2007, providing indirect and direct livelihoods for over 12,000 workers. This work is supported by the aforementioned econometric study of co-operative formation in France by Pérotin (2006), in which she showed that co-operative formation increases as unemployment increases. This evidence from a number of countries and many different time periods shows how co-operatives can be important sources of employment creation and lay-off prevention during times of economic downturn and crisis.

Co-operatives and long-term growth

Co-operatives and innovation In general, there are multiple strategies that firms can follow to get the new technology that they need in order to compete and to grow. For example, firms can develop new patents or license new technology from another company. Co-operatives can and do pursue these strategies, but, in addition, co-operatives have comparative advantages in certain types of innovation.

Smith (1994) discusses these comparative advantages, which include smaller-size innovations that are contributed by individual members. For workers' co-operatives, observations that the workers make in the course of their daily work – whether in the context of building craft products, working on an assembly line or service work – may be more likely to be mentioned, recorded and built upon by the co-operative. In this way, the co-operative can introduce improvements and new methods of production and organisation with incentives to do so and with the more direct line of communication that their management structure facilitates. This is clearly a comparative advantage of co-operatives over conventional firms.

Because monitoring effort and work quality can be costly, producing goods that require high quality or increased effort can be expensive. Conventional firms may have difficulty in monitoring and incentivising high-quality work. Co-operatives may therefore have a benefit in specialising in quality or artistic versions of goods within a broader sector, as their incentive structure is better suited to worker engagement and effort. At least indirect and anecdotal evidence suggests that this is the case, for example in Italy (Restakis 2010; Smith 1994).

In the consumer co-operative sector, once again, co-operatives have a special advantage in member suggestions. Members have more incentive to suggest and develop new ideas that may benefit them. They have more encouragement to experiment and to learn from experimentation; and perhaps most importantly, members have a built-in voice to get their ideas a 'fair and open hearing'. Co-operatives that build on these special advantages may be successful – almost certainly they will be more successful than those that do not. This could be a fruitful and valuable area for further research on co-operative innovation.

Co-operatives in the agricultural sector have also had an important and well documented history of innovation. Deller et al. (2009) discuss how agricultural co-operatives pioneered the organic and natural food movement in the US in the 1970s. Drivas and Giannakas (2006) studied how agricultural co-operative product innovation affects the agri-food system. There are many examples of agricultural co-operatives that drive innovation, including Ocean Spray (cranberry juice blends and 'craisins'), Land O'Lakes (no-fat sour cream, spreadable butter, and flavour-preserving food packaging), Limagrain (new vegetable varieties and improvements in vegetable and wheat varieties) and Cebeco (improved seeds), among many others. Drivas and Giannakas have constructed a model that shows that co-operative involvement in a market where those co-operatives introduce quality and input innovations can increase the overall innovation activity in the market and enhance welfare, when compared with a market with no co-operatives.[6]

Groupings, or leagues, of co-operatives often provide services that may have high fixed costs or network effects, thereby helping achieve economies of scale and scope for the co-operative sector, even while individual co-operatives tend to remain small (often intentionally).

Such services can help co-operatives remain at the cutting edge in their industries. Various sorts of leagues are found among most types of co-operatives, including consumer co-operatives that jointly source goods, workers' co-operatives that share marketing activities, agricultural co-operatives that share infrastructure, and credit unions that share credit card and service centres.[7]

Co-operative leagues can also have important direct roles to play in innovation. A well-known example is the Mondragon system of co-operatives in Spain, which have formed research and development (R&D) technology centres to study such sectors as machine tools, metallurgy, appliances, the automotive sector and packaging. The Mondragon R&D arm had a budget of €61.5 million in 2011, up from €49.6 million in 2007 (Mondragon 2007; 2011). Lopez, Lopez and Larrañaga (2009) state that, in 2005, new products (fewer than five years old) accounted for 19 per cent of total sales in the Mondragon co-operative network. In Italy, the Institute for Co-operative Innovation (ICIE) is also very involved with technology transfer to their member co-operatives, in areas including energy-efficient construction in the construction sector, pollution and cultural heritage sites, and high-performance construction materials (Smith 2001).

Given the importance of co-operative leagues for innovation, the question is: how and why do they form? We often observe workers' co-operatives in particular clustering together in a single region. So how can this be explained? On the one hand, formal and informal co-operative leagues help provide the scale economies that make co-operatives viable – scale economies for innovation and scale economies for production sales. But, on the other hand, you cannot easily have leagues unless you have co-operatives to start and help maintain them, so the result can be a classic chicken-and-egg problem: which comes first? The co-operatives can be supported by the leagues, but the leagues need the co-operatives to operate. So even if co-operatives can be successful, and the contributions to this book present many cases in which they can be very successful, there is no reason to believe that they will appear 'magically' on their own, just because they can be efficient; they need an adequate number of co-operatives around them in a network to help facilitate their entry and survival (Joshi and Smith 2008; Smith 2001). Similar arguments should also apply to other types of co-operative as well, such as consumer and agricultural co-operatives, and this constitutes an important frontier for empirical research on co-operatives.

The participation of women, competitiveness and productivity Another area where co-operatives may have a role to play is in encouraging the inclusion of women in the decision-making process of the firm. Evidence from a variety of countries – including Australia (Adams et al. 2011; Ali et al. 2011), Denmark (Smith et al. 2006), Spain (Campbell and Mínguez-Vera 2007; 2009) and the United States (Anderson et al. 2011; Carter et al. 2003; Peni 2014) – suggests that increasing the role of women in leadership positions in firms can have a positive impact on those firms' profits. Moreover, female chief executive officers were shown to positively affect the performance of micro-finance institutions (MFIs) in a study of over 278 MFIs in sixty countries (Mersland and Strøm 2009).

In addition to the direct effects of women decision-makers on firms, studies show that, when women control income or assets, child health and education outcomes improve. Studies have also shown that the involvement of women in the political process can affect policy priorities and improve the aspirations and educational attainment of girls (Duflo 2011). Employment and income generated outside the home can play an especially important role in women's empowerment (Anderson and Eswaran 2009).

The social mission of co-operatives gives them a comparative advantage relative to other firms in utilising the productive capacity of women, at least in principle. Therefore, co-operatives have an integral role to play in each of the dimensions mentioned above. They can help place women in positions of leadership in firms, provide women with income and assets that they control, and generate employment for women outside the home. In each of these ways, co-operatives can contribute to the growth and empowerment of women in both the short and the long term.

Conclusion

In this chapter we have discussed how co-operatives can generate employment, especially in times of economic crisis. We have also discussed the comparative advantages that co-operatives and co-op-erative leagues have in generating innovation, and how co-operatives can help empower women and foster economic development. We would like to close by discussing questions and areas of research into co-operatives that can help us understand how co-operatives can continue growing, creating employment and innovating into the future.

When studying co-operatives, one should take into account not just whether a firm is a co-operative or a conventional firm; the kind of co-operative it is may be at least as important. We can learn a lot by looking at different kinds of co-operative patterns. First, is the co-operative part of a league or not? There are many benefits to being in a league. While co-operatives that are not in leagues can be, and in some cases are, quite successful, we still need to better understand how and why the performance of league member and non-league member co-operatives differs.

How innovative are co-operatives? There may be innovative and non-innovative co-operative styles of management and operation. It may be possible to continue to be successful without innovating; but innovation can be, and is increasingly likely to be, of great importance for continued co-operative survival and successful new co-operative entry. Further study of innovative co-operatives is a clear research priority.

What form does the internal governance take? Types of internal co-operative governance can matter, and the existing evidence shows that this area is very important in workers' co-operatives. It seems reasonable to conjecture that it is significant in other forms of co-operative as well. But this is another important research priority.

Finding ways of encouraging employment and investment is also important. There are differences between co-operatives and between co-operative leagues.

And last, but certainly not least, there are new issues concerning environmental sustainability coming to the fore. This is an exciting new area for co-operatives of all kinds going forward, and an obvious area for further research.

Notes

1 This chapter is based on a presentation at the International Conference on Co-operative Economics – Imagine 2012, held on 6–7 October 2012 in Quebec.

2 The Organisation for Economic Co-operation and Development (OECD) notes that 'Only Turkey, Greece, France, Hungary, and Belgium recorded no increase or small declines in their Gini coefficients' (OECD 2011: 22).

3 Leagues can be federations, second-tier co-operatives, or associations and networks.

4 Table 12.1 presents data relating to co-operatives and co-operative employment in selected countries. Strikingly, Italy is the country with the largest co-operative sector, approaching 6 per cent of total employment, while some countries, of course, have a far smaller sector. There is some evidence that, historically, Italian co-operatives have put some weight on employment as an objective (see, for example, Smith 1984). Table 12.1 also includes a list of the sources for the co-operative data for each country used in this chapter.

5 Half of those 82 per cent were at the initiative of workers, compared with 80 per cent of co-operatives that were formed from scratch at the initiative of workers.

6 For the example of Fairtrade, see Lacey (2009).

7 Credit union leagues can help support credit union formation and provide services that may have high fixed costs or network effects, such as credit card processing, ATM networks and shared service centres, so their roles are analogous to functions of other types of co-operative leagues.

References

Adams, R., S. Gray and J. Nowland (2011) 'Does gender matter in the boardroom? Evidence from the market reaction to mandatory new director announcements'. *Social Science Research Network*, 2 November.

Ali, M., C. T. Kulik and I. Metz (2011) 'The gender diversity–performance relationship in services and manufacturing organizations'. *International Journal of Human Resource Management* 22(7): 1464–85.

Anderson, R. C., D. M. Reeb, A. Upadhyay and W. Zhao (2011) 'The economics of director heterogeneity'. *Financial Management* 40(1): 5–38.

Anderson, S. and M. Eswaran (2009) 'What determines female autonomy? Evidence from Bangladesh'. *Journal of Development Economics* 90(2): 179–91.

Arpaia, A. and N. Curci (2010) *EU Labour Market Behaviour During the Great Recession*. Economic Paper 405. Brussels: European Commission, Directorate-General for Economic and Financial Affairs.

Birchall, J. and L. Hammond Ketilson (2009) *Resilience of the Cooperative Business Model in Times of Crisis*. Sustainable Enterprise Programme. Geneva: International Labour Organization (ILO).

Burdín, G. (2012) *Does Workers' Control Affect Firm Survival? Evidence from Uruguay*. Working Paper 641. Siena: Università degli Studi di Siena.

— and A. Dean (2009) 'New evidence on wages and employment in worker cooperatives compared with capitalist firms'. *Journal of Comparative Economics* 37(4): 517–33.

Campbell, K. and A. Mínguez-Vera (2007) 'Gender diversity in the boardroom and firm financial performance'. *Journal of Business Ethics* 83(3): 435–51.

— (2009) 'Female board appointments and firm valuation: short and long-term effects'. *Journal of Management and Governance* 14(1): 37–59.

Carter, D. A., B. J. Simkins and W. G. Simpson (2003) 'Corporate governance, board diversity, and firm value'. *Financial Review* 38(1): 33–53.

Censis (2012) *Primo rapporto sulla cooperazione in Italia*. Rome: Fondazione Censis.

CEPES (2012) *The Social Economy in Spain*. Madrid: Confederación Empresarial Española (CEPES).

Clément, M. and C. Bouchard (2008) *Taux de survie des coopératives au*

Québec. Quebec City: Ministère du Développement Économique, Innovation et Exportation, Direction des Coopératives.

Confecoop (2012) 'Evolución de las principales variables: sector cooperativo colombiano'. Bogotá: Confederación de Cooperatives de Colombia (Confecoop).

Co-operatives UK (2013) Homegrown: The UK co-operative economy, 2013. Manchester: Co-operatives UK. www.uk.coop/sites/storage/public/downloads/homegrown_coop_economy_2013_final_o.pdf.

Decoop (2006) 'Estadísticas y cifras del sector cooperativo'. Santiago de Chile: Departamento de Cooperativas (Decoop), Ministerio de Economía, Fomento, y Turismo de Chile.

Deller, S., A. Hoyt, B. Hueth and R. Sundaram-Stukel (2009) Research on the Economic Impact of Cooperatives. Madison, WI: Center for Cooperatives, University of Wisconsin.

DGRV (2003–08) 'Geschäftsbericht'. Berlin: Deutscher Genossenschafts- und Raiffeisenverband (DGRV).

Drivas, K. and K. Giannakas (2006) 'The effect of cooperatives on product innovation in the agri-food system'. American Agricultural Economics Association Annual Meeting, Long Beach, 23–26 July.

Duflo, E. (2011) Women's Empowerment and Economic Development. NBER Working Paper 17702. Cambridge, MA: National Bureau of Economic Research (NBER).

Elsby, M. W., B. Hobijn and A. Sahin (2010) The Labor Market in the Great Recession. NBER Working Paper 15979. Cambridge, MA: National Bureau of Economic Research (NBER).

Estrin, S. (1985) 'The role of producer co-operatives in employment crea-tion'. Economic Analysis and Workers' Management 19(4): 345–84.

Howarth, M. (2007) Worker Co-operatives and the Phenomenon of Empresas Recuperadas in Argentina: An analysis of their potential for replication. Manchester: Co-operative College.

INSEE (2012) 'L'économie sociale'. Paris: Institut national de la statistique et des études économiques (INSEE). www.insee.fr/fr/themes/detail.asp?ref_id=eco-sociale.

Jones, D. C. (1984) 'American producer cooperatives and employee-owned firms: a historical perspective'. In R. Jackall and H. M. Levin (eds), Worker Cooperatives in America. Berkeley, CA: University of California Press, pp. 37–56.

Joshi, S. and S. C. Smith (2008) 'Endogenous formation of coops and cooperative leagues'. Journal of Economic Behavior and Organization 68: 217–33.

Lacey, S. (2009) Beyond a Fair Price: The co-operative movement and fair trade. Paper 14. Manchester: Co-operative College. www.co-op.ac.uk/wp-content/uploads/2010/07/4157_coop-booklet-fair-trade.pdf.

Lopez, U., S. Lopez and I. Larrañaga (2009) 'Innovation in industrial cooperatives: special features and potential of the Mondragon model'. International Journal of Technology Management and Sustainable Development 8(1): 39–56.

Martin, T. H. (2000) 'The impact of worker ownership on firm-level performance: a comparative study'. PhD dissertation, Yale University.

MDEIE (2011) 'Évolution des coopératives non financières par secteur d'activité'. Montreal: Ministère du Développement Économique, Innovation et Exportation (MDEIE), Direction des Coopératives.

Mersland, R. and R. Ø. Strøm (2009)

'Performance and governance in microfinance institutions'. *Journal of Banking and Finance* 33(4): 662–9.

Meschi, E. and M. Vivarelli (2009) 'Trade and income inequality in developing countries'. *World Development* 37(2): 287–302.

Mondragon (2007) *Informe Anual*. Mondragón: Corporación Mondragon.

— (2011) *Informe Anual*. Mondragón: Corporación Mondragon.

OECD (2011) 'An overview of growing income inequalities in OECD countries: main findings'. In OECD, *Divided We Stand: Why inequality keeps rising*. Paris: OECD Publishing, pp. 21–45.

Pencavel, J., L. Pistaferri and F. Schivardi (2006) 'Wages, employment, and capital in capitalist and worker-owned firms'. *Industrial and Labor Relations* 60(1): 23–44.

Peni, E. (2014) 'CEO and chairperson characteristics and firm performance'. *Journal of Management and Governance* 18(1): 185–205.

Pérotin, V. (2006) 'Entry, exit, and the business cycle: are cooperatives different?' *Journal of Comparative Economics* 34(2): 295–316.

Restakis, J. (2010) *Humanizing the Economy: Co-operatives in the age of capital*. Gabriola Island, Canada: New Society Publishers.

Rural and Co-operatives Secretariat (2010) *Co-operatives in Canada (2007 Data)*. Ottawa: Rural and Co-operatives Secretariat, Government of Canada. www.ic.gc.ca/eic/site/693. nsf/vwapj/coops_in_canada_2007. pdf/$file/coops_in_canada_2007.pdf.

Smith, N., V. Smith and M. Verner (2006) 'Do women in top management affect firm performance? A panel study of 2,500 Danish firms'. *International Journal of Productivity and Performance Management* 55(7): 569–93.

Smith, S. C. (1984) 'Does employment matter to the labor managed firm? Some theory and an empirical illustration'. *Economic Analysis, and Workers Management* 18(4): 303–18.

— (1994) 'Innovation and market strategy in Italian industrial co-operatives: econometric evidence on organizational comparative advantage'. *Journal of Economic Behavior and Organization* 23(3): 303–20.

— (2001) *Blooming Together or Wilting Alone?* Discussion Paper 2001/27. Helsinki: United Nations University, World Institute for Development Economics Research (UNU-WIDER).

— (2003) 'Network externalities and cooperative networks: a comparative case study of Mondragon and La Lega with implications for developing and transitional countries'. In L. Sun (ed.), *Ownership and Governance of Enterprises: Recent innovative developments*. New York, NY: Palgrave Macmillan, pp. 202–41.

Stringham, R. and C. Lee (2011) *Co-op Survival Rates in Alberta*. Port Alberni, Canada: BC-Alberta Social Economy Research Alliance.

Waldmann, R. and S. C. Smith (1999) 'Investment and supply effects of industry-indexed bonds: the labor managed firm'. *Economic Systems* 23(3): 245–68.

13 | A ROLE FOR CO-OPERATIVES IN GOVERNANCE OF COMMON-POOL RESOURCES AND COMMON PROPERTY SYSTEMS

Barbara Allen

When Elinor (Lin) Ostrom won a Nobel Prize in economics in 2009, practitioners who employed her theories and researchers who had demonstrated their truth shared in the triumph of an idea: democratic self-governance could sustain a commonly held resource. Ostrom challenged the idea that shared resources (e.g. 'the commons') would inevitably suffer from overuse, resulting in the infamous 'tragedy of the commons' coined in 1968 by Garrett Hardin. Until her pioneering work on cases of commons governance, the conventional wisdom had held that prevention of the 'tragedy' of overusing and destroying a resource held in common required one of two actions: a private property right that enabled individual owners to manage their individual share or a 'state' management system that governed the resource in the name of the community. Lin Ostrom showed that people could transcend the dichotomy of privatisation or state to govern and manage their commons on their own.

But what is a 'commons'? Lin Ostrom and her life companion and the scholar on whom her work built, Vincent Ostrom, defined common-pool resources as goods or resources where it was technically, economically or physically impossible to prevent people using them, but that were diminished by each use. In short, if a common-pool resource existed for one to use, it existed for all, but every use left less behind for the next user.

Lin and Vincent Ostrom's work established a middle category between what economists had called 'pure public goods' and 'private goods'. Private goods are defined as resources from which a potential user could be barred – by private rights to a property, for example – and for which a use subtracted from what remained. The 'pure public good', on the other hand, was defined as a resource that if available for one was available for all, and for which use of the good had no impact on what was left behind. Air was often given as an example of the pure public good. But anyone who has travelled to Delhi or Beijing, or Los Angeles circa 1970, or Paris today knows that use by automobiles, point source polluters and householders for cooking, heating and so forth can considerably decrease the safely breathable air in a given 'airshed'. The 'problem' with public goods, it was said, amounted only to convincing everyone to contribute to producing them – for why would anyone contribute to create a good that, once it was available to one, was also available to all? But with one environmental catastrophe after another, scholars soon realised that use as well as creation could plague a public good. Or, put another way, perhaps some public goods were really common-pool resources – airsheds and watersheds were not wholly safe from depletion.

My goal in this chapter is to present some of the ideas of Lin and Vincent Ostrom, co-founders of the Workshop in Political Theory and Policy Analysis (known colloquially as the Workshop). After outlining the conventional wisdom at mid-century about the commons and our hopes for co-operation, I turn to earlier studies that offered ideas that Elinor Ostrom brought to her study of the commons. I will then outline the frameworks used at the Workshop that help us think about 'what works' and why. But what does it mean to 'work' well in governing the commons?

The Workshop

The Workshop's primary value, principle and focus of study is self-governance. More than democracy, thought of as a voting rule, self-governance means that individuals have an ongoing opportunity to constitute themselves as a community, an association. They have an ongoing capacity to organise and establish the rules for their associations, particularly rules about how subsequent decisions will be made. Individuals have ongoing opportunities to make decisions and act individually and collectively.

Individuals form many types of associations. The ideas about self-governance developed at the Workshop emerged from studies of municipal governments. These studies showed how 'top-down' thinking and administration often cost more and produce less in the way of public services on which a city's inhabitants might depend. They also suggested that the increasingly centralised governments of the United States (including metropolitan-wide consolidation plans) diminished citizens' capacity for self-governance. The Ostroms' early work, undertaken in the 1960s, advanced an alternative form of organising called 'polycentricity'.

The word may seem like social science jargon, but it has the virtue of saying exactly what it is: many centres – in this case, the term applied to many centres of authority, each acting concurrently and independently, sharing authority and responsibility for the results. Polycentricity differed from the catch-all 'decentralisation'. A polycentric system was not one in which a centre had given out a bit of authority (and could presumably take it back); a polycentric system was *un*-centralised. Polycentricity described accurately the kind of governance structure operating at the deepest level of organisation to create the opportunities for self-governance that people in a self-governing society could experience in their daily lives.

When Elinor Ostrom turned specifically to studying common-pool resources and common property regimes, 'the commons', polycentricity was a guiding principle of organisational health. After nearly twenty years of studying co-operation in the realm of government administration, Workshop colleagues turned to the study of governance in the commons. The shift was logical and natural because governance of a commons often meant governance by (or among) the village(s) of a shared resource.

The Ostroms applied what they learned about co-operation from 'public entrepreneurs' to the many situations where ordinary citizens as well as citizen-officials created associations, often crossing jurisdictional boundaries to handle a shared resource. Vincent Ostrom spoke of the citizen-sovereign as the forgotten, but critical, authority for self-governance. The most basic lesson they took from studying successes and failures is that there is no 'cookie cutter' method; there is no one single organisational form or rule; there is no panacea when it comes to achieving self-governance or the sustainable relationship of self-governing people to their physical environment. By studying the patterns of successful co-operation, Elinor Ostrom described *principles* that worked. Above all she found that co-operative behaviour can become a norm under conditions supplied by several specifiable arrangements of constitutional choice and collective choice.

Co-operatives, as well as co-operation, are an important organisational form in governing a commons – and, as it turns out, many of our resources and ways of life either are commons or touch upon them. The principles and ideas that emerge from Elinor and Vincent Ostrom's work, including equity, self-governance, participation, sustainability, preservation and choice, are a part of co-operative economics and the co-operative movement. Not every co-operative arrangement has been able to adhere to these ideas, however. Not every co-operative arrangement has been sustainable or beneficial to those outside the arrangement or to the commons itself. The ideas that emerge from the Ostroms' work suggest a variety of arrangements, each of which may fit some, but usually not all, of the variety of commons contexts.

The assumption and the *finding from research* are that self-governing associations wish to govern themselves and live in their world in a sustainable way. Human beings are not perfect, however. A foundational teaching from Workshop colleagues concerns our ability to diagnose the causes of social failures and to do something with what we have learned. Their emphasis on *diagnosis* as the key element in any effort towards human well-being reflects the importance of individual and social creativity, learning and adaptation. This mental stance in itself challenged much of the thinking of mid-twentieth-century economic theory.

The challenge: how to frame the problem

In showing that self-organisation is possible, Elinor Ostrom's work challenged not only the 'tragedy of the commons' belief but also the conventional wisdom associated with the '(il)logic of collective action'. The logic was straightforward: people often fail to produce a resource or good to which each would have access for their individual benefit. Instead, they take advantage of those who do their part for the common good; they 'free ride' at the expense of those who have contributed, and they hope to do so until they are forced to contribute. As Mancur Olson (1965) asserted, a rational individual will contribute to a shared benefit only if there is a 'selective' incentive – a benefit available only to contributors – associated with producing the resource to be shared in common. In experiments, Ostrom showed that the archetypal model of commons tragedy, the canonical game theory example of mutually destructive behaviour known as the 'prisoner's dilemma', is not inevitable. In field research she found:

> Under the right circumstances, people are willing to accept additional efforts and costs. It all depends on trust in the fact that others will also act. Humans have the capacity to engage and see that their own long-term future is harmed if they don't change their lifestyles. Under the right circumstances they understand: It's not me against you. It's all of us against ourselves, if we don't act. So trust really is the most important resource.[1]

In challenging the tragedy of the commons narrative, Ostrom argued that individuals using an existing commons could organise as commons users (a user-group) to manage collectively held properties or govern the use of common-pool resources. In challenging the logic of a collective action dilemma, she argued that individuals could form a 'producer-group' to provide the shared good, or by, for example, contracting with the producer of the good, they could create a 'provider-group', making the good available to the group or to other users. Perhaps most profoundly, she showed that the conventional wisdom about regulating the use, provision or production of a commonly held resource had limited the 'solutions' to either a commons or a collective action dilemma to two, simplified abstractions: 'the market' or 'the state'. In the prevailing theories, either an invisible hand solved these dilemmas by dividing the commons into private properties, or authorities took control, tutoring the inexpert commons user in sustainable resource management and lawfully coercing wayward non-contributors with the threat of punishment.

In the abstract modelling of 'economic man', 'rational actors' and self-interested, if not selfish, behaviour, orthodox economic theory had failed to consider what people might be doing to organise and, perhaps, govern themselves for a sustainable future.

Elinor Ostrom asked what fishermen, herders, farmers and urbanites actually did when they faced a commons or a collective action dilemma. She found that individuals can co-operate in taking the collective action necessary to create the governance structure to create or use a commons for their mutual benefit. But what factors helped in creating trustworthy members of an association?

Describing the successful (or failing) approaches to commons governance is a first step, but analysing why a group of fishermen, for example, have responded to each other and to their commons requires questions to be asked about the context in which their responses and choices were made. Self-interest, altruism and other motivations might produce observable patterns of behaviour, but what rules promote or hinder a particular motivation?

Rules as institutional arrangements

Actions take place within a context of what is permitted, prohibited or demanded – what we may, must not and must do, according to rules, norms and so forth. The starting point for analysing what worked (or failed) was an understanding of 'rule-ordered relation-ships' for a given context: what actions were authorised and who could give an authorisation as an authoritative, accepted condition? At the heart of the Workshop thinking was the study of rules and how rules ordered our relationships. The aim of an analytical framework was to offer a way to think about rules and rule-ordered relationships or, in short, 'institutional arrangements'.

Institutions 'are the sets of rules governing the number of decision makers, allowable actions and strategies, authorised results, transfor-mations internal to decision situations, and linkages among decision situations' (Kiser and Ostrom 1982: 64–5). Institutional arrangements are not 'given' in the manner that is often assumed in, for example, economic theory or the analysis of public policies; rather, they are the results of 'rules, events, and community' as they interact over time (ibid.: 65). Institutions create the opportunities and constraints that transform individual action into results. Although the ideas about governing the commons emerged from the study of specific cases, the goal was to consider institutions at the most general level to see how the institutional foundation of order shapes relationships in a variety of contexts – from families, commons, voluntary associations, co-operatives and the market to legislatures, government agencies and political 'systems'.

In thinking about the institutional arrangements in any of these contexts, it turned out that the category of permitted action – what may be done – proved especially helpful in understanding co-operative actions (Crawford and Ostrom 1995; E. Ostrom 2005). The arena of 'may' is a site of creative possibility. Some systems of ordering activity by rules and norms are more conducive than others when it comes to creativity, learning, adaptation and innovation.

In his earliest work, Vincent Ostrom found that a particular institutional environment encouraged creative responses to problems: a 'polycentric order' that offers many centres or sites for experimenting with a variety of solutions that address a variety of problems. A polycentric, as contrasted with a monocentric or 'top-down' way of organising relationships, acknowledged the diversity of contexts, physical environments, cultures and ways of thinking about problems and solutions found in our diverse, complex worlds.

'Discovering' polycentricity[2]

In 1961, Vincent Ostrom, Charles Tiebout and Robert Warren developed a theory of how urban services such as electricity, water, police and fire protection, street cleaning and sanitation might be delivered to a community's inhabitants. Their fieldwork focused on homeowners' actions in 'Lakewood', a housing development in southern California. Their findings held broad implications for how we think about collective choice, our capacity for self-government, and how we create and consume shared resources. Their study of the Lakewood project resulted in two important changes in economists' understanding of the provision and evaluation of 'public' goods. First, their investigation of the institutional requirements that enabled co-operation and contracting identified a *polycentric* system of relations as the framework enabling the contracting and co-operative arrangements. Second, they underscored the importance of criteria other than economic efficiency in evaluating public policy and public choice.

Framing urban services: collective action problems and economies of scale At mid-century, economic theory generally classified the shared production and maintenance of infrastructure elements and services as public goods. Public goods were arguably difficult to produce through voluntary contributions. Once the good existed, anyone could use it, so why should any single individual contribute to producing it? In the logic of collective action dilemmas, every potential user must be forced to contribute to the production of public goods, for example by taxation. As a result, the classification seemed to necessitate government ownership and administration of the resource.

Many of the services that urban dwellers expected were also subject to 'economies of scale': the great investment required for production facilities and their operation, maintenance and administration *might* be less costly to individual users if a larger operation produced more units of the good and served more people. When the production of a public good was conceptualised as a mega-scale project, costs were presumed to be beyond the capacity of entrepreneurs (including social entrepreneurs), co-operatives or consortiums. When assumptions about large-scale enterprises (especially the idea of 'capturing' economies of scale) motivated policy-makers, other important criteria for evaluating public service delivery often received far less attention.

Equity could become a significant issue for individuals who were paying but not benefiting or benefiting but not paying for the large-scale production of a public good. If a community could not raise boundaries around the good (e.g. limit a service area) to prevent use by those who did not pay their share, then the tax burden fell unfairly on only a portion of the good's beneficiaries. If the group of individuals paying for the good was larger than the group benefiting, that also could cause inequities. In the conventional wisdom of Ostrom et al.'s contemporaries, large-scale governments (minimally metro-wide, and frequently state and in some cases federal regimes) offered the *only* way to deal with such 'spill-over effects'.

For Ostrom et al., such a conclusion seemed unduly limited, even counterintuitive. Not all urban concerns were metropolitan-wide – a neighbourhood park might better fall under the jurisdiction of a smaller, local, perhaps neighbourhood, government (V. Ostrom et al. 1961). In the classic economic description, the world of human enterprise divided into two realms, public and private, with public and private goods mapping neatly on to government and market producers. Ostrom et al. challenged the idea that public goods necessarily require government provision and bureaucratic administration; the people using public goods often shared in (co-)producing the good. Ostrom ultimately challenged the entire frame within which we think about 'public goods', demanding a new understanding and expansion of the typology of goods beyond the public/private dichotomy.

As a starting point, Ostrom, Tiebout and Warren (1961) conceptualised public goods as existing in a 'public economy' that complemented a market economy. Activities by leaders in a public economy necessitate thinking about issues of oversight, accountability and representation, which, in Ostrom et al.'s discussion, must be handled in transparent, democratic processes. Indeed, democratic self-governance, a value that Vincent Ostrom would later develop more fully, stands out as a criterion for policy evaluation throughout Ostrom et al.'s analysis. The inhabitants of a community needed a voice in the activities of *their* public economy, they argued. Community leaders (whether elected or in some other way emergent) could function as public or social entrepreneurs in working out arrangements for the common good. In opposition to the centralised, 'top-down' authority advocated by mid-twentieth-century economists and urban planners, Ostrom et al. imagined a public service 'industry' comprised of many ways to produce, provide and use public goods. Their study of Lakewood, California's approach to founding a political community and providing its inhabitants with public services, suggested that such an alternative was possible.

The Lakewood example Lakewood, a housing development in Los Angeles County, epitomised southern California's post-war housing boom and 1950s suburban migration. Soon after completion, Lakewood's houses, shopping centres and parking lots became the focus of an annexation proposal launched by the City of Long Beach. Anticipating dramatic increases in property taxes and a loss of community authority from annexation, Lakewood residents pioneered a different approach from joining a mega-municipal institution. They incorporated as a smaller city and gained access to large-scale public service production by contracting with Los Angeles County.[3]

In the later language of Elinor Ostrom, the inhabitants of Lakewood formed a user-group, the individual members of which committed themselves to share the cost of obtaining public goods – in this case the public services of police and fire protection, street sweeping, road repair, water and other utilities. As a user-group, Lakewood residents obtained these goods by contracting with another public entity, the County of Los Angeles. Residents of Los Angeles County produced services that the residents of Lakewood could not afford to produce for themselves. Lakewood residents did not need to raise money to create their own power plant to get electricity. They did not need to fund the construction of the west coast power grid, of which they were a very small part. They only needed to organise as a legal entity – a city, in this case – to buy such goods from an organisation with the capacity to sell them.

The Lakewood collaboration among residents demonstrated how resource users can move from a voluntary co-operation among home-owners in a housing development to an enforceable agreement among citizens in an incorporated community. The collaboration between the user-group (the City of Lakewood) and the public goods producer (Los Angeles County) represented, in the language of Ostrom et al. (ibid.), a quasi-market arrangement in which the user-group would be free to seek services from an entity of its choice at a negotiated price. The insight that Ostrom et al. took from Lakewood – that public service production and public service provision are different activities – opened up a new intellectual frontier for thinking about how consumers, clients and citizens can provide themselves with a shared resource.

The response of Lakewood's residents to their potential collective action dilemma defied the conventional wisdom. It also underscores the crucial message that Elinor Ostrom delivered in every post-Nobel Prize lecture: there is no panacea; there is no 'one and only one' way. Entrepreneurial leadership can take a variety of forms in various 'sectors' that exceed the public/private dichotomy, as Vincent and Elinor Ostrom's studies suggest. A polycentric order had enabled the Lakewood homeowners' new institutional arrangement (ibid.).

From Lakewood: a theoretical description of polycentricity Ostrom et al. (ibid.) defined polycentricity as 'many centres of decision-making which are formally independent of each other'. They observed that such decision-making centres might compete, contract or enter into voluntary co-operative relations. Conflicts could arise in any of these types of relationships. When many authorities (for example, different government bodies in a metropolitan area) could take their conflicts to a mutually acceptable authority for resolution, the whole arrangement worked as a 'system' in which 'the jurisdictions in a metropolitan area ... function in a coherent manner with consistent and predictable patterns of interacting behavior' (ibid.: 831). Breaking down this definition underscores several important points.

First, why have a diversity of 'jurisdictions', many different official boundaries that overlap and divide authority? Why have precincts and parishes, villages, small cities, counties, metropolitan areas, special districts, state or provincial governments, regional governments, and so on? Why should inhabitants have so many identities as members of this or that governed group? Equity requires that those affected by a given decision have a say in decision-making. Each person is affected by numerous issues *of diverse scale*; we need many arenas of choice if we hope to match the scale of an issue to the scale of the decision-making authority (Ostrom and Ostrom 1965). What was true regarding multiple avenues for using government authority also applied to other types of associations (Allen 2005; V. Ostrom 1972; E. Ostrom 1973). Second, Ostrom et al. (1961) view conflict as inevitable; Vincent Ostrom (see, for example, 1975; 1983; Ostrom and Ostrom 1965) later emphasised the possibility for conflict to produce information (particularly bringing inequities to light), learning, correction and innovation. Third, to be *productive*, conflict must be open to resolution. Ostrom et al. describe polycentric orders as those with several possible forums for addressing grievances, at least some of which will be accessible to all, and that have sufficient ability to hold all parties to a resolution. Fourth, productive conflict must occur in the open – we can observe the behaviour and patterns of activity of the authorities (in this case governments) (V. Ostrom 1991; 1993). The authority may be shared and benefits may be mutual, but some barriers to collusion exist. The people who are to receive a service need to be either directly involved in the process or have sufficient oversight and ways to hold authorities responsible and take action to stop irresponsible or dishonest behaviour.

These were among the important aims and values that polycentricity was theorised to achieve. Most broadly, the idea of polycentricity underscored the relational aspect of actions, whether they are explicitly collective actions or individual deeds, bringing us back to the motivators of motivations – rules. All relationships are ordered by rules that create motivations and obligations (to act) and capacities (for action). Rules may be enforced by the parties to the relationship themselves, by a third party in which those in the relationship have vested this authority, or by a multiplicity of vested third parties that share authority in ways that permit them to address shared problems of various scope and scale. A monocentric order means that the authority and power for defining and enforcing rules are vested in 'a single decision structure that has an ultimate monopoly over the legitimate exercise of coercive capabilities'; in a polycentric system, 'many officials and decision structures are assigned limited and relatively autonomous prerogatives to determine, enforce and alter legal relationships' (V. Ostrom 1972, reprinted in McGinnis 1999: 55). The Lakewood example demonstrated that neither hierarchy nor a monocentric order necessarily deliver public goods more efficiently than could a number of other approaches; these were empirical questions worthy of investigation. In fact, a close examination of the goods in question might lead policy-makers to conclude that the 'default' approach should be a polycentric order. In evaluating public goods provision, policy-makers might also find that several criteria should be added to their customary concern, 'efficiency'.

From Lakewood: new ideas about evaluating public goods and public choices 'Efficiency' is generally understood as a relevant measure for evaluating exchanges of private goods, but the concept may not reveal inadequacies in transactions that produce or provide public goods. Equity, which economists conceptualised in terms of 'spill-over', is also an important value in thinking about the provision of public goods. Ostrom, Tiebout and Warren (1961) used the word 'fit' in thinking about equity. They distinguished between the 'public' and the 'political' community – the former being those affected by the provision of a public good, and the latter those who are taken into account (that is, whose interests are in some manner represented) when making decisions about public goods provision. 'Fit' between the public and the political community was among the most important criteria for evaluating whether and how to provide a public good (ibid.: 836). A public organisation or authority such as a city often contained multiple political communities and publics, raising an empirical question of whether the political community seeking a public good coincided with the public that was authorised to decide or to bear the costs. If we cannot expect to find a near equivalence between the potentially *numerous* political communities and *numerous* publics, we cannot assume that a governance frame-work comprised of a single dominant authority will perform well. Differences in the scale of publics and political communities require us to pay attention to such criteria as fairness and fit between the distribution of benefits and the costs of public goods. Ostrom et al. argued that it was counterintuitive to assert, for the sake of equity, that 'spill-over' would be contained by enlarging a provision area *for all services*. The concept of 'fit' reflected the complex nature of equity issues and emphasised the importance of participation in a decision-making process. Decision-makers and the beneficiaries of a good must coincide; beneficiaries must be prevented from shifting the costs not only to those who receive no benefits from a public choice but also to those who have no voice in that choice.

Thinking about choices in a public economy raises questions about the methods of regulation and oversight, and about other aspects of the relationships between producers, providers and consumers. Whether authority is structured in a polycentric manner that produces a quasi-market, or in a monocentric way, public organisations must address these concerns. The redundancies, checks and balances of polycentric organisation offer an important alternative to vesting monopoly authority in the unitary command structure of a monocentric order.

In Ostrom et al. (ibid.), considerations of equity align closely with principles of self-determination and self-governance. Equity demands adequate representation of diverse public interests. Co-operative ventures among user-, producer- and provider-groups must serve a public interest as well as the interest of the co-operating entities. As Ostrom et al. concluded, the impact of public goods provision on representative governance arrangements is a practical as well as a normative criterion for evaluating decision-making processes and the delivery of public goods.

Adequate (i.e. democratic, self-governing) representation in a polycentric governance system suggested that 'choice' itself was an important indication of performance (Ostrom and Ostrom 1965; E. Ostrom 1983). On what basis are public choices made? The many dimensions of the 'common good', which public goods enhance, cannot be converted to a single measure of value (Ostrom and Ostrom 1965). Ideas of preference and price, well understood in market exchanges, may have uncertain meaning in public economies. As later work made clear, a value scale may include not only equity and democratic participation but also such important factors as use and preservation, tradition and innovation, as well as other relevant matters that go beyond one-dimensional measures of utility, efficiency and price. The consequences of a community's decisions may last longer than a human generation, and some values and objects may in fact be priceless (V. Ostrom 1993). A polycentric order characterised by openness and transparency and by adequate ways of resolving conflicts, identifying errors, and diagnosing the causes of failure and success could go a long way when considering many values and evaluating the various possible ways of achieving common and individual good.

Empirical studies of polycentric order: citizens as co-producers of urban services Polycentricity developed conceptually as Elinor Ostrom and her colleagues at the Workshop in Political Theory and Policy Analysis began observing and measuring urban service delivery empirically in the hotly contested era of police and school consolidation (E. Ostrom 1976; 1983).[4] At that time, public administration experts viewed 'overlapping' authority (when authorities from several political jurisdictions had a say) and 'fragmentation' of authority (when no one political authority had the 'last word' because several shared the decision-making power) – in short, the essence of polycentric arrangements – as the *cause* of most urban problems. Ostrom studied polycentricity by comparing the police service 'industry'. She evaluated the efficiency and effectiveness of smaller, independent city departments with adjacent neighbourhoods that depended on consolidated metropolitan police departments. The evidence collected on the police services in Indianapolis and Chicago showed that small- to medium-sized departments in cities performed at least as well as, and in many cases outperformed, the large consolidated departments – and at a lower cost (E. Ostrom 1976; E. Ostrom et al. 1973). More complex studies in St Louis, Rochester and Tampa–St Petersburg corroborated these findings, demonstrating that small departments performed at least as well as medium-sized departments, while medium-sized departments often outperformed both their larger and smaller counterparts (E. Ostrom and Parks 1976; E. Ostrom and Smith 1976).

High-performing departments often achieved an appropriate fit between the scale and scope of service boundaries and decision-making authority, as well as citizens' positive evaluations of effective service delivery by forming co-operative producer- and provider-groups. Using voluntary and contractual arrangements, co-operating agencies crossed jurisdictional boundaries and shared technical resources and personnel. Eventually the study covered eighty US metropolitan areas, finding that well performing police agencies depended on a number of co-operative producer–provider inter-organisational arrangements that included contracts, mutual aid agreements and joint operations (E. Ostrom et al. 1978).

These studies demonstrated empirically what Ostrom et al. (1961) had deduced and had offered as theory: polycentric orders make it possible for a variety of public goods providers to take effective independent, co-ordinated and co-operative actions. Polycentricity enables choice, self-determination, adaptation and innovation among diverse communities seeking a variety of public goods. Small municipal governments could act as a buyers' association, representing their constituents (V. Ostrom 1973); providers and producers could pool resources to share costs in providing services fit for specific needs. Policies for providing or consuming shared resources must be evaluated according to the effect on a political community comprising many 'publics'. Polycentricity may appear as federated associations and networks. To evaluate such *un*-centralised institutional designs we must look at the strength of relationships among the participant associations rather than judge an organisational form that has avoided centralising power as being simply diffused and weak.

By looking more closely at the term 'public good', Elinor and Vincent Ostrom fundamentally changed our understanding of the governance of resources used in common. Indeed, building on this early work, they introduced the concept of common-pool resources, common property regimes – the commons – into the vocabulary of several disciplines. Their work had been conducted in the arenas of *government* authority, but, for the Ostroms, the concepts applied broadly to *governance*. All associations used rules – a governance structure. Families, colleagues in a workplace, a business co-operative, or voluntary associations that read books or made quilts together – all associations had worked out institutional arrangements of 'how things are done around here'. In the view of Elinor and Vincent Ostrom, governments were associations, and an individual or a voluntary association could be a member of many governments simultaneously. Governments, like all associations, might be of differing scales and, on a given question, more or less universal in their reach (Allen 2005). These ideas could apply broadly to a variety of problems that fall under the umbrella of 'the commons'.

Polycentricity and the commons: beyond the dichotomy of public versus private goods Early efforts to characterise public goods emphasised the impossibility of excluding anyone from consuming the good (*exclusion*) and the impact that one unit of use had on the remaining supply (*subtraction*, which may or may not be capable of being *separated* into packaged units, or, as noted in the Samuelson (1954) definition, *rivalrous consumption*). A good characterised by low subtraction (non-rivalrous consumption), in which the consumption of the good by one person does not subtract from the supply, was termed a public good. The difficulty of excluding non-contributors was identified as the 'free rider' problem of public goods provision. Subtraction (separable-ness, non-rivalrous consumption) and exclusion went hand in hand.

Elinor and Vincent Ostrom recognised another concern by viewing exclusion and subtraction as distinct attributes: a good might be characterised by the difficulty of excluding non-contributors and by *separable* consumption in which each use subtracted from the remaining supply. By emphasising both attributes of goods, the Ostroms expanded the dichotomy of 'private' and 'public' goods to a four-part typology that included a new term, *common-pool resources*. By expanding the typology of goods beyond the dichotomy of public or private, they directly challenged the idea that the only options available in dealing with the dilemmas of commons governance were 'market' or 'state/government'.

Ostrom and Ostrom brought reality to bear on speculation about 'the commons'. They showed that individuals facing a 'commons dilemma' could resist the logic of mutual destruction. Consumers of common-pool resources need not be viewed as rivals (although they may become so), but as users whose actions affect others and who have the capacity to design strategies that benefit all users (V. Ostrom

1975). They also found that people had developed many methods of dealing with collective action and commons dilemmas, advancing beyond prescriptions of government-coerced compliance or market arrangements based on individual property rights (V. Ostrom 1983; E. Ostrom 1977; 1990). They found producer co-operatives that pooled resources in bringing a product to market exchange, consumer co-operatives that pooled individual buying power, and providers and co-producers (for example, co-operation between consumer and producers or 'self-help') in public and market economies. Their aim was to describe a framework that encouraged long-enduring institutions, and to do so at the most generally applicable level possible (E. Ostrom 2005).

Their framework of institutional analysis looked to the terms and conditions of law – rule-ordered relations – as well as to the physical and social circumstances determining the attributes of goods. They studied the nexus of relationships occurring in the operation of collectivities, while insisting that prior collective choices, processes that are regulated by antecedent constitutional choice, set the terms and conditions of operational decision-making (V. Ostrom 1989; 1993; 2012b; 2012c). The choices that a community makes about how to choose – constitutional choice – determine what is possible for everyone engaged in later collective choices.

Constitutional choices are often ignored in analysing why a group makes a decision to move forward in a particular way. Questions about how collective decision-making is constituted are vital. Who is eligible to participate? What is the scope of their authority as a group? What happens if the scope is defined inaccurately? Are there ways to hear opposing views? Are there ways to measure consequences? Are there ways to amend choices, including those about who is eligible to participate? Constitutional choice is not necessarily a matter of grand occasions, major discussions and ratification (although these are all possible).

Constitutional choices may be ongoing (and in resilient self-governing groups they are continuous) and may guide subsequent action with far less ceremonial but no less authoritative 'that's just how it is' statements. As important as they are, questions about 'how it is' that 'it got to be' often are *not* asked when collective choices take a group down the wrong path. Operational decisions concern day-today activities that occur according to the collective choices about how action and choice are to take place. Again, when things go wrong, questions might be similarly advanced about the governing collective choices.

To understand how to look at such questions, Elinor Ostrom and colleagues developed first the Institutional Analysis and Development (IAD) and subsequently the Social-Ecological Systems (SES) frameworks (E. Ostrom 2009).

When the worlds of action are described in terms of linked and overlapping arenas of action, of constitutional, collective and operational choices, and of the encompassing social-ecological system, it becomes obvious why Elinor Ostrom insisted that there are no panaceas that will address micro, meso and macro issues and problems (E. Ostrom 2007). Recognising the importance of a polycentric order (E. Ostrom 2010) and understanding its constitutional structure is a starting point; a vital aspect of such an order is the community's understanding of how that order is constituted. Co-operative relations among commons users and common resource producers and providers also depend on institutions based on principles of equity and effectiveness. In addition to equity, effectiveness and efficiency, the criteria for evaluating such institutional arrangements include representation, possibilities for self-organisation and self-governance, methods of holding authorised actors accountable, conformity to norms and values (in Ostrom's terms, 'general morality'), and choices of sufficient variety to enhance the capacity for adaptation to new circumstances (E. Ostrom 2005: 66–7; V. Ostrom 2012a). In light of these principles, a polycentric order offers a complex framework in which to address the complex reality that characterises self-governance. Each 'solution' to a problem establishes a next context, which inevitably reveals new institutional weaknesses, calling for further learning, choice and adaptation – responses that may be possible if we maintain the sufficient variety, alternatives and 're-dundancy' (the 'backup' system) in a polycentric order.

Conclusion

Lin Ostrom's work connected to a new era in thinking and doing when it came to collective action and self-governance. For those who listened, her ideas spoke to the intuitions of many – including economists, natural resources scientists, activists and policy-makers

– that the received wisdom of the either/or of top-down management versus laissez-faire had for centuries taken humanity in the wrong direction. And for many, the Nobel Prize brought a sense of urgency to enter the new millennium with a different understanding. Practices based on the either/or of 'hierarchy or market', as it was put by Oliver Williamson, the co-recipient of the 2009 prize, seemed surely to have brought us to the brink: the calamities brought about by climate change, abject poverty and myriad gross inequalities pressed theorists and practitioners alike to campaign for a new approach. For Lin Ostrom, the urgency of any situation necessitated thought as much as – perhaps more than – immediate action.

Understanding institutional diversity was Lin Ostrom's life work. She found that local voluntary co-operative arrangements, federated associations, competitive markets, government agencies, government and voluntary association partnerships and multi-government federations were among the many possible forms that people imagined could work 'best' in a given situation. However, Lin Ostrom put it simply: *there are no panaceas.* She meant at least two things in this statement: 1) stop looking for someone or something to fix a problem for you; and 2) stop looking for the one and only absolute solution.

The Ostroms' work demonstrated that many different property regimes could be effective in dealing with shared needs among resource users and resource producers and providers. Often, the collective action that individuals might take to provide or use a commonly held resource called upon competitive markets. Collective buying occurred by voluntary arrangements between individual and corporate producers and providers, including co-operative producers and providers of goods. Co-operatives could be organised in many ways, including as direct democracies, federated democracies or hierarchies. Effective organisational forms could not be judged according to labels, but only through careful evaluation. In a sense, the differences between property regimes were somewhat eclipsed by the degree to which governance of a resource was accomplished in a multi-tiered, integrated way that engaged local knowledge and the sharing of authority among local parties, the more encompassing physical and social environments in which a local community was embedded, and the communities and authorities in between the narrowest and most universal scales of governance. Lin Ostrom's work built directly on Vincent Ostrom's discovery of the concept of 'polycentricity', the key to self-governance and to sustainably governing the commons.

Notes

1 'Nobel Laureate Elinor Ostrom: "Climate rules set from the top are not enough"'. *Spiegel Online*, 16 December. www.spiegel.de/international/world/nobel-laureate-elinor-ostrom-climate-rules-set-from-the-top-are-not-enough-a-667495.html (accessed 25 June 2013).

2 The term 'polycentricity' has emerged in several grammatical and denotative forms in disparate academic disciplines and social contexts. In the late 1950s, Italian communist party leader Palmiro Togliatti (1893–1964) described the working relations among post-Stalinist communist parties, countries and regimes as a unified, yet diverse, 'polycentrism'. In 1951, Michael Polanyi offered scientific knowledge and the economy as examples of 'polycentric systems', ordered spontaneously by the interactions between several 'centres.'

3 Interview by Barbara Allen with Robert Warren, 2006, Newark, Delaware.

4 In the United States, the school consolidation movement, which began with a professionalisation movement in the 1930s, decreased the number of independent school districts from about 130,000 in 1930 to fewer than 16,000 (a reduction of about 90 per cent) by 1980. More than 100,000 schools closed and school size increased about five-fold. The largest percentage change occurred after 1950, when the number of school districts fell from 83,642 to 15,987 in 1980. As Elinor Ostrom said in an interview, 'We would have studied schools, but they had already been destroyed. Police and fire were coming next.' (Interview with Elinor Ostrom by Barbara Allen, 13 February 2012.)

References

Allen, B. (2005) *Tocqueville on Covenant and the Democratic Revolution: Harmonizing earth with heaven*. Lanham, MD: Lexington Books.

Crawford, S. E. S. and E. Ostrom (1995) 'A grammar of institutions'. *American Political Science Review* 89(3): 582–600. Reprinted in M. D. McGinnis (2000) *Polycentric Games and Institutions: Readings from the Workshop in Political Theory and Policy Analysis*. Ann Arbor, MI: University of Michigan Press, pp. 114–55.

Hardin, G. (1968) 'The tragedy of the commons'. *Science* 162(3859): 1243–8.

Kiser, L. L. and E. Ostrom (1982) 'The three worlds of action: a metatheoretical synthesis of institutional approaches'. In E. Ostrom (ed.), *Strategies of Political Inquiry*. Beverly Hills, CA: Sage Publications, pp. 179–222. Reprinted in M. D. McGinnis (2000) *Polycentric Games and Institutions: Readings from the Workshop in Political Theory and Policy Analysis*. Ann Arbor, MI: University of Michigan Press, pp. 56–88.

— (1987) *Reflections on the Elements of Institutional Analysis*. Working Paper W87-22. Bloomington, IN: Workshop in Political Theory and Policy Analysis.

Olson, M. (1965) *The Logic of Collective Action: Public goods and the theory of groups*. Cambridge, MA: Harvard University Press.

Ostrom, E. (1973) 'The need for multiple indicators in measuring the output of public agencies'. *Policy Studies Journal* 2(2): 85–92.

— (1976) *The Delivery of Urban Services: Outcomes of change*. Urban Affairs

Annual Reviews Vol. 10. Beverly Hills, CA: Sage Publications.

— (1977) 'Collective action and the tragedy of the commons'. In G. Hardin and J. Baden (eds), *Managing the Commons*. San Francisco, CA: W. H. Freeman, pp. 173–81.

— (1983) 'A public service industry approach to the study of local government structure and performance'. *Policy and Politics* 11(3): 313–41.

— (1990) *Governing the Commons: The evolution of institutions for collective action*. New York, NY: Cambridge University Press.

— (2005) *Understanding Institutional Diversity*. Princeton, NJ: Princeton University Press.

— (2007) 'A diagnostic approach for going beyond panaceas'. *Proceedings of the National Academy of Sciences* 104(39): 15181–7.

— (2009) 'A general framework for analyzing the sustainability of social-ecological systems'. *Science* 325(5939): 419–22.

— (2010) 'Beyond markets and states: polycentric governance of complex economic systems'. *American Economic Review* 100(3): 641–72.

— and R. B. Parks (1976) 'Suburban police departments: too many and too small?' In L. H. Masotti and J. K. Hadden (eds), *The Urbanization of the Suburbs*. Urban Affairs Annual Reviews, Vol. 7. Beverly Hills, CA: Sage Publications, pp. 367–402.

— and D. Smith (1976) 'On the fate of Lilliputs in metropolitan policing'. *Public Administration Review* 32(3): 192–200.

— R. B. Parks and G. P. Whitaker (1978) *Patterns of Metropolitan Policing*. Cambridge, MA: Ballinger Books.

— W. Baugh, R. Guarasci, R. B. Parks and G. P. Whitaker (1973) *Community Organization and the Provision of Police Services*. Sage Professional Papers in Administrative and Policy Studies 03–001. Beverly Hills, CA: Sage Publications.

Ostrom, V. (1972) 'Polycentricity'. Workshop Working Paper Series, Workshop in Political Theory and Policy Analysis. Presented at the Annual Meeting of the American Political Science Association, 5–9 September. Reprinted in M. D. McGinnis (1999) *Polycentricity and Local Public Economies: Readings from the Workshop in Political Theory and Policy Analysis*. Ann Arbor, MI: University of Michigan Press, pp. 52–74.

— (1973) 'Can federalism make a difference?' *Publius* 3(2): 197–237.

— (1975) 'Competition, monopoly, and the organization of government in metropolitan areas: comment'. *Journal of Law and Economics* 18(3): 691–4.

— (1983) 'Nonhierarchical approaches to the organization of public activity'. *Annals of the American Academy of Political and Social Science* 466: 135–47.

— (1989) 'Some developments in the study of market choice, public choice, and institutional choice'. In J. Rabin, W. B. Hildreth and G. Miller (eds), *Handbook of Public Administration*. New York, NY: Marcel Dekker, pp. 861–82.

— (1991) *The Meaning of American Federalism: Constituting a self-governing society*. San Francisco, CA: ICS Press.

— (1993) 'Epistemic choice and public choice'. *Public Choice* 77(1): 163–76.

— (2012a) 'Conceptualizing the nature and magnitude of the task of institutional analysis and development'. In B. Allen (ed.), *The Quest to Understand Human Affairs: Essays on collective, constitutional, and epistemic choice*. Vol. 2. Lanham, MD: Lexington Books, pp. 181–217. (Originally published 1985.)

— (2012b) 'Some ontological and epistemological puzzles in policy analysis'. In B. Allen (ed.), *The Quest to Understand Human Affairs: Essays on collective, constitutional, and epistemic choice*. Vol. 2. Lanham, MD: Lexington Books, pp. 253–96. (Originally published 1991.)

— (2012c) 'Interpreting social experiments: an agenda for critical reflections and inquiry about a research program in comparative institutional analysis and development'. In B. Allen (ed.), *The Quest to Understand Human Affairs: Essays on collective, constitutional, and epistemic choice*. Vol. 2. Lanham, MD: Lexington Books, pp. 297–321. (Originally published 1993.)

— and E. Ostrom (1965) 'A behavioral approach to the study of intergovernmental relations'. *Annals of the American Academy of Political and Social Sciences* 359(1): 137–46. Reprinted in M. D. McGinnis (1999) *Polycentricity and Local Public Economies: Readings from the Workshop in Political Theory and Policy Analysis*. Ann Arbor, MI: University of Michigan Press, pp. 107–18.

— C. Tiebout and R. Warren (1961) 'The organization of government in metropolitan areas: a theoretical inquiry'. *American Political Science Review* 55(4): 831–42.

Samuelson, P. A. (1954) 'The pure theory of public expenditure'. *Review of Economics and Statistics* 36(4): 387–9.

14 | IS THE DEBT TRAP AVOIDABLE?

Claudia Sanchez Bajo

Introduction[1]

In this chapter we briefly review the path that has led us up to the latest debt trap, with some recent considerations on the still evolving global crisis. We will focus on issues of resilience and sustainability. Not surprisingly perhaps, the Davos World Economic Forum Annual Meeting 2013 placed *resilience* and '*resilient dynamism*' at its centre. No doubt the issues discussed at the Imagine 2012 conference in Quebec were showing the way forward. The argument here is that co-operatives are part and parcel of a new trajectory to be charted, not only because they are resilient and dynamic, but also because they steer away from debt traps, freeing up forces for development and enabling community change.

A truly global crisis

The global crisis began in 2007 following accounting changes that led to the bursting of the bubble in the US subprime housing market. After stalling the financial sphere, it turned global with the Lehman Brothers' collapse and then went into a new phase with states that found themselves ridden with debt after giving aid packages to banks and industry in 2009.

Let us just highlight a few key points. In February 2007, Freddie Mac, in view of changes in accounting stemming from both the IASB and the FASB (respectively the London-based International Accounting Standards Board and the US Financial Accounting Standards Board), made the public announcement that it would stop its practices relative to lending for subprime mortgages. The bursting of the great bubble was linked to securities used in relation to the housing market in the United States, called collateralised debt obligations (CDOs).[2] Such securities were a major part of the asset base of large banks, which, after hoarding cash, were saved either with the support of the US Federal Reserve (the Fed) or by other governments or sovereign wealth funds (St Louis Federal Reserve Bank 2013). With the crash, financial assets were wiped out. By early 2010, US citizens had lost 35 per cent of their financial wealth and those of the Eurozone 25 per cent. But the global crisis was not only financial. One example was the drastic fall in trade and enterprise investment in 2008 and 2009: the 2009 United Nations Conference on Trade and Development (UNCTAD) report showed that global foreign direct investment (FDI) inflows fell by 44 per cent and mergers and acquisitions by 76 per cent in early 2009, compared with the same period in 2008. In developing countries, inward FDI declined by 39 per cent in early 2009. The drop was so pronounced that it showed beyond doubt that firms were using financial mechanisms to sustain trade. On the one hand, with the just-in-time system of lean management practices, firms' inventories were kept to the necessary minimum. On the other hand, as global chains competed for volume to maintain low pricing, an excess capacity gave individual firms little pricing power. This system is based on open credit lines and, since global trade and finance work together in a loop of interwoven credit and debt, if the system of payments gets blocked, implosion may follow. The use of short-term financial products in money markets amplified volatility and, since this financial activity was not shown on balance sheets, a corresponding lack of accountability. For the first time, most developed countries found out that not only financial institutions but also all actors in the real economy were highly indebted: households, firms, and public institutions from local authorities to nation states. The downturn spread further, as so many actors have had to confront the leverage of debt obligations, namely the debt relative to assets or income. Credit contracted, except in cases with a healthier equity base, such as credit unions and co-operatives. Credit unions and co-operatives have shown strong resilience to the crisis because they were either not leveraged at all or only slightly, they had built a healthier equity basis, and, generally, they did not engage in toxic financial instruments.

In the very beginning, once the financial sphere stalled and a liquidity trap took place, politicians cried out about capitalism imploding and being brought to its knees. In this phase of the crisis, governments intervened heavily. The global crisis and recession that followed would have surely been far more dramatic without governmental intervention but it is still very difficult for a rapid recovery to take place, considering the amount of debt. Five years on, even though some positive signs arise here and there, the world economy is still suffering from the fall in activity, credit, employment and consumption. In late 2012, the toll on growth reached the European Union's (EU's) core: Germany and France. Meanwhile, the US recovery has been going back and forth.

During the first phase of the crisis, there was much talk of a return to Keynesian ideas. Yet, after the first phase, the earlier ideological consensus among policy-makers has regained predominance: adjustment policies, fiscal consolidation, privatisation and strong pressure on restructuring under the threat of losing credit rating and funding. In this way, the influence of financial markets, so decried at the start of the crisis, remains in force. In the EU, austerity has been imposed, bringing about prolonged recession and in some cases outright deflation, coupled with very high unemployment rates, especially affecting the young, women and ethnic minorities.

The social impact and suffering have been widespread: in the USA, there were still 23 million unemployed in 2012 (Lam 2012). Worldwide, the number has officially reached 202 million in 2013, according to the International Labour Organization. Nation states have faced revolts and strains (including on constitutional agreements, as in Spain). Regional entities such as the EU are faced with their own limits and they are experiencing rising internal divergence and citizens' disaffection. Labour disputes continue unabated, some lasting years. Thousands of companies and farms are going bust in many European countries every year, with the exception of some Nordic countries and Germany, where there is no prescribed minimum wage. Many delocalise, while some truly slave-like labour practices such as debt bondage are booming. For example, Belgian ministers lodged an EU complaint against Germany for employment practices of very low pay without benefits, calling them unfair social dumping. Used in agriculture, food-processing and abattoirs, such practices push Belgian companies into bankruptcy (Laurence 2013). Besides, the UN has published a conservative estimate of 21 million trafficked people with about half of the £20 billion profits made out of human trafficking in developed countries (Nelson 2013). In another example, even bank representatives became worried about policies that reflate already overpriced houses and build a new debt trap, this time for youth in the UK (Elliott 2013).

Yet, considering the debate at Imagine 2012 on ecological overshooting (see Chapter 4), namely that we are using our planet's resources and ecosystem in a way that exceeds its carrying capacity, which we may not be able to recover or replace, this depressing picture still seems possible to redress. But where to start?

The work of international entities and decision-making frameworks established at the height of the crisis, such as the G20 and Basle III, so active in 2009, appear today rather subdued. Suffice here to mention the 2012 and 2013 G20 meetings in Mexico and Russia[3] or the delay in the implementation of Basle III in early 2013.[4]

The Securities and Exchange Commission in the US encountered some setbacks in its attempts at regulation. As a preferred solution, the USA has released an enormous mass of money at zero or very low interest rates injected to both prop up the financial situation of banks and enterprises and to purchase assets and resources across the world; similar measures are being implemented in Japan and the UK. Indeed, the business buzz word is 'to go out': export, consolidate and acquire foreign assets. This phenomenon sounds reminiscent of the 1880s and the 1890s, when this took place after the big financial crises of the nineteenth century. As a result, since 2010, countries such as Indonesia, Mexico, Brazil, Russia, Taiwan, Colombia and others have either passed capital controls or introduced banking regulation to restrain international capital movement, in particular short-term speculative flows, in order to shield themselves from an unfair context that carries the risks of inflation and asset bubbles, and hinders their export competitiveness due to exchange rate appreciation (Evans-Pritchard 2010). Even for the International Monetary Fund (IMF), capital controls now have a positive role to play (IMF 2012). The other side of the coin will be a sudden reversal of flows once the Fed ends its 'quantitative easing'.

At the macro level, between austerity and recession in the EU and others' efforts to maintain export competitiveness, global aggregate demand will continue to be a key concern. Connected to this key question, inequality, the outrageous gap in income distribution and the growing income concentration have finally been recognised by the

IMF in 2012 as major causes of instability and household indebtedness, with significant macro-economic consequences. Here again, the links between the micro and the macro in economic theory are slowly being recognised. In turn, the IMF, which had become almost irrelevant with very little capital in 2003, has received a new life with large inflows of fresh capital and a series of new countries to supervise. On the other hand, mathematical and statistical models creating systemic risk (such as Li's 'Gaussian copula' function) are now under scrutiny (Forslund and Johansson 2012). This is the mathematics that allowed the CDOs to be rated as totally secure and sold in vast quantities. Finally, there is raging debate in economic theory. The EU consensus remains a strong advocate of monetarist policies targeting inflation, but monetary policy per se is ceding the ground to institutional economics (both classic and new institutional economics, Keynesian theories, and even market monetarists who propose targeting the level of nominal income instead of inflation).

Technological change has brought an epochal shift in finance: since August 2012, more than half of the money invested on the stock market is placed through highly automated machines and high-frequency trading (HFT). These computers do a great deal of trading off-exchange into so-called 'dark pools', surfing on trends for milliseconds before inverting the bets to cash in. It is no longer about the stock markets, but the dark markets of stocks. Stocks are now held on average about two months, compared with two years in the 1980s. The EU has singled out fast trading for favouring speculation and price volatility, requesting that 'share orders would have to be posted for at least half a second, far longer than HFT firms currently stay in the market' (Guardian 2012), and that a new type of trading platform should be created where HFT would come out in public. There is tension between the older system, which is led by stock markets and banks, and another led by wealth institutions, namely rich individuals and government funds composed of a very concentrated shareholder base that takes top-down decisions. The former – stock markets and banks – usually have a much larger shareholder base and have tended to operate as platforms of exchange. The difficulties of Banca Monte dei Paschi di Siena (MPS) are very symbolic in this respect. This case, far from being the only one in finance, is paradigmatic because MPS is the oldest bank in the world, founded in 1472 as a 'mount of piety' by the authority of the city state of Siena in Italy. Present in the USA, Russia, China and European countries, among others, it became the third most important bank in Italy after acquiring Banca Antonveneta at the start of the global financial crisis. This acquisition was the straw that weakened MPS's capital. Previously a safe institution devoted to the development of the real economy, and having survived through centuries, it was brought into turmoil by the financialised, unregulated and shadowy system that most in the bank and its foundation were not aware of. The bank received state aid after approval by the European Commission for fear that, if MPS fell, Italy would have to request EU financial aid. Yet, the state aid from the Monti government was a loan that needed to be repaid, making MPS's situation worse! Italy's economy became even more uncertain.

Finally, there is a sentiment in most countries that change is necessary, and that sentiment is shared by the majority of the population, be they the youth or the elderly, women and families, entrepreneurs, farmers and artisans, the Occupy movement or the 15 March movement in Spain voicing 'Ya basta!' ('Enough!'). This strong sentiment is expressed in some countries through new political parties and movements, moving away from existing political institutions, including the EU, and in the polarisation of politics in others. This crisis carries a sense of historical change with a trajectory not yet stabilised.

The global financial crisis as a debt trap

Most reactions to the global financial crisis have focused on macro-economic issues and on governance and supervision. But what has the crisis been about? Lots of interlocked debt put entire socio-economic systems at risk. Keynes distinguished between risk and uncertainty: risk could be controlled privately, while governments' role was to deal with uncertainty. But can risk be managed when control does not accompany ownership any longer? In the book *Capital and the Debt Trap* (Sanchez Bajo and Roelants 2011), our main hypothesis is that a debt trap and the toxic context we suffer are linked to a shift in control in relation to ownership. The two have been disconnected in economic and social institutions.

Ownership has been blurred by both financialisation and technological change, and control does not necessarily match ownership any more. Earlier debates on control versus ownership rights focused on the relationship between shareholders and managers in a firm. Now, the International Financial Reporting Standards (IFRS) that are replacing the old accounting system clearly distinguish between both: control means power over the investee (privileged access to resources, and 'exposure, or rights, to variable returns from its involvement with the investee'[5]); ownership is expressed in equity as the claim to the residual net assets of the entity (the IFRS see owners and entrepreneurs as financial investors).

In banking, opaque and informal lending have loaded debt on to both private and public entities, building bubbles in the prices of assets. By its nature, such lending makes those with less information its prey. When an unexpected event happens, loan conditions change and refinancing becomes difficult or impossible, a crisis breaks up. As with the CDOs (the financial debt leverage instrument that inflated the subprime bubble, dispersing toxic 'poison' that interlocked banks and financial institutions throughout the world), many continue to entertain the illusion that risk could be passed on to others. But in the current system, not only do institutions lend to each other, some also bet against their own clients. Fast computers and secretive dealings augment the chances of unexpected events and add to the current system's unsustainability. In the end, the common citizen ends up paying the bill, with Cyprus being the latest casualty at the time of writing, in March 2013.[6]

Many firms are inserted into a financialised system that hails absentee investors and allows top managers to reward themselves for takeovers and/or closure of plants, furthering a shift of control away from real economy stakeholders. This shift has taken place within a broader process of state deregulation or light public regulation. Not enough attention has been paid to the risk built within entities that carry systemic risk for all, leaving each entity vulnerable to risk and deception, and neglecting issues of accountability and ethics towards both the stakeholders in the same entity as well as the economy and society at large. It is clear now that uncertain activities with large impacts need better regulation in the public interest. The 2013 Swiss referendum has been an important first step to redress the situation.[7]

The large leading firms in global chains of production and distribution have in turn strengthened structural control along chains due to the setting of standards, timing, logistics and finance. In contrast, owners of small- and medium-sized enterprises (SMEs), workers and policy-makers have lost control and it has become very difficult for them to negotiate conditions. For example, in a global chain, the owner of a subcontracting firm may not control production standards, timing, type of product or spare parts, or intellectual property. The firm can also be replaced by another subcontractor. The subcontracting firm must adapt swiftly to change and orders; it takes risk but it may not have control over its own production and distribution process.

Therefore, to understand the crisis we need to shed light on the links between the micro and the macro, and between the financial economy and the real economy. To do so, three mechanisms leading to and deploying the crisis can be observed as traps: a consumption trap, a liquidity trap and a debt trap, each one feeding into the other.

The first trap is that of consumption, as its growth continues even when households' purchasing power and income are diminishing, and financial institutions, through deregulation and speculation, inflate asset bubbles based on credit frenzy. This was the case in the US subprime crisis. Yet, it should not be forgotten that investing in housing was also connected to the lack of general health and pension coverage. Households turned to bricks and mortar to face old age and sickness, as well as to pay for daily necessities. Predatory practices promoting unsustainable 'growth' are responsible for systemic risk in a highly interconnected global economy and finance. Once the trap closes in, households lose heavily and the economy initiates a process of deflation. Thence, a debt trap is first and foremost the consequence of systematic recourse to debt that thrives in contexts of increasing inequality and reduced government regulation.

The second trap is that of liquidity, once the crisis bursts out and the interbank lending is halted due to panic. Since credit (and debt), more than cash, is today's global currency, trade, investment and even production in global chains were almost immediately halted as well. Only those with cash and secure assets prove more resilient. From then on, a downward spiral begins, in consumption, employment, sales and general prices. All these aspects together, part and parcel of the current financialised and technical phase of capitalism, create the debt trap.

Why so much debt in the real economy?

A question needs asking: why so much debt? Household debt was briefly mentioned above. In the case of firms, why would firms prefer to use debt mechanisms rather than equity financing? A first argument relates to managers, who hold key information and know whether their shares are correctly priced or not. If they are, they would be unlikely to issue new equity shares because that would signal lower future returns.

Other major reasons relate to globalisation and world restructuring. Debt has been useful as a disciplinary tool in particular in relation to labour issues as well as a tax shield (Buettner and Wamser 2009). The outrage in the UK against Starbucks, Google and Amazon at the end of 2012 makes the point (Barford and Holt 2013).

Debt leverage has been upheld as worthy because, under financial pressure, managers were expected to obtain shareholder value more aggressively. The penalty for managers who are not aggressive enough has not been the loss of management benefits but the firm's takeover or delocalisation. Private equity guides have introduced leveraged buyouts to managers as a way of becoming owners of the enterprise (BVCA and PWC 2003). This concerns top managers only, turning the agent into a principal,[8] with power in the restructuring of the firm. In such an evolution, labour movements and trade unions lost bargaining power. A major reason for the latter was that acquired firms were usually given as collateral for the loans used to buy them. Loaded with debt, acquired firms not only had to repay the loans but at the same time distribute dividends, bonuses and other rewards to top managers and absentee investors. To equal the amount of debt leverage and rewards, firms soon had to look for further borrowing. In March 2013, the Bank of England warned of a systemic threat posed by private equity buyouts as from 2014, given the 'need over the next year to refinance firms subject to heavily leveraged buyouts' (Bank of England 2013). Indeed, refinancing in the current context is much harder, if possible at all. This could be the next phase of the global crisis. On the other hand, some financial institutions could have the opportunity to convert debt into equity, extending their influence in the real economy. With the unfolding crisis, the high, and rising, rate of unemployment reduces further trade unions' bargaining power.

The strategies of debt leverage and shift in control are connected to the building of global industrial chains in which the Fordist mode of production has given way to the Toyotist one. In the Toyotist logic of outsourcing and vertical de-integration, debt inter-linkages are common. Toyotist firms generally own only a minority of their operating capital. Under Toyotism, debt to equity ratios of 80 per cent are not exceptional. These debts are usually shared by several banks. As debt financing grows, control along supply chains is increasingly exercised through decisions and supervision focusing on financial flows and profits, the reputation of the global brand and access streaming.

Now let's turn to the state. As with Greece's CDOs – among other off-balance-sheet practices that have triggered the EU member states' crisis – many public–private investment projects are actually a debt practice. Many hospitals and roads have been financed by private investment and are regulated by long-term contracts lasting up to thirty years that include all aspects of the project, from design to construction, maintenance to management, and the provision of the service. Although they appear private to the citizen, it is the state that is being charged with the debt incurred, and it is the citizen who should foot the bill through their use of the services. Analyses of public–private partnerships have been unfavourable, resulting in debt now shifting to the states' balance sheets, on the basis that the latter control expected future income even though they may not own the investment. The high leverage buyout deals undertaken in the period of loose credit conditions potentially present a significant risk to the financial system, due to the leveraged loan exposure of banks, as well as through the effects of leveraged buyouts on corporate indebtedness, which is more susceptible to default. Why now? Leveraged buyouts use acquired companies as collateral, and the majority are structured as 'bullet' repayments, namely the principal is repaid at the end of the maturity period, on average seven years. Large lump sums must be repaid when loans used to buy the companies mature. If not refinanced, the financial institutions, the investors and the indebted companies get into trouble. There are £160 billion of UK leveraged loans with a maturity in 2012 or later, with a peak in maturities in 2014.

Before, banks, just like the CDOs, sold their leveraged loan exposures as collateralised loan obligations to other entities. But the banks are focused now on repairing their balance sheets, the Bank of England explains, and loan exposures will become fixed from 2014 onwards. The loans will not be refinanced in the future. The Bank talks thus of a refinancing cliff, as there is a shortage of options to deal with the risk. Will they invent something new in about a year's time? Or will the state save those that are too big to fail with more public money? Are citizens aware of what they might be paying next? Good questions.

What happens to institutions lost in the debt trap? The first sign is a loss of autonomy and timing in reacting to the changing conditions, in the face of external shocks and events. Since the institution was neither capable of preventing leverage nor prepared for the consequences, growing internal divergences flare up under pressure, especially when there are no appropriate compensatory institutions (special funds, monitoring schemes, etc.). The outcome then rests on individual leadership and short-termism, which can take precedence over the long-term vision, including the 'common interest'. As trust evaporates, the lack of transparency and debt leveraging that built the bubble in the first place feed general suspicion. Either new behaviour or institutional patterns rebuild trust through more transparency, equality and justice, or decay sets in, because, with neither trust nor institutional mechanisms to face a crisis together, each stakeholder and participant will try to save themselves on their own. The case of the EU bears a resemblance to this unfortunate scenario.

Resilience of co-operatives in times of crisis and their contribution to the future

Many studies by international organisations (Birchall and Hammond Ketilson 2009) and government reports have confirmed that, in both developed and developing countries, co-operatives not only contribute strongly to socio-economic development and generate more equality and social cohesion, but are also a significant actor to consider in responding to the challenges of climate change, biodiversity and a green transition. These and other studies acknowledge that co-operatives have also shown relatively higher resilience to the global crisis (CICOPA 2012). In the case of co-operative groups and consortia, innovation is already under way to respond to future socio-economic needs. During the last few years, due to their achievements and resilience, co-operatives have received more attention in public debates and the media. Unfortunately, more has not meant much, as yet. Throughout the economic and financial crisis, co-operatives have become more topical, but they are rarely considered an essential partner to build a path that steers away from future debt traps.

In what sense can co-operatives help us avoid a debt trap? And, once we end up suffering one, in what way can co-operatives help resist its worst effects? How do they react and manage the impact of such debt crises?

By their nature, when co-operatives' stakeholders take the risk of starting a common venture that aligns control with ownership, their standpoint and interest are tied into the long term. To achieve their common aims in a sustainable and lasting manner, co-operatives tend towards a more balanced generation and distribution of wealth. Information within co-operatives tends to flow in a more transparent manner than in conventional firms because members have more equal access to it, on the basis of their values and principles. Decisions, responsibility and accountability are more equally shared, thus carrying a higher degree of acceptability and legitimacy. This point becomes extremely important when confronted with a stark crisis.

Another characteristic of co-operatives is that, being owned and controlled by locally embedded members, they do not delocalise, placing the issue of trust and accountability at the heart of their business model. It is only natural and normal that they develop a strategic long-term vision. Co-operatives tend to distinguish between strategic investment in the real economy and financial risk, and thus are logically interested in responding to inequality and steering away from a consumption trap (relentless, ostentatious consumption that falls into indebtedness), as their aim is to develop the community and have a healthy equity basis. Co-operative banks with thousands of common people as stakeholders and owners concentrate on developing the local economy and its SMEs. Consumer co-operatives and credit unions do not typically engage in predatory practices that lead to their members' indebtedness. Workers' co-operatives will not engage in risky financial mechanisms, as members are both workers and owners of the business.

In the global crisis, 'the type of ownership and methods of

capitalization are two of the key factors that have created the disparity in the financial positions of credit unions and banks, to the advantage of savings and credit co-operatives or credit unions' (Coombes 2008). Credit unions and co-operative banks usually form regional or national banking networks and continue to control upwards what the central institution is doing, while the latter has a downward monitoring role. In the very few cases where co-operative banks have flirted with international finance, sanctions have come in swiftly. One example has been the central unit of Crédit Agricole (BBC News 2008). Soon after the trouble, the managers were sacked by the grass-roots local co-operative banks.

Co-operatives, credit unions and mutuals have contributed neither to bubble-making nor to bubble-bursting. Many savings and credit unions and co-operative banks have continued lending because they have a more thoughtful and sparing[9] vision of growth, therefore being in better health, which allows them to be forward looking and focus on the needs stemming from the real economy and society. The case of German regional banks, many of which are co-operatives, show how important this aspect is for providing credit to SMEs, especially in uncertain times. In workers' co-operatives, where workers are also joint owners and controllers, diverse management strategies help the latter remain in the enterprise. Skilled workers who are ready to take up commands once the economy picks up somewhere in the world, and global chains start to function again, are an absolute necessity. Otherwise, firms lose competitiveness and contracts. The German government has spent a great deal to keep workers in companies, even if they remain at home for some time. Co-operatives have done that without public money. This measure avoids job losses, allowing the country to remain competitive, ready to take up global orders as soon as global chains' activity restarts.

Especially in the first phase of the crisis (2008 and 2009), nation states took unprecedented steps to prop up ailing banks, insurance companies and major enterprises. In a shared decision, many countries subsidised the automotive sector and promoted purchases of new cars. Yet, in general, shareholders of the state-funded bankrupt enterprises were not touched and neither shareholders nor managers were sacked or replaced. Much of that public money was repaid in the following years. Such a state role had more to do with short-term financing facilities than with investment in the real economy with a long-term strategy. One important exception would be General Motors in the USA, where the government supported both restructuring and product innovation. In the case of the EU, Germany used all types of measures to prop up its national economy while other EU countries used only one or two types of measures.

At the core of the financial breakdown, the US, the UK and now Japan, in particular, have provided enormous liquidity to financial markets and institutions to fight potential deflation, but the idea of fiscal consolidation and austerity policies remain predominant. But stable growth and healthy credit available to the real economy, including to the SMEs that provide most of the employment in every country, are still missing. The monetary base is significant but the monetary supply to the real economy is not. Financial institutions are hoarding it, as they 'deleverage' their debt condition. Government priorities have geared bailouts to the financial sector and a few large companies, while public services and jobs shrank at the local and municipal level. To 24 November 2008, governments' commitments to financial bailouts (US$4.1 trillion) were forty-five times the sum allocated to development aid in 2007 and 313 times the sum given to respond to the climate crisis (Anderson et al. 2008). Meanwhile, the privatisation of public services – water and transport industries – has proceeded apace (Zacune 2013).

Co-operatives are one of people's responses to increasing inequality and loss of access to services. In times of crisis, in particular in the face of a debt trap, and as exclusion and poverty mount following job losses, income reduction and home evictions, new co-operatives begin to spring up in an élan of self-help and solidarity to avoid or confront indebtedness. In the field of personal and community services, social co-operatives have maintained and even increased their labour force, thus enlarging the quantity and quality of services. Closer to the needs of their members and users, co-operatives seem to better heed social needs while being less of a burden on public budgets.

Despite all their positive points, why is it still difficult to see any acknowledgement of co-operatives by public authorities? The late Nobel Prize Laureate in economics Elinor Ostrom suggested an answer to this. There is first the need to mainstream collective action theory among the instruments of policy analysts and in theories about human action, by which a group of interested participants can voluntarily organise by themselves and retain the residuals of their efforts. She wrote that 'Examples of self-organized enterprises abound ... Most co-operatives are also examples' (Ostrom 1990: 214; see Chapter 13). Continuing in Ostrom's footsteps, institutional analysis should acknowledge on the one hand the links between the micro and the macro, and on the other the 'normality' and value of horizontal co-ordination. Vertical command without checks and balances ends up taking concentrated bets that risk systemic failure.

Conclusions

We have reached a dangerous peak not only in terms of environmental damage but also in terms of indebtedness and predatory finance. The practice of joint control, which co-operatives' stakeholders uphold in a democratic manner, is appropriate for a transition that builds a new trajectory towards a sustainable economy. Many characteristics of co-operatives can come in handy: more transparent information circulating on a real-time basis, democratic accountability, checks and balances, a systematic building of common capital reserves, enterprise education of common citizens, and sustainable employment and horizontal systems of entrepreneurship with horizontal co-operation dynamics. Such an organisation tends to steer away from high-risk strategies, high-debt leverage and short-termism. This also means that co-operatives are forward looking to the long term, not only in good times but also, and most importantly, in bad times!

Resilience is, in fact, built *in advance*. Resilience is not a mere question of good ethical values and sharing participation. When a shock arrives, or a crisis breaks out, a timely reaction and general trust are essential. And this is the case in most co-operatives, where trust has been built in advance due to the fact that social capital was high and the organisation had generated higher equality and general wealth. If, on top of this, stakeholders had built reflexive monitoring mechanisms with effective cross-control in checks and balances within the organisation, legitimacy is largely shared. Painful decisions can then be taken because members know that the share is fair and that they are all in it together. Their various common funds allow them to breathe, resist the shock of the crisis and think ahead, in terms of innovation and community needs.

At the time of writing these lines, the four empirical cases studied in the book *Capital and the Debt Trap* (Sanchez Bajo and Roelants 2011: the Natividad divers' co-operative in Mexico, the Ceralep industrial co-operative in France, the Desjardins financial co-operative group in Quebec and the Mondragon co-operative group in the Basque country) are doing fine. We cannot delve further into this here, but it confirms the resilience and innovation capacity of co-operatives throughout the global crisis, on which there are now many studies, surveys, news reports and documentary films. Yet such resilience has its limits in the face of systemic decisions that impose deflation or long-lasting recession on entire economies, weakening trust and social cohesion in the end, imposing undue suffering and opening the door to increasing indebtedness, especially among the weakest and the poorest. In turn, these negative outcomes open the door again to future traps in consumption, liquidity and debt, a vicious circle that has to be broken.

The crisis has shown the centrality of debt interweaving the financial and the real economy together and being used to attain various objectives; these include to be a disciplining tool; to avoid taxes; to develop global chains; to solve the chronic underfunding of pension funds through buyouts and takeovers; and to redesign entire sets of bargaining relations, in particular labour pay and working conditions. With each debt crisis, more wealth is destroyed than has been generated during the building of the bubble.

Globalisation has reached its limits under the following contradiction: 'too big to fail' firms that need constant enlargement of business scale, doing so with little equity and capital reserves, with just-in-time management of reduced stocks, and highly dependent on a tightly interlinked and fast electronic financial system running across the globe, day and night. In this circular context, the generalised use of debt is no longer sustainable. Due to interconnectedness, any event can magnify systemic risk that can easily lead to implosion. Is it a coincidence that the word 'toxic' is so often used in relation to this global crisis? It is not only the environment of the planet but also the present global financial-economic system that are increasingly falling out of balance. The old ideal of rapid and high rates of growth on the basis of debt leverage and consumers' indebtedness should be considered outdated, and a trajectory towards a more equitably generated and distributed general wealth should be built.

The micro builds an accumulated impact on the macro. We need to pay greater attention to social and economic entities, their organisation and accountability, their values and practices, their resilience and preparation for bad times, if these ever come. The rapport between ownership and control is absolutely essential in assessing resilience. Co-operative cases we have studied serve as a source of inspiration in terms of resilience to crises – resilience that is best when built in advance. One is not resilient and innovative just by having good ideals and values (although this is certainly key to organisational building) but by building mechanisms and dynamics that deliver legitimacy, rapidity, flexibility and accountability within a framework of joint ownership and democratic control with checks and balances.

Beyond the significant resilience of co-operatives and similar types of enterprise, it would be desirable to undertake more studies on their capabilities and mechanisms to co-operate in order to innovate and to respond to the prospective needs and aspirations of citizens and communities, as well as to generate further specialisation. Such knowledge could be very useful not only to other co-operatives but also to SMEs, social movements, non-governmental organisations and local communities. We move here from the micro level towards the idea of building meso-economies with sustainable pools of resources, flows and affinities that both respond to the needs and aspirations of local people and communities and are able to enhance the sustainability of all life on the planet.

In terms of specialisation, two aspects may be considered. We enter here the old debate on the division of labour from the point of view of a long-term rationale that is not individualistic. First, when co-operatives consider scaling up or reacting to new or more complex social, economic and cultural needs, they can respond with organisational innovation without having to become one huge vertical unit. Thanks to their characteristics, type of model and governance, they can encourage spin-offs of members to form new co-operatives; create secondary level and/or multi-stakeholder co-operatives; and establish networks and consortia with other co-operatives and stakeholders. As co-operatives comprise members, some of them may leave the original co-operative to set up a new one or may be detached to another existing co-operative. It is not about specialising by task but by area or field of activity. In the case of a workers' co-operative, it is not about working in an assembly line under vertical control but about self-organising work in an enterprise where workers are both members and owners. Some co-operatives promote internal task specialisation but others implement multi-task skilling with shifting roles. Specialisation within a co-operative grouping where primary co-operatives remain autonomous is done via areas of activity, while solidarity within the grouping is exercised through solidarity mechanisms. These could include savings, cross-checks, monitoring and/or consultancy, training, support services, guarantees, and social, innovation and restructuring funds, among others. Indeed, co-operatives can replicate their co-operative model with other stakeholders. Through the multiplication of primary co-operatives, they can remain rather small and embedded across the territory and society. Through co-operative networks and consortia, they are able to mutualise support resources. Through spin-offs and higher-level co-operatives, they can innovate, specialise in specific activities, enter new ones or upgrade skills and knowledge.

As a call for further debate and engagement, a debt trap is similar to an ecological overshoot, displaying a systemic trajectory that is no longer sustainable, but rather leads to systemic failure. To avoid it, we must imagine and chart another trajectory, distinguishing markets and capital from capitalism, analysing how capital in all forms (social, human, cultural, intellectual, financial, natural and environmental) is truly valued. We need to discuss new ways to sustainably generate genuine value leading to general and common wealth. To achieve this, we need to be critically aware of, and focus on, how we organise our economic lives.

Notes

1 This chapter is grounded on the research published in the book *Capital and the Debt Trap* (Sanchez Bajo and Roelants 2011). The book provides an explanation of the global crisis that broke out in 2007 and why co-operatives have been showing a relatively higher degree of resilience compared with other types of enterprise, generating genuine value and general wealth in a sustainable manner.

2 The CDOs were the trigger of the financial crisis (see Sanchez Bajo and Roelants 2011: Box 1.1, Chapter 1).

3 The G20 summit held in Los Cabos, Mexico, on 18–19 June 2012 was very light in results, and the G20 meeting of finance ministers and central bankers in Moscow in mid-February 2013 included a heated debate about exchange rates being utilised to further exports. The latter meeting recognised the lack of global demand and high unemployment.

4 On 7 January 2013, it was decided to let EU and US banks meet only 60 per cent of their liquidity coverage ratio by 2015 and 100 per cent in 2019, instead of 2013. Other countries that were pressed to implement Basle III find implementation uneven. It signalled that the crisis was not over, stringent rules affected recovery, and banks cannot deleverage at this stage.

5 See the concept of control in IFRS 3 and IFRS 10 at www.iasplus.com. For an alternative view to the IFRS conceptual framework, see Whittington (2008).

6 On 17 March 2013, Cyprus agreed to the terms of a €10 billion bailout (RTE News 2013).

7 The 'Minder' solution approved by the Swiss vote was 'to give the general assembly of shareholders the power to approve all compensation packages to board members and the company leadership' (Sydney Morning Herald 2013).

8 In economics, the principal–agent theory is linked to the differentiation between ownership and control, and the difficulties in motivating one side (the 'agent', in this case the manager) to act in the best interests of another (the 'principal', in this case the shareholder or owner of the firm).

9 I use 'sparing' instead of austere, since 'austere' is now a euphemism for structural reforms.

References

Anderson S., J. Cavanagh and J. Redman (2008) *Skewed Priorities: How the bailouts dwarf other global crisis spending*. Washington, DC: Institute for Policy Studies.

Bank of England (2013) 'Private equity and financial stability'. *Quarterly Bulletin* 2013 Q1. www.bankofengland.co.uk/publications/Documents/quarterlybulletin/2013/qb130104.pdf.

Barford, V. and G. Holt (2013) 'Google, Amazon, Starbucks: the rise of "tax shaming"'. BBC News Magazine, 21 May. www.bbc.co.uk/news/magazine-20560359.

BBC News (2008) 'Credit Agricole hit by sub-prime'. BBC news, 5 March. http://news.bbc.co.uk/2/hi/business/7278702.stm.

Birchall, J. and L. Hammond Ketilson (2009) *Resilience of the Cooperative Business Model in Times of Crisis*. Sustainable Enterprise Programme. Geneva: International Labour Organization (ILO).

Buettner, T. and G. Wamser (2009) *Internal Debt and Multinationals' Profit Shifting: Empirical evidence from firm-level panel data*. WP 09/18. Oxford: Oxford University Centre for Business Taxation.

BVCA and PWC (2003) *A Guide to Private Equity*. London: BVCA and PricewaterhouseCoopers (PWC).

CICOPA (2012) *The Resilience of the Cooperative Model: How worker cooperatives, social cooperatives and other worker-owned enterprises respond to the crisis and its consequences*. Brussels: CICOPA. www.cicopa.co-op/IMG/pdf/raport_cicopa_2012_en_v06.pdf

Coombes, A. (2008) 'Given turmoil at banks, time may be right to try a credit union'. *Market Watch*, 27 April. www.marketwatch.com/story/given-turmoil-at-banks-time-may-be-right-to-try-a-credit-union.

Deloitte (2013) 'International GAAP Holdings Limited: model financial statement for the year ended 31 December 2013'. www.iasplus.com.

Elliott, L. (2013) 'George Osborne's Help to Buy scheme "a moronic policy"'. *Guardian*, 4 June. www.guardian. co.uk/business/2013/jun/04/george-osborne-help-to-buy-moronic.

Evans-Pritchard, A. (2010) 'Capital controls eyed as global currency wars escalate'. *Daily Telegraph*, 29 September. www.telegraph.co.uk/finance/economics/8031203/Capital-controls-eyed-as-global-currency-wars-escalate.html.

Financial Times (2010) 'West inflates EM super bubble'. *Financial Times*, 30 September. http://video.ft.com/v/620158442001/West-inflates-EM-superbubble.

Forslund, E. and D. Johansson (2012) *Gaussian Copula: What happens when models fail?* Gothenburg: Chalmers University of Technology. www.math.chalmers.se/~rootzen/finrisk/gr15_forslund_johansson_gaussian_cop.pdf.

Guardian (2012) 'EU group votes to curb high-frequency trades'. *Guardian*, 26 September.

IMF (2012) 'The liberalization and management of capital flows: an institutional view'. International Monetary Fund (IMF), 3 December. www.imf.org/external/np/sec/pn/2012/pn12137.htm and www.imf.org/external/np/pp/eng/2012/111412.pdf.

Lam, T. V. (2012) '22 million Americans are unemployed or can't find full-time work'. Planet Money, 4 May. www.npr.org/blogs/money/2012/05/04/151936447/23-million-americans-are-unemployed-or-cant-find-full-time-work.

Laurence, P. (2013) 'Belgium protests over German low pay in EU complaint'. BBC News, 9 April. www.bbc.co.uk/news/world-europe-22080862.

Nelson, F. (2013) 'Slavery, not horse meat, is the real scandal on our doorstep'. *Telegraph*, 14 February. www.telegraph.co.uk/foodanddrink/foodanddrinknews/9870692/Slavery-not-horse-meat-is-the-real-scandal-on-our-doorstep.html.

Ostrom, E. (1990) *Governing the Commons: The evolution of institutions for collective action*. New York, NY: Cambridge University Press.

RTE News (2013) 'Cypriot president says bankruptcy was alternative to €10bn bailout terms'. RTE News, 17 March.

Sanchez Bajo, C. and B. Roelants (2011) *Capital and the Debt Trap: Learning from co-operatives in the global crisis*. Basingstoke: Palgrave Macmillan.

St Louis Federal Reserve Bank (2013) 'US map of failed banks: 2007 to present'. Economic Research. http://research.stlouisfed.org/maps/failed_banks.php (accessed 6 March 2013).

Sydney Morning Herald (2013) 'Swiss vote in favour of golden parachute ban'. *Sydney Morning Herald*, 4 March. www.smh.com.au/business/world-business/swiss-vote-in-favour-of-golden-parachute-ban-20130304-2ff46.html#ixzz2OBcckB2O.

Tietz, J. (2011) 'Loophole for cheap labor: Amazon accused of systematic job subsidy abuse'. Spiegel Online, 28 November. www.spiegel.de/international/business/loophole-for-cheap-labor-amazon-accused-of-systematic-job-subsidy-abuse-a-800408.html.

Whittington, G. (2008) 'Fair value and the IASB/FASB conceptual framework project: an alternative view'. *Abacus* 44(2): 139–68.

Zacune, J. (2013) *Privatising Europe: Using the crisis to entrench neoliberalism. A working paper*. Amsterdam: Transnational Institute.

CONCLUSION

Sonja Novkovic and Tom Webb

The co-operative form of organisation is markedly different from the investor-owned enterprise. It is based on the needs of a group of people who seek the necessary resources to jointly address particular issues (employment, access to finance, access to markets, risk reduction, service provision, etc.) through a business enterprise. The co-operative firm is therefore people-centred,[1] as opposed to capital-centred; democratically governed and controlled; and a long-term collective problem-solver, rather than a short-term means to amass financial wealth. Members have an interest in securing the viability of the business in the long run, as their communities often depend on it.

In an economy such as ours, prone to crisis and guided by policies and institutions that foster short-term economic goals, what is the role for co-operatives? Where and how can they survive, and what corrective roles can they play in a market economy?

Setting the stage

The dominant economic model and global institutions supporting it are facing challenges that are difficult to solve with the policies of the 'Washington consensus' or the post-consensus austerity measures producing 'jobless recoveries'. Our understanding of the aggregate demand-induced growth fuelled by consumerism has also been brought into question as evidence mounts that this is not the road to progress, or happiness. Reliance on fossil fuels has caused irreparable damage to the environment and has impoverished natural resources, with dramatic effects on societies and indigenous cultures as well as social and biological diversity. Depletion of the regional and global commons has been accompanied by speculative financial bubbles, exceeding the real economy fifty-fold (see Max-Neef, Chapter 1). The neoclassical economic paradigm relying purely on monetary incentives to induce 'rational' economic behaviour, with ensuing built-in measures of progress and success, resulted in policies that hindered economic development (Max-Neef, Chapter 1; Colman 2012); created and exacerbated income inequality (Wilkinson and Pickett 2009); jeopardised job creation (Goodwin, Chapter 2); resulted in an ecological and financial overshoot (Rees, Chapter 4; Victor, Chapter 5; Fullerton, Chapter 7); and deepened the ongoing debt crisis (Sanchez Bajo, Chapter 14). Steadily increasing and more concentrated wealth and entrenched power fed inequality and exacerbated poverty traps. For many decades now, a false comfort in capitalism's provision of 'equality of opportunity' as the mechanism to reach economic success has enabled the status quo, with blind trust in unfettered markets that have reduced government ability to regulate the economy to its bare bones. Yet it was precisely the stifling of government action that led to the 2008 economic collapse and the demands that governments had to bail out the banks and corporations grown too big to fail. Neoliberal policies produced a system for privatising profits and socialising losses for the wealthiest 20 per cent but are increasingly paralysed when it comes to the provision of the common good.

The tide seems to be turning, although, arguably, not fast enough. The global civil society is demanding change specifically with respect to social justice, democracy and the relevant economic and political institutions. Citizens are 'occupying' public spaces; they are also occupying jobs and the right to work. There is an underlying understanding that human meaning and dignity derive from self-realisation through meaningful work, and from sufficient income to meet basic material needs coupled with the ability of individuals to contribute to their families, communities and society.

Citizens around the world demand true political and economic democracy, with decision-making directed to meeting people's needs and based on the one person one vote principle, rather than one dollar one vote. There is also a developing understanding that political democracy will deteriorate in the absence of economic democracy, with calls to redraft the social contract and redefine the role of government.

Lastly, social economies, grass-roots systems and institutions are being developed around the globe. People are establishing social economy institutions, including co-operatives, barter economies, local alternative currencies and trading blocs built on solidarity, partly as a result of open spaces left by crippled governments pulling out of their traditional welfare provision role, and partly due to the rejuvenated push to change the institutional status quo. In light of the evidence that private ownership of the limited natural resources (the 'policy of choice' during the decades of neoliberal fundamentalism) does not result in socially optimal solutions, a re-examination of ownership regimes is demanding renewed access for people to the common resources of the planet. This means increased reliance on the control of the commons by the people who depend on them for their livelihood, as well as an increasing share of the global economy in the hands of co-operative and other democratic social economy enterprises (Allen, Chapter 13). Against this backdrop, there is a renewed interest in the co-operative form of organisation and an opportunity to 'humanise the economy' with the co-operative model at its centre (Zamagni, Chapter 8).

Shaping the new economy

The new economic paradigm would rest on some key principles (see below) that would steer the economy away from the current separation of social from economic spheres of influence and towards socio-ecological economics that recognise that 'The economy is a subsystem of a human social system; and that, in turn, is a subsystem of the ecological context. Each of these systems affects, and is affected by, the others' (Goodwin, Chapter 2).

'Asking what a sustainable economy and social system would look like if they were designed to maximise human well-being' (Wilkinson and Pickett, Chapter 3), the new economic paradigm needs to be built for a human-scale economy (Max-Neef, Chapter 1). With a growing need to shift from existing economic systems to systems that are socially and environmentally just and sustainable (Goodwin, Chapter 2), suggestions for the underlying principles of such an economy include the following:

- people-centred;
- steady-state growth;
- localised;

- built on social relationships;
- reducing inequality;
- economic democracy;
- ethical finance; and
- sustainability and resilience.

What can co-operatives contribute to such an economy?

Co-operatives and the 'new economy'

Co-operatives fill many of the gaps required for the functioning of the new economy and have a great deal to contribute to the new economic thinking. Their purpose and organisation serve as a stabiliser of current economic trends (see, for example, Pérotin 2012). Co-operatives can be the leaders of change in partnerships with like-minded organisations, since they are satisfying member needs rather than pursuing a return on investment for shareholders, and since their shares are not traded in increasingly dysfunctional financial capital markets. Their underlying values unify across geographical, religious, linguistic, ethnic and social divides.[2] A set of principles and interconnectedness rooted in solidarity, equity and equality form the framework for productivity gains coupled with positive social impacts, but, to achieve that effectively, co-operatives need to use measures of progress and accounting based on their identity and that feed into the measures of well-being, rather than measures of just the economic value-added (Colman 2012).

Following the underlying principles of the new economic paradigm highlighted by the authors of chapters in this volume and by presenters at the Imagine 2012 conference in Quebec City, we illustrate the aspects of co-operative organisation that fit well with the new economic paradigm.

People-centred It has become clear that one aspect of the economy has been neglected in the global policies of the twentieth century – the economy needs to serve people and their needs, not the other way around. Manfred Max-Neef (Chapter 1) adds the underlying value of the new economic paradigm that: 'No economic interest, under any circumstance, can be above the reverence for life.' In a world where economic relationships are defined by the supremacy of private property rights over the common resources, with grave social implications, this aspect of our lives has been shifting into uncharted waters.

Co-operatives, as champions of collective ownership and democratic problem-solving, are people-centred by their very nature, and can contribute to the effective management of the commons. Besides, capital plays the supporting role rather than being a driving force of the business. Personal benefit is secured through the collective gain, and the latter cannot be just the sum of its parts, as assumed in neoclassical economics.

Steady-state growth paradigm Permanent exponential growth is impossible given the limits of the economy as a subsystem of a finite biosphere (Max-Neef, Chapter 1; Goodwin, Chapter 2; Rees, Chapter 4; Victor, Chapter 5; Fullerton, Chapter 7). It has become clear that our global economy needs to reduce the use of non-renewable resources. Moreover, the evidence points out that economic growth in the rich countries is no longer a source of increases in well-being (Wilkinson and Pickett, Chapter 3), and development is not necessarily correlated to growth (Max-Neef, Chapter 1). National income as a measure of market activity is, therefore, not necessarily a good measure of progress. Alternative measures have been developed, such as the Genuine Progress Indicator, and measures of well-being and happiness (Colman 2012; Max-Neef, Chapter 1).

The driver of growth is the pursuit of scale economies and profitability on the supply side, and consumerism feeding the economy from the demand side, with pervasive pressure from financial markets. Both these effects can be mitigated by co-operatives through ethical business practices on both sides of the market – producers securing jobs, remaining small,[3] and correcting market imperfections (the 'competitive yardstick' effect of co-operation: Nourse 1992); and consumer co-operatives increasing consumer surplus rather than the return on investment. These behaviours do not exert growth pressure on the economy in the way that the investor-driven model does; because co-operative shares are not publicly traded, they are not under the constant pressure to show increased short-term profits. The co-operative firm can, therefore, be successful without growth.[4] The measure of success for co-operatives is not their extent of market activity, but the impact of their activities on their members and society. As such, positive and negative externalities[5] of co-operative business ought to be measured and reported. Ideally, they would feed into the macro-economic calculation of well-being that includes social and ecological impacts of economic activity.

Localised economy A locally entrenched economy is more likely to internalise the externalities, provide long-term jobs, and secure a quality of services that cannot be matched by absentee business owners. Small businesses in general are likely to fit the bill, but co-operatives are rooted in their local community by definition.[6] Democratic governance of co-operatives and their community focus often give them an edge as community enterprises. However, co-operatives can also form partnerships with diverse democratic businesses in the social and solidarity economy to create a vibrant local economy. The agility and adaptability of a co-operative often depend on its networks, from the level of social capital and community support it can draw on, through solidarity systems and mechanisms that rest on social relationships. The spreading of risk is realised through second-tier networks of enterprises rooted in the community.

Social relationships Features of a localised economy feed into the requirement that the economy should be built on social relationships in order to shift from overdependence on consumption and material sources of satisfaction to having community and relationships as the main sources of well-being and happiness (Wilkinson and Pickett, Chapter 3; Layard 2005; Helliwell 2001). The Erdal study (Chapter 11) suggests that 'conventionally structured firms are at odds with human nature, both in the social relationships involved and in the distribution of wealth ... while workers' co-operatives and employee-owned firms suit human nature in ways that lead to widespread prosperity, healthier communities, deeper individual satisfaction and longer lives'. The question of what is measured and what outcomes are pursued comes to the fore. Investor-ownership (coupled with consumerism) is fed by the need to increase demand and revenues in order to register economic growth – the be-all and end-all of our perceived economic success.

Reducing inequality Wilkinson and Pickett (2009; Chapter 3) point out research findings that show the alarming increase in income inequality and a direct correlation between inequality and social externalities, such as increased crime, reduced life expectancy, health issues and many others. To the extent that inequality arises due to misguided corporate incentives, co-operatives by design set a more equitable pay ratio than investor-owned firms. There is extensive literature on the small gap between the highest- and lowest-paid workers in the large and successful Mondragon industrial co-operative group in the Basque country in Spain, and income inequality is significantly lower among the co-operative communities of Emilia-Romagna than in other Italian regions (Erdal, Chapter 11). However, a market economy, co-operative or otherwise, is bound to create some inequalities and regional and sector discrepancies in wealth accumulation. Supportive income redistribution policies are therefore necessary to ensure a more equitable society, although a strong presence of co-operatives would no doubt reduce inequalities caused by intra-firm income differentials.

Economic democracy[7] The theoretical underpinnings of behavioural economics (Altman, Chapter 9) suggest that democratic workplaces increase productivity and offset the potentially higher costs of ethical practices in co-operatives.[8] An abundance of evidence further supports the notion that employee-owned systems increase productivity; however, democratic control is necessary for a long-term positive effect of ownership (Sanchez Bajo, Chapter 14).

Member-owned and -controlled enterprises draw on the social capital of their members for innovation, direction (risk-taking or risk avoidance), cost reduction and creation of social value. More importantly, democratic governance of firms is more likely to result in transparency and accountability that is increasingly demanded by civil society, in light of the abuse of power and misappropriation of resources by the entrepreneurial elite in both publicly traded investor-owned companies and non-democratic social enterprises (Bateman and Novkovic 2013).

Ethical finance for the new economy The current global financial system is in overshoot (Fullerton, Chapter 7; Rees, Chapter 4), having morphed from a system that supports the real economy to one with a life of its own. The new economic paradigm needs a finance with a role 'as servant to, not master of, an economy that operates within finite ecological boundaries' (Fullerton, Chapter 7).

At the same time, co-operative finance ought to satisfy the co-operative purpose: it serves as the means rather than an end of production (Robb et al. 2010; Scalvini 2011); it is subordinated to human needs; the nature of investment is long term, patient capital; and maximising the return on capital cannot be the aim of the co-operative.[9] Evidence in the aftermath of the global economic crisis shows that:

> co-operatives tend to distinguish between strategic investment in the real economy and financial risk, and thus respond to inequality and steer away from a consumption trap as their aim is to develop the community and have a healthy equity basis ... Consumer co-operatives and credit unions do not typically engage in predatory practices that lead to their members' indebtedness. Workers' co-operatives will not engage in risky financial mechanisms, as members are both workers and owners of the business (Sanchez Bajo, Chapter 14; Sanchez Bajo and Roelants 2011).

Co-operatives need to access capital to significantly increase their economic presence and impact, especially in capital-intensive sectors; to do this effectively and to maintain member control they will need to develop new forms of capital with different behaviours and characteristics than those of investor-driven capital. Rather than being speculative, co-operative capital must be of a 'patient' kind – seeking a fair, limited return while at the same time respecting co-operative values and principles (Robb et al. 2010). With the growing interest in responsible investment and with more than a billion co-operative members around the world, this is an area of opportunity that the co-operative movement has to seize.[10]

Sustainability and resilience

> 'Getting better is better than getting bigger.' (William Rees, Chapter 4)

The sustainability imperative highlighted in many of this book's chapters clearly points out the reasons why we need a shift in economic paradigm. Measuring economic growth does not set off the alarm bells that would sound in the presence of stress leading to economic crisis if we used measures of genuine progress, which include externalities and non-market assets (Colman 2012; Max-Neef, Chapter 1). The issue is systemic, and therefore the requirements of new economic thinking for a sustainable economy and society include more than just a change in metrics. Some of the required changes in the way we think about the economy are the consideration of equity, rather than efficiency; pursuing an optimal scale under socio-ecological constraints, rather than the maximum scale; qualitative improvements rather than capital accumulation; understanding complementarities between different types of capital (natural, social and physical); and preserving adequate physical stocks of capital (Rees, Chapter 4: Table 4.2).

But the proverbial 'elephant in the room' is the untouchable and unchallenged private gain from ownership of natural resources stimulated by the neoliberal economic paradigm. Until our global economies put a ban on market trading of land, fossil fuels, minerals, water, air and the natural commons, our chances for a paradigm shift are slim. Co-operative ownership can be a part of the solution, under the assumption that common resources cannot be demutualised or depleted.

Considering that our socio-ecological systems are complex and poorly understood (Homer-Dixon, Chapter 6), the potential damage that could be caused by excessive resource extraction and, as a result, by a crisis-prone economic and political system is immense. Creating resilient systems with flexible components is therefore an essential part of building sustainable economies. Community ownership of common resources, we argue, would reduce risk and increase resilience (see Allen, Chapter 13).

Co-operatives can clearly thrive within the sustainability paradigm; however, they operate in hostile capitalist markets under the pressure of competition, predatory pricing and lack of appropriate regulation. Not unlike their counterparts in the investor-owned world, co-operative managers face uncertainty and deal with risk. Playing a leadership role in the global society and economy by using co-operative values and principles as guidelines through complex adaptation[11] is one component of the co-operative advantage that has, to date, been only partially realised. Increasing complexity, risk and uncertainty require agile system components held together by a common purpose and values.

Conclusion

While co-operatives are a flexible model fit for the micro-economic foundation of the new economy, the co-operative movement is not without its challenges. Among them, we highlight the treatment of co-operatives in economic theory, co-operative growth, and governance for the new economy.

Co-operatives in economic theory Neoclassical dominance in twentieth-century economics resulted in the use of inadequate assumptions to build the economic theory of co-operatives, causing serious damage to the study and understanding of the co-operative economic model. Starting from the self-centred individual decision-maker, the theory of the day assumed that individuals only cared to maximise their own incomes (Vanek 1970; Ward 1958). This was later supplemented with agency theory and transaction costs to explain why co-operatives form or fail (Dow 2003). The collective nature of ownership and decision-making in co-operatives was often blamed for their inefficiency and ultimately their failure,[12] despite contrary evidence (see Bonin et al. 1993 for an overview of decades of research on this issue).

More recently, findings in behavioural economics and economic psychology have offered concepts such as trust, reciprocity and intrinsic motivations that help us to better understand co-operative organisations (Altman, Chapter 9; Negri Zamagni, Chapter 10), their formation, success or failure, but they also offer findings of behavioural diversity that are suggestive of a need for the right 'fit' between a co-operative organisation and its members (Ben-Ner and Ellman 2013). Concepts such as the 'dual motives' theory (Lynne 2006) are valuable in defining the co-operative difference (Novkovic 2012) in light of the overlapping social and economic goals of co-operatives. New policy options are also available as there is increasing evidence that people take other interests into consideration when they make their economic decisions, and that they are 'predictably irrational' (Thaler and Sunstein 2008) when making long-term decisions. Based on those findings, 'nudging' individuals into behaviours that benefit society in the long run is often a more viable solution, and one that is typically embedded in the co-operative structure.[13]

Besides behavioural economics, the work of Elinor and Vincent Ostrom brought to the fore a need for diversity in governance and decision-making, particularly with commonly owned or used resources (Allen, Chapter 13). Importantly, they posited the notion of multi-layered and self-defined governance by resource users as being key to successful collective decision-making, countering private ownership as a panacea for efficiency.

Co-operative growth The particular challenge for co-operatives and their long-term viability is how they approach growth. While co-operatives engage in organic growth, opt for a spin-off model or enlarge their member base by mergers, they also pursue aggressive, highly capitalised growth strategies, especially when faced with increased competition. Increasingly, large co-operatives go beyond the 'traditional' member-capitalisation methods and tap into capital markets. This strategy carries the danger of undue influence of capital, since democratic control by user-members of a co-operative implies a supporting role for capital as a means to fulfil the purpose of the co-operative.

This risk is especially true if the capital employed has the characteristics of traditional investor capital and seeks, solely or primarily, maximum return. The growth strategy we suggest, in light of the wide-ranging challenges raised in this volume, is for co-operatives globally to commit themselves to enlarging the co-operative share of the total economy using capital whose behaviour and characteristics are consistent with co-operative identity. This means creating pools of 'co-operative capital' (Robb et al. 2010) that are sufficient to expand their share of economic activity and enable the use of the co-operative business model in capital-intensive industries.

As part of this effort, systems and rules have to be in place to secure member control, and to avoid isomorphism, or demutualisation. Preventing a focus on the 'return on investment' at the expense of 'user (purpose)' focus and ensuring control by (user-)members are the implications of successful governance and management of change in co-operatives. They are also imperatives in the context of a new economic paradigm, and a sustainable economy.

Effective democratic governance Co-operative governance must reflect the co-operative's democratic nature and member control, but also ensure its long-term viability as a co-operative (see the International Symposium on Co-operative Governance 2013).

Co-operatives experience tremendous competitive, regulatory and educational pressure to emulate the business and governance practices of investor-owned firms. Not surprisingly, they are exposed to strong oligarchic tendencies.[14] Strong governance that engages members ensures that co-operatives stay focused on meeting member and community needs, and that in turn increases the likelihood of co-operative success. However, much work needs to be done internally, as well as with educational systems, to promote innovation in co-operative business practice that is consistent with the co-operative model.

Co-operation among co-operatives, which is one of the principles, includes the formation of federations, second-tier co-operatives, supply chain networks, and other complex co-operative networking arrangements (Novkovic 2013). A co-operative hallmark, networking is a means to an agile, sustainable economy. Network governance is, of course, a challenge. Democratic processes on a large scale need to be carefully weighed (Birchall 2014), but overall the key aspect of the co-operative network governance model is the principle of subsidiarity, with decisions made at the lowest possible level in the hierarchy. A polycentric system of self-governance, as argued by Ostrom (see Allen, Chapter 13) enables democracy and fits well with co-operative values.

This tendency to liaise, built on the relations of trust, solidarity and reciprocity, should, in theory, facilitate co-creation of policy and links with other democratic social economy organisations and community enterprises that share the co-operative values. In line with Vincent Ostrom's thinking (Allen, Chapter 13; Wagner 2005), governance is a bottom-up construct, and a must for resilient local economies. Self-defined rules in co-operatives present the potential foundation of a 'model of participative government in place of an interventionist one' (Ostrom 1991) as an appealing building block of the new economy.

Co-operative economics?

In order to build a convincing co-operative economic paradigm, the co-operative movement will have to devise institutional solutions to some of the issues discussed in this volume. The strategy outlined in the *Blueprint for a Co-operative Decade* (ICA 2012) is a good start.

Some components of co-operative economics outlined by various authors in this volume rest on common ownership of resources; user control; polycentric (network) governance; 'de-incentivised' capital for investment in common pool resources; enabling an institutional set-up for the development of social capital, trust and reciprocity; and 'nudging' to induce socially optimal behaviour. The outcomes of these settings are greater income equality; a socially just allocation of resources; the creation of more meaningful jobs; business longevity; induced care for the environment and community; sustainable growth; and a transformation of economic goals and outcomes (see Erdal, Chapter 11; Smith and Rothbaum, Chapter 12).

But, as most co-operatives have developed in capitalist economies, with increasingly more concentrated markets, some current institutional developments in co-operatives promote the status quo in the economy. Therefore, some challenging questions for the co-operative movement remain relevant. Is 'labour for hire' acceptable in co-operative economic systems or should workers share in membership? Is venture capital an acceptable investment form? Co-operative economics needs supporting institutions, from legal frameworks to norms and self-governing rules. Until these questions are answered, a unifying co-operative economic paradigm may remain an elusive goal.

Notes

1 'People-centred' implies a focus on human needs as consumers, service users, workers or producers rather than as owners of capital.

2 Co-operatives have been built on the organisational values of solidarity, equity, equality and mutual self-help, and the personal member values of honesty, openness, social responsibility and caring for others (International Co-operative Alliance statement of co-operative identity at www.ica.coop). By accepting the co-operative organisational form, they are expected to follow the co-operative principles of: voluntary and open membership; democratic

member control; member economic participation; autonomy and independence; education, training and information; co-operation among co-operatives; and concern for community.

3 Co-operative growth strategies can be markedly different from the investor-owned model, as they reach scale through networks, or through new, spin-off co-operatives.

4 Growth in this context is understood as expansion based on capital.

5 Externalities are the unintended effects of economic activity on various stakeholders.

6 Exceptions to this rule are virtual

co-operatives, and co-operatives whose members share a 'community of interest' rather than a location.

7 See Erdal (Chapter 11), Altman (Chapter 9), and Wilkinson and Pickett (Chapter 3).

8 These include practices such as the living wage policy, increased employee benefits, and the purchase of fairly traded inputs.

9 This is already the purpose of the investor-owned business model.

10 The *Blueprint for a Cooperative Decade* was launched in November 2012. One of the pillars of the blueprint is access to co-operative capital (see www.ica.coop).

11 Homer-Dixon (Chapter 6) describes complex adaptation as adjustments that happen between shocks, when societies develop new ideas and experiment with new forms of economic and social arrangements they might want to implement during the next shock.

12 This is in line with Hardin's infamous 'tragedy of the commons', where a lack of 'well defined' or private ownership supposedly causes resource overuse (see Allen (Chapter 13)).

13 As an example, the non-divisible capital reserves are a default option in many co-operatives, indicating that members care about the long-term viability of the co-operative, as opposed to pursuing the short-term personal gain claimed by the neoclassical paradigm.

14 Vincent Ostrom noted: 'Beyond a very small threshold, deliberative bodies depend upon someone to preside and exercise control over an agenda and maintain ordered deliberations ... All democratic assemblies are subject to strong oligarchic tendencies that increase with size' (Ostrom 1991: 205).

References

Bateman, M. and S. Novkovic (2013) 'Cooperatives as agents of collective entrepreneurship: reflections on the rise of the social enterprise phenomenon'. Paper presented at the 43rd Atlantic Schools of Business conference (ASB), Antigonish, Nova Scotia, 27–29 September.

Ben-Ner, A. and M. Ellman (2013) 'The contributions of behavioural economics to understanding and advancing the sustainability of worker cooperatives'. *Journal of Entrepreneurial and Organizational Diversity* 2(1): 75–100.

Birchall, J. (2014) *The Governance of Large Co-operative Businesses: A research study for Co-operatives UK*. Manchester: Co-operatives UK. www.uk.coop/sites/storage/public/down loads/the_governance_of_large_cooperatives_o.pdf.

Bonin, J., D. Jones and L. Putterman (1993) 'Theoretical and empirical studies of producer cooperatives: will ever the twain meet?' *Journal of Economic Literature* 31(3): 1290–320.

Colman, R. (2012) 'Are we better off? Can our current measurement and accounting system answer that question?' Paper presented at the Imagine 2012 conference, Quebec City.

Dow, G. (2003) *Governing the Firm: Workers' control in theory and practice*. Cambridge: Cambridge University Press.

Helliwell, J. (2001) *How's Life? Combining individual and national variables to explain subjective well-being*. NBER Working Paper W9065. Cambridge, MA: National Bureau of Economic Research (NBER).

ICA (2012) *Blueprint for a Co-operative Decade*. Geneva: International Co-operative Alliance (ICA). http://ica.coop/sites/default/files/media_items/ICA%20Blueprint%20-%20 Final%20version%20issued%207% 20Feb%2013.pdf.

International Symposium on Co-operative Governance (2013) *Themes and Recommendations from the International Co-operative Governance Symposium*. Halifax: Saint Mary's University. www.smu.ca/webfiles/Report_InternationalSymposium_CooperativeGovernance-2013_SSBSMU_Web.pdf.

Layard, R. (2005) *Happiness: Lessons from a new science*. London: Penguin Books.

Lynne, G. (2006) 'Toward a dual motive metaeconomic theory'. *Journal of Socio-economics* 35: 634–51.

Nourse, E. G. (1992) 'The place of the cooperative in our national economy: reprint from American Cooperation 1942 to 1945'. *Journal of Agricultural Cooperation* 7: 105–11.

Novkovic, S. (2012) 'The balancing act: reconciling the economic and social goals of co-operatives'. In E. Molina and M. Robicheaud (eds), *The Amazing Power of Cooperatives*. Quebec City: International Summit of Cooperatives, pp. 289–300.

— (2013) 'Co-operative networks and organizational innovation'. In C. Gijselinckx, L. Zhao and S. Novkovic (eds), *Cooperative Innovations in China and the West*. Basingstoke: Palgrave Macmillan.

Ostrom, V. (1991) *The Meaning of American Federalism*. San Francisco, CA: ICS Press.

Pérotin, V. (2012) 'Workers' cooperatives: good, sustainable jobs in the community'. Paper presented at the Euricse-ICA international conference 'Promoting the Understanding of Cooperatives for a Better World', Venice, 15 March.

Robb, A., J. Smith and T. Webb (2010) 'Co-operative capital and why our world needs it'. Paper presented at the Financial Co-operative Approaches to Local Development Through Sustainable Innovation conference, Euricse, Trento, 10–11 June.

Sanchez Bajo, C. and B. Roelants (2011) *Capital and the Debt Trap: Learning from co-operatives in the global crisis*. Basingstoke: Palgrave Macmillan.

Scalvini, F. (2011) 'Keynote address'. CICOPA North America conference: 'Cooperation without Borders', Quebec City, 13–15 October.

Thaler, R. and C. Sunstein (2008) *Nudge: Improving decisions about health, wealth, and happiness*. New Haven, CT: Yale University Press.

Vanek, J. (1970) *The General Theory of Labour-managed Market Economies*. Ithaca, NY: Cornell University Press.

Wagner, R. (2005) 'Self-governance, polycentrism, and federalism: recurring themes in Vincent Ostrom's scholarly oeuvre'. *Journal of Economic Behavior and Organization* 57: 173–88.

Ward, B. (1958) 'The firm in Illyria: market syndicalism'. *American Economic Review* 48: 566–89.

Wilkinson, R. and K. Pickett (2009) *The Spirit Level: Why more equal societies almost always do better*. London: Allen Lane.

ABOUT THE CONTRIBUTORS

Barbara Allen is Ada M. Harrison Distinguished Teaching Professor of the Social Sciences, professor and former chair of the Department of Political Science, Carleton, and Director of Women's Studies at Carleton College, Northfield, MN. She is also Senior Research Fellow of the Vincent and Elinor Ostrom Workshop in Political Theory and Policy Analysis at Indiana University.

Morris Altman is Professor of Behavioral and Institutional Economics and head of the School of Economics and Finance at Victoria University in Wellington, New Zealand. He is also Professor of Economics at the University of Saskatchewan, Canada. A former visiting scholar at Cambridge, Cornell, Duke, Hebrew and Stanford universities, he served as editor of the *Journal of Socio-economics* for ten years and is currently the editor of the *Review of Behavioral Economics*.

David Erdal was born into a family that owned a paper manufacturer and in 1985 took over as head of the 1,500-employee firm, Tullis Russell, and led its full employee-buyout in 1994. His most recent book is *Beyond the Corporation: Humanity working*.

John Fullerton is the founder and president of the Capital Institute. He had an eighteen-year career at JPMorgan during which he managed multiple capital markets and derivatives businesses and venture capital investment activity. He is currently a director of Investors Circle and New Day Farms, Inc., and an adviser to Natural Systems Utilities. He is a participant in and author of the United Nations Environment Programme's Green Economy report.

Neva Goodwin is co-director of the Global Development and Environment Institute at Tufts University. In her books (*Microeconomics in Context*, *Macroeconomics in Context*, and *Principles of Economics in Context*) and in other publications, she is developing theories of economics that will have more relevance to real-world concerns than does the dominant economic paradigm.

Thomas Homer-Dixon holds the Centre for International Governance Innovation Chair of Global Systems at the Balsillie School of International Affairs in Waterloo, Canada. He is author of *The Upside of Down* and *The Ingenuity Gap*.

Manfred Max-Neef began his career as Professor of Economics at the University of California, Berkeley, served as rector of the Universidad Austral de Chile and teaches and lectures globally. He received the Right Livelihood Award in 1983. In 1981 he published *From the Outside Looking In: Experiences in barefoot economics* and in 1991 *Human Scale Development*.

Vera Negri Zamagni is Professor of Economic History at the University of Bologna and a visiting professor of European Economic History at the Bologna Centre of the Johns Hopkins University. His recent publications include *Cooperative Enterprise: Facing the challenge of globalization*, co-authored with Stefano Zamagni, *L'industria chimica italiana e l'IMI* and *Finmeccanica*.

Kate Pickett is Professor of Epidemiology in the Department of Health Sciences at the University of York in the UK. She was a UK National Institute for Health Research Career Scientist from 2007 to 2012 and is a fellow of the Royal Society for the encouragement of Arts, Manufactures and Commerce and of the UK Faculty of Public Health. She is co-author of *The Spirit Level* and a co-founder of the Equality Trust.

William E. Rees is Professor Emeritus at the University of British Columbia's School of Community and Regional Planning and is the originator of 'ecological footprint analysis' set out in *Our Ecological Footprint*, co-authored with Mathis Wackernagel. He is a member of the Global Ecological Integrity Group, a fellow of the Post-Carbon Institute, a founding member and past president of the Canadian Society for Ecological Economics and founding director of the One Earth Initiative.

Jonathan Rothbaum is a labour economist whose work includes research on intergenerational income mobility, spatial econometrics and co-operative enterprises. He currently works as an economist in the Social, Economic and Housing Statistics Division of the US Census Bureau.

Claudia Sanchez Bajo is currently chair of Co-operative Enterprises and an assistant professor at the University of Winnipeg. She has published *The Debt Trap*, co-authored with Bruno Roelants, and *The Political Economy of Regionalism: Business actors in Mercosur in the petrochemical and steel industrial sectors*.

Stephen C. Smith is Professor of Economics and International Affairs at George Washington University, where he is the director of the Research Programme in Poverty, Development and Globalisation, and a former director of the Institute for International Economic Policy. He serves on the Advisory Council of BRAC USA, is Non-resident Senior Fellow of the Brookings Institution, and IZA (Institute for the Study of Labour) Research Fellow.

Peter A. Victor studied at the University of Birmingham and University of British Colombia. He is one of the founders of the discipline of ecological economics and the first president of the Canadian Society for Ecological Economics. Among his books are *Managing without Growth: Slower by design, not disaster* and *The Costs of Economic Growth*. In 2011, he was awarded the Molson Prize by the Canada Council for the Arts for his lifetime contribution to economics and the environment.

Richard Wilkinson studied economic history at the London School of Economics before training in epidemiology. He is Professor Emeritus at the University of Nottingham Medical School and Honorary Professor at University College London. In 2009 he co-authored, with Kate Pickett, *The Spirit Level*.

Stefano Zamagni is vice-director of the Bologna Center, Senior Adjunct Professor of International Economics and Professor of Economics and former dean of the economics faculty at the University of Bologna. He has taught at the University of Parma, University of Bocconi (Milan) and Johns Hopkins University. His publications include: *Economics: A European text*; *Relational Complexity and Economic Behaviour*; *A Civil Economic Theory of Cooperative Firms* and *Cooperative Enterprise*.

INDEX

greed, as fundamental value, 17
Green Economy Macro-model and
    Accounts (GEMMA), 113
greenhouse gas emissions, 104, 106, 108,
    112
Greenpeace, 80
gross national happiness, 72
Gross National Income per capita
    (GNIpc), 63
Gross National Product per capita
    (GNPpc), 61
growth, economic, 45; alternatives to,
    103; and scale, 41–3; biophysical
    constraints on, 102; costs outweigh
    benefits, 30; creates poverty, 88; co-
    operatives' approach to, 295–6; drivers
    of, 289; end of, 41, 101–14; limits to,
    83, 140; misnomer, 65; myth of, 92;
    not the same as development, 22,
    27–31; obsession with, 17; permanent,
    impossibility of, 34–7; relation to well-
    being, 61; turning away from, 17
guaranteed income, 110
Gulf War, 119

Hansen, James, 123–5
Hardin, Garrett, 242
harmful work, avoidance of, 56
health: related to employee ownership,
    210–20; related to economic growth,
    64–5
Heinberg, Richard, *The End of Growth*,
    43–4
hierarchical governance, 201–4
hierarchy, 190, 206, 211, 213, 296
high-frequency trading, 268
Hirschman, A. O., 162
HIV/AIDS, in Africa, 21
holism, 137
Holling, Buzz, 131
Homer-Dixon, Thomas, *The Upside of
    Down*, 121
Homo economicus, 199, 246
Homo sapiens, 84–5, 88, 92, 94
human appropriation of the net products
    of photosynthesis (HANPP), 101
human nature, modelling of, 210–20
human needs: categories of, 25; definition
    of, 25; matrices of, 27; satisfaction of, 25
human potential, subversion of, 88–91
human resource management, 5
human rights, principle of, 24
humiliations of servitude, 217

hunter-gatherer bands, 212

ideal economy, 39, 51–3
illegal immigrants in USA, 54
Imagine 2012 conference, 10, 264, 267
immigration, as source of population
    growth, 110
Imola, workers' co-operatives in, 214
import substitution, 18
incentive to work harder and smarter,
    181, 191
income redistribution policies, 291
incomes: differentials of, 70; equality of,
    297; preference for stability of, 221
Index of Health and Social Problems,
    66–7, 70
Index of Sustainable Economic Welfare,
    30, 66
individualism, 7; as base for economic
    activity, 194; culture of, 171; self-
    centred, 294
Indonesia, Nike Corporation in, 20
Industrial Revolution, 61
inequality, 222, 267–8; of incomes, 221,
    286; reduction of, 76, 288, 290–1;
    social, 221
infant mortality, 64
informal work, 56
information technologies, 127
Initiatives for Renewal, 1
innovation, 115–33, 291; co-operatives and,
    234–7, 238, 274, 280, 296; in promoting
    growth, 222–3
Institute for Co-operative Innovation
    (ICIE) (Italy), 236
Institutional Analysis and Development
    (IAD) framework, 259
intellectual property, 18
interest, compound, 138
Intergovernmental Panel on Climate
    Change (IPCC), 58
International Accounting Standards Board
    (IASB), 264
International Co-operative Alliance, 1, 179
International Energy Agency, 140
International Expert Working Group
    (Bhutan), 74, 80
International Financial Reporting
    Standards (IFRS), 270
International Labour Organization (ILO),
    20, 266
International Monetary Fund (IMF), 18,
    267, 268